Ruth Livesey
Department of English
Royal Holloway, University of London
Egham, UK

Peter Adey
Royal Holloway, University of London
EGHAM, UK

Nicholas Daly
School of English
Trinity College Dublin
Dublin 2, Ireland

Lindsey Green-Simms
American University
Washington, DC, USA

Tim Cresswell
Institute of Geography
University of Edinburgh
Edinburgh, UK

Jonathan Grossman
UCLA
Los Angeles, CA, USA

This series represents an exciting new publishing opportunity for scholars working at the intersection of literary, cultural, and mobilities research. The editors welcome proposals that engage with movement of all kinds – ranging from the global and transnational to the local and the everyday. The series is particularly concerned with examining the material means and structures of movement, as well as the infrastructures that surround such movement, with a focus on transport, travel, postcolonialism, and/ or embodiment. While we expect many titles from literary scholars who draw upon research originating in cultural geography and/or sociology in order to gain valuable new insights into literary and cultural texts, proposals are equally welcome from scholars working in the social sciences who make use of literary and cultural texts in their theorizing. The series invites monographs that engage with textual materials of all kinds – i.e., film, photography, digital media, and the visual arts, as well as fiction, poetry, and other literary forms – and projects engaging with non-western literatures and cultures are especially welcome.

Kai Syng Tan

# Neuro-Futurism and Re-Imagining Leadership

## An A-Z Towards Collective Liberation

Kai Syng Tan
Winchester School of Art
University of Southampton
Southampton, UK

ISSN 2946-4838          ISSN 2946-4846   (electronic)
Studies in Mobilities, Literature, and Culture
ISBN 978-3-031-55376-9        ISBN 978-3-031-55377-6   (eBook)
https://doi.org/10.1007/978-3-031-55377-6

This Palgrave Macmillan imprint is published by the registered company Springer Nature
Switzerland AG.
The registered company address is: Gewerbestrasse 11, 6330 Cham, Switzerland

Paper in this product is recyclable.

*For Dare-devil dreamers and do-ers. Ballsy fishes out of water, under-dogs and scape-goats. Impatient workers of culture, tired-of-fakers, risk-takers. Hopeful makers of art, trouble, meaning, change, and futures.*

# Praise for *Neuro-Futurism and Re-Imagining Leadership*

*Neuro-Futurism* tackles the myriad of concerns around injustices, mobility, creativity and community, with a spotlight on what neurodiversity brings to the table. The book is a commentary on neurodiversity, the foregrounding of the neglect of scholarship that takes neurodiversity seriously as a mode of interacting with the world, and the potential for neurodiverse creatives, scholars and activists, and their communities, to contribute to the growth of research on artistic methods, community engagement, resistance, and mobility justice projects.

The book takes the reader on a whirlwind tour around these issues, through an alphabetically structured series of chapters that lead readers through the relations across seemingly disparate phenomena. This is carefully and thoughtfully done. It forces the reader to upend their assumptions and allows Kai to build momentum and unravel this self-described 'manifesto' for the reader. This 'unconventional' structure is part of the book's clever manoeuvre—it urges the reader to consider their own assumptions and prejudices and carefully encourages a re-learning and call-to-action for creative, innovative and diverse practices to have space to breathe in the academy and beyond. It will ruffle feathers of (perhaps mostly neurotypical) scholars due to its structure and tone of writing, but that is, I think, part of the point. It is meant to disrupt and energise—asking for change and urging us to question assumptions and poor habits we find ourselves easily dismissing under excuses of institutional frameworks. It questions academic agency and integrity, urging to confront difference and diversity, and using the artistic and creative as one mechanism to push for better leadership in this space. This is bold and inspiring—and I cannot wait to use this as an exemplar in my own methods and teaching—which, I hope, is exactly the kind of inspiration and action that the author has strived for.

The book draws on contemporary issues and recent worldly events, but is also attentive to foundational texts and theories. Engagement with literature across disciplines and topics is ambitious and impressive, and there are plenty of avenues for further readings in the footnote-commentary too. By mid-way through the book, the reflection and examples drawn from her own work really start to shine through as illustrative of some of the concepts and resistances that are set up earlier in the book.

The book will appeal to a broad audience. Kai is a well-connected and respected scholar across mobilities, creative arts, social sciences, and more—with an international network of colleagues who I know will engage with the book in their research and teaching. It will also feed out into other disciplines that are engaged with disability studies, neurodiversity, postcolonial/decolonial scholarship, and more.

—Dr Kaya Barry, Artist-Geographer

Astonishing, daring, pioneering, and much, much needed, Kai Syng Tan's *Neuro-Futurism* is a remarkable achievement both in form and in content. Through a journey of 26 powerful reflections and calls to action, it shows how leadership has become enmeshed with inequality, injustice, consumerism, and exploitation of people and the planet. It reveals that, more often than not, leaders act in the service of maintaining vested systems of interest and the legacies of colonialism. With a style that is at once inspirational, creative, subversive, and at times hilarious, Kai Syng Tan gives us multiple strategies to disrupt and reclaim ideas and spaces. In her unique vision for the future, by 2050 neurodivergence and, more generally, difference become the grounds for new ways to think about and *do* leadership that can move the world in an equitable and sustainable fashion.

—Dr Mohammed Abouelleil Rashed, Philosopher-Psychiatrist

# ACKNOWLEDGEMENTS

The endurance, courage and creativity of marginalised body-minds who are on the move, who have moved us and who are moving the world have kept many going, especially during our troubled times. Why we haven't discussed many of these movers and shakers in leadership terms, and why we continue to canonise individuals and systems that trip, trick, maim or murder puzzled me. My curiosity has driven my endeavour since at least 2016 to find out more about the conceptual and imaginative possibilities of leadership as a critical and creative study and practice. *Neuro-Futurism and Re-Imagining Leadership: An A-Z Towards Collective Liberation* is my collage at this juncture.

This book maps together exemplars of what I consider as *better* definitions and models of leadership, and *better* role models, and proposes a new way to think about and do leadership. It critically appropriates, elevates and celebrates the Dirty, Demeaning and Dangerous labour of those in the margins as a leadership discourse. After all, having survived and even *thrived* within hostile systems, aren't the resource-Poor often already resource-*ful* and *leader-ful* by nature and design?

This book expresses my solidarity with larger efforts of abolition, emancipation, transformation and liberation. I'm particularly grateful to many teachers, mentors, collaborators and students who have guided and pushed me.

I am not able to feature or thank every-body in this book. I put my hands up with regard to my biases and blind-spots and welcome feedback and learnings. Furthermore, I acknowledge the privilege, luxury and luck

I've been afforded to be able to put my musings, sketches and speculations down and for them to be shared. If your teacher, colleague, institution or other frameworks you function within require proof or precedence for the anti-oppression labour you are engaged in, please cite book-books like this one. Instead of having to apologise or explain again and again, I hope that you can get on with what it is that you care about.

Last but not least, I thank my critics, trolls and detractors. You've made it clear why efforts like *Neuro-Futurism* are necessary.

*Attention: All views expressed here, when not that of others referenced, are that of the author's alone and not that of any institution or individual they are affiliated with.*

# ABOUT THE BOOK

Power imbalance. Prisons. Police brutality. Pogrom of Palestinians. Plutocracy. Pollution. Public service that ignores 'public' and 'servitude'. Practices that Persecute the Poor or Peculiar. Policies that execute non-white body-mind-worlds. Performative allies. The Popular Pre-occupation in autistic cartoon tycoons. Pipe-line Problems, not just for oil—thanks Putin—but for fresh Prototypes of Power. Poverty—of imagination. Have pale/stale approaches to 'leadership' Produced and Perpetuated our world of problems with a capital P? If standard approaches to 'leadership' suck, can the creative, 'non-standard' animate new Path-ways forward, beyond the Perma- and Poly-crises?

*Neuro-Futurism and Re-Imagining Leadership: An A-Z Towards Collective Liberation* is a rip-roaring manifesto that re-claims ways to think about and do 'leadership' in more equitable and energising ways. Colliding mobilities, social justice, neuro-queering, critical leadership studies, futurity and creative research for the first time, the book proposes 'neuro-futurism' as a beyond-colonial, heuristic change-making practice for individuals and institutions. Across 26 short chapters and 39 images, and celebrating the Dirty, Demeaning and Dangerous labour of marginalised culture workers, movers and shakers otherwise side-lined in (leadership) scholarship, *Neuro-Futurism* outlines a repertoire of riotous strategies towards dismantling and liberating from white-supremacist cis-het-neuro-normative-capitalist-patriarchal approaches to power. Punching up, punchy and pulling no punches, this sweaty hand-book is a call to arms, feet, sole and soul for body-minds of all ilk and from all walks, to re-imagine a world where diverse beings can thrive alongside other humans, nature and more-than-humans, including one Octo-Pussy. The deadline is 2050 so we're running out of time. Are you ready for an awesome adventure?

# CONTENTS

# ABOUT THE AUTHOR

**Kai Syng Tan**, PhD PFHEA (she/they) is an award-winning artist-academic-agitator known for her trademark 'eclectic style & cheeky attitude' (*Sydney Morning Herald*). Tan's unique vision of leadership draws on her portfolio as a sought-after hyper-active mover and shaker, as well as background as a neuro-divergent migrant from a working-class upbringing. Tan is a change-maker (as Yamagata International Documentary Film Festival juror, awarding the top award to an anonymous filmmaker formerly imprisoned by the Myanmar military junta; as trustee of a charity for detained asylum-seekers, drove its radical transformation by embedding co-creation and anti-oppression practices, leading to the appointment of its first, Black neuro-divergent female Artistic Director), curator and creative director (leading programmes ranging from £0 to £4.8m, including a Black History Month celebration that reached 18.2 million worldwide, and the opening and closing ceremonies of Asia's Paralympics praised as 'game-changing' by disability groups), trans-disciplinary innovator (first artist on a Royal College of Psychiatrist's editorial board), artist (San Francisco International Film Festival Golden Gate Film Award; National Coordinating Centre for Public Engagement Culture Change Award; Young Artist Award conferred by the president of Singapore; showcases in Museum of Modern Art (New York) (MoMA), Guangzhou Triennial and Royal Geographical Society), provocateur (regularly delivering keynote lectures; expert advisor for UK and Singapore government bodies, international research councils and even a ministry of defence), research instigator (acknowledged as 'absolutely instrumental' in re-framing running as creative discourse, through her curated RUN! RUN!

RUN! Biennale, as well as Running Cultures and Running Artful Networks; founded and/or (co-)led six global research networks, including the 420-member Neurodiversity In/& Creative Research Network), creative theorist/writer (publications include BBC, Guggenheim, *Frontiers Psychology* and *The Manila Times*), and mentor, teacher and academic developer (awarded Principal Fellowship; taught in 200 universities worldwide; regularly delivers masterclasses, such as for Royal Society of Arts, and 870 brain and mind experts from 17 countries, 14th International Conference on ADHD in Berlin). Tan is Associate Professor of Arts and Cultural Leadership at Winchester School of Art, University of Southampton. *Neuro-Futurism* is her first—and certainly not last—book.

# List of Figures

# CHAPTER 1

# T: Turn the Table of Dis-Contents

*Tired of how the world is moving—or* not *moving? Had enough of being taken for a ride by those in power? Join me, in my movement, to become movers and shakers for 2050 and beyond. Instead of quaking in fear, let's shake things up, and co-curate ways to think about and do 'leadership' together.*

## Bat-Shit

Hi, I'm Kai. I'm a chimera. I'm a tentacular, part AI-run-octopus-slash-pussy-cat-slash-hair-less-chimp: an *Octo-Pussy*.[1] I've been chewing over leadership, the future, and the future of leadership ever since I felt peculiar.

Was it long Covid?

Unlikely, as I've been queasy long before humans ate bat soup.

Could the revolting turn of events cause my motion-sickness?

Probably. If the world is 'on the move' and is an 'oyster' for the mobile, as sociologist John Urry argues,[2] the ~~motion~~ *commotion* has become frenetic, and the oyster rancid for many.[3]

That's if plebs can afford oysters—or oyster-mushrooms—to begin with.

© The Author(s), under exclusive license to Springer Nature Switzerland AG 2024
K. S. Tan, *Neuro-Futurism and Re-Imagining Leadership*, Studies in Mobilities, Literature, and Culture, https://doi.org/10.1007/978-3-031-55377-6_1

## MINDING OUR Ps

Power-imbalance underpins how 'leadership' works—or *doesn't*. Think 'leadership', and you picture the precious few exercising control over creatures and cosmoses with rules and structures that they sit above. Those with resources occupy and guard the top of the food-chain as 'leaders', and manipulate the story, practice and knowledge of 'leadership'—and everything else—at the expense of everybody else. To pump-up its status and to up-hold the status quo, the ruling elite starve others of access, autonomy and agency. In the name of 'progress', they invent imperialism, agriculture, war, slavery, mining, zoos, capitalism and other blood-sports and systems that im-prison us, from the personal to planetary.

No wonder we're Plied with Problems with a capital P:

- Protectionism and Plutocracy. Public service that turns its back to 'Public' and 'servitude'. Poshos Peddling Policies to Paralyse the Precariat. Peppa Pigs, Party-gate and the sunken billionaire's toy Ocean-gate. Push-backs—including literally—of boats of refugees. Titanic unremitting taunts of the Passengers and Progeny of HMT *Empire Windrush*. ~~Provide~~, Polarise, rule and ridicule.
- Police brutality. Procedures criminalising difference. People who're queer, of the wrong colour/class/conduct Penalised. Despite being a colourful, critical mass, the global majority being marginalised and *minoritised* by the ruling minority. Post-George Floyd's murder, a Proliferation of Public Pledges of diversity, equity and inclusion (EDI or DEI), which are Performative and pre-maturely DIE.[4] We Protest—and face back-lash, including by those playing Poundshop versions of their oppressors. In their desperation for approval, they become more extreme and evangelical Parodies of former masters, double down and Punch-down harder.[5] Sponsorship of the holocaust of Palestinians via tax-payers' money. The exclusion of Rohingyas—the world's largest stateless Population[6]—from our mind and land.
- Those with queer, neuro-divergent bodies—or body-minds-worlds, since they're entangled—are fetishised as 'competitive advantage',[7] the next talent opportunity',[8] and drivers of Progress for 70,000 years,[9] with autistic cartoon-tycoons as Poster-Boys. Weird but Pale or Prosperous? Charming! All other oddballs remain

Pathologised, demonised, infantilised, ventriloquised, silenced and out-cast.[10]

- It gets weirder: The Perpetuation of normative Play-books within Purportedly Pro-diversity communities. Many Prohibit those from the Global South, or those not 'high-functioning' (sic) to join the Party and ignore calls for decolonisation.[11] The queerness of how one thought-leader of neuro-diversity—the co-existence of many minds—can't grasp gender-diversity, or that many transgender people are also autistic,[12] and aired trans-exclusionary views *during Pride Month*, while continually recentring their own victimhood.[13]

- Hungry for more crying-wolf and gas-lighting? Let's have the carbon-hungry 'kinetic elites' monopolise 'shared' resources[14] and cover up predictions of climate disaster in the 1970s.[15] Want more shitty magic? Potable water becomes diarrhoea when firms dump sewage into seas and canals. Let's escalate (fecal) matters: Apart from lording over (social) media, supply chains,[16] the cloud and governments,[17] or openly maiming and murdering the Poor,[18] the hyper-mobile 'Fauxlanthropists'[19] are colonising the low earth orbit, mars, moon and more, although there's already 'no more space'.[20]

- Despite consulting or inventing theories, we find no respite. Plot twists and turns Pervade—neuro, spatial, (new) mobilities, creative—but many turn out to be Pontifications un-fit for Purpose. Even the boffins agree that leadership remains one of the 'least understood phenomena on earth' such that 'one of the most universal cravings of our time' is the 'hunger for compelling and creative leadership,[21] and that 'moving leadership forward' demands 'multidisciplinary and inter-disciplinary collaboration' and a 'broad lens'.[22]

- Pre-Pandemic, the Promotion of creativity and cross-Partisan collaboration to solve wicked global challenges, particularly for the AI-governed era of 'Industry 4.0'.[23] Still, we revert to nostalgia, walls, silos and segregation. We ~~Plunder~~ Protect barbarians' arts and artefacts, mock minoritised scholars for being 'niche'—even, or *especially* by areas Pre-fixed with 'critical' or purport to be 'constructivist' which often Prioritise their struggles on single issues and blindsides others—and report them to the Prevent anti-terrorism hotline, then re-Package their ideas as 'Post-' this or that. We spend billions[24] on courses on 'Personal growth', but find no re-course, only finger-Pointing at individuals for not being 'resilient[25]' or 'responsible.[26]

Meanwhile, Pipeline issues Persist, not just for oil—thanks Putin—but for fresh Prototypes of Power, and new Paradigms and Paragons of leadership.

- Poverty—of imagination.

What a loopy loop.

## A Non-Consensual Hallucination

Why should 'leadership' be about throwing the weaker under moving buses? Why are Porsche SUVs speeding on the Pavement, running over Pedestrians with wooden Prosthetics, then extorting 'compensation' from the grieving relatives for their PTSD? Isn't it bat-shit if being a 'leader' is about fixing systems to put others in a fix, while you make yourself fixed, fixated with power, un-movable and un-moving, making others (feel) un-fit, including for leadership, and Peddling Placebos to fix us?

I feel ill. Did I consent to this? I don't think I was even asked. Didn't I squeal in Protest when excreted from another Primate's birth canal, drenched in fetal/fecal jelly?

Then why did I pop up one month Pre-maturely?

Also, although ill-fitted to much of the established order, I haven't Purged myself from it.

Aren't I as guilty for Pooing into Uranus, and my own?

*It's Pants. I'm Panting. I'm going to Puke.* (Fig. 1.1[27])

**Fig. 1.1**  Motion-Sickness (Self-Portrait)

# CHAPTER 2

# P: Pivot. Play Havoc

*Are you throwing up too? But don't throw in the towel. Here's mine to wipe our sick.*

## Minding Our Qs

First, the bad news: There are no quick fixes for our Plight.

The good news, however, is that we *can believe* that we can make things *better*, and share *better* news.

I'm an artist. It's my job to think that.

Buddha hit the nail on its head by saying that we live in an illusion. So did bell hooks (1952–2021). The poet-slash-teacher clarifies that the value of art isn't to 'tell it like it is', but to 'imagine what is possible'.[28]

We'll spurn nihilism and nirvanas. Instead, we'll Play a Part in Proposing Pathways to the Possibility of *better*, im-Perfect and hole-y as our Plans must be.

That we can Pose *better* questions, like:

- How have Pale, stale Practices of and thinking around leadership Produced and Perpetuated our Perma- and Poly-crises?
- How to knock, mock, unlock and dismantle or abolish harmful monuments and master (sic) narratives around leadership?

K. S. Tan, *Neuro-Futurism and Re-Imagining Leadership*, Studies in Mobilities, Literature, and Culture, https://doi.org/10.1007/978-3-031-55377-6_2

- As 'leadership' has been in hot soup, what could it be(-come)? Since the 'norm' has been sub-standard, what could the 'non-standard' or 'ab-normal' reveal for the 'new normal'?[29] In a world in motion and commotion, how to activate body-minds in motion as modes of creative intervention?[30]

## TENTACLES AND TRAILS, TRIALS AND TRIBULATIONS

These lines of inquiry run through this book. The lines are squiggly, more like tentacles. *Neuro-Futurism and Re-Imagining Leadership: An A-Z Towards Collective Liberation* is a manifesto of my motions and moves, to re-imagine leadership as a (co-)creative (ad-)venture. I'm corralling fellow odd-balls, creatures, collectives, classrooms, (under-)classes, communities, composites and cosmoses, to con-join forces and curate change together—and here's hoping that you adore words starting not just with 'P', but 'C', as there're more to come. Being critical friends, we'll comfort and challenge one another, and celebrate wins of any scale. We'll lock hand-in-hand, and with heads, hearts with horns, and soul with sole, and Perform *better* Possibilities of leadership, and shape a *better* future, together.

Am I punching above my weight?

Definitely. I have many blind spots and biases. I've also made more missteps than hits than I can count. I am as responsible as others of my generation and upbringing for the systemic damages committed.

That's also why I must now clean up after myself and others.

Having been a teacher for three decades, I also believe that humans—myself included—can un-learn and re-learn. And nope, I didn't see teaching as my grand vocation. Being poor, giving tuition allowed me to make a living from the age of 17.

Furthermore, as a former endurance runner, I'm also a die-hard optimist fuelled by long-range vision.[31] I'd begun imagining futures—one generation away in 2050—when I got sick and tired of feeling sick and tired. I want to not be part of the Problem, and instead contribute to efforts to take us towards spaces with less struggle, danger or pain, and more creativity, love and joy, where we can thrive.

Being hyper-active, I don't sit still. Nor do I take things lying down. I'm animated and always wandering/wondering by default/design (Fig. 2.1[32]). Therefore, we'll run through spectra of courses and discourses, sprinting across time, space and our imagination.

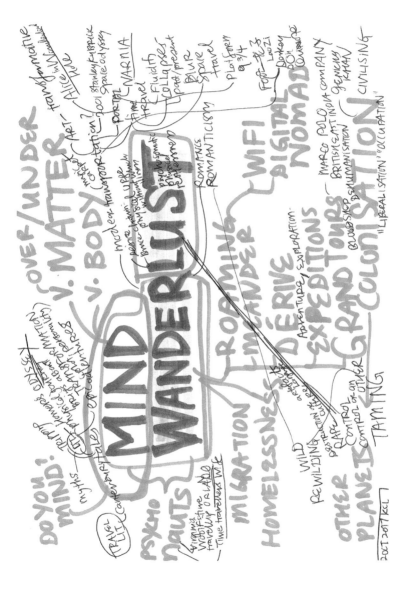

**Fig. 2.1** Wandering/Wondering

To *Pivot*—like this book, and like many businesses during the Covid pandemic—and generate systemic change, we can't Pussy-foot around. After all, the Chinese and Latin root words of 'discourse'—'*dao*' and '*discursus*'—con-joins the head and thinking, with feet that are moving—specifically *running*—from place to place.[33] In fact, the Old English and Old Dutch origins of 'leadership'—'*loedan*' and '*lithan*'—refer to travelling, endurance and guidance.[34]

We'll run with this grounding of leadership because it evokes the toil, blood, sweat and tears of those working towards change. Framing leadership as the action or process of 'travelling' rather than destinations or individuals also runs with how those in 'Critical Leadership Studies' (CLS) broadly understand leadership. Instead of something fixed, in-born, or centred on individuals. CLS approaches leadership as a socially constructed process constituted by meaning-making and embedded in context and culture.[35] Power is confronted, to highlight the 'dependent, messy, paradoxical and partial ways of the relational and contextual dynamics of leadership'.[36] That said, nuanced discussions about difference, resistance and emancipation still often remain side-lined.

## FOOTINGS FOR OUR GROUND-CLEARING EXERCISE

Thus, we'll seek *guidance* by fearless forerunners and fugitives who've *endured* hardship to out-play dominant, oppressive systems. Like other body-minds on the move, their ground-clearing work have often epitomised the infamous 3D's: Dirty, Demeaning and Dangerous. These Deviant, Defiant Dare-Devils have Paved the way for others like myself to now run our own expeditions.

Two such guides are Linda Tuhiwai Smith and Chijioke Obasi. Smith, of Māori heritage, warns that Western imperialism still destroys, and is reforming itself constantly, such as positioning itself as the source of 'civilised' knowledge, and judges what counts as knowledge.[37] To decolonise knowledge and our mind, we must interrogate *what, how* and *why* knowledge is produced, advises Obasi, who proposes 'Africanist sistahood' in her own research to critique (white) feminism.[38]

That's why *Neuro-Futurism* clears the murky air and ground, re-turns to the drawing board. We'll collage building blocks to propose new forms—and knowledge-formations—of leadership. This book is a mapping of our tools *in progress*. We'll invent magical and messy entanglements across diverse and divergent body-minds, and bodies of knowledge and Practices. We'll collide leadership studies with fields it hardly rubs shoulders with.

This includes the study of how humans, ideas and things move (or not)[39]—which is the field of 'mobilities studies'. The future seems 'murky', announces mobilities co-founder John Urry.[40] That's also why this Project is urgent, and why leadership must be about Projecting *ahead*.

Since making art is often about making futures through visualisation[41]—seen not least in movements like Afrofuturism—the arts, culture and creativity will Propel our voyage. Even leadership scholars admit that any meaningful scrutiny of the field of leadership cannot run away from the arts and humanities, since leadership is a 'creation of our imaginations—forged from human relationships that encompass the hopes, fears, dreams, passions, wants, and needs of our individual and collective experiences'[42]. We've also learnt that to fight novel viruses and crises, creative, novel approaches are key.[43] Thus, we'll entangle creativity with mobilities, which will Permit us to be 'Promiscuous', 'experimental', and flirt with scale,[44] con-joining the planetary[45] with the parasitic.[46]

Besides taking inspiration from artistic outputs like fiction and film, we'll explore what I have termed 'artfulness'.[47] This involves *artistry* and craftiness as a-typical interventions into the wider world beyond that of 'art'. In particular, we'll highlight artworks and artful approaches by those in the margins. After all, having survived and even *thrived* within hostile systems, aren't the resource-Poor often already resource-*ful* and *leader-ful* by nature and design[48]? The extra-ordinary impact and legacies of the many Black feminist culture workers who will guide us in our journey— bell hooks for instance—exemplify the potential of what I term 'artful leadership'.

This runs with hooks' invitation to re-claim the 'margin' as an 'inclusive space' of 'radical openness' and 'resistance', 'creativity and power'.[49] Those in the margin 'see things differently', and can battle the 'interlocking systems' of 'white-supremacist capitalist patriarchy'.[50] Making those in the Periphery call the shots for our future hits back at 'victors' who'd white-washed history. It also contests Perspectives that are far from 'universal' as claimed,[51] but are steeped in Patriarchal, First world Problems, like the Probable, Plausible, Possible and Preferable[52] framework favoured by those in design.

In particular, we'll shine a spotlight on the neuro-divergent, who're incidentally over-represented in the arts[53]—hence the prefix 'neuro-' in the 'neuro-futurism' of this book's title. My arguments are doubly a-typical for spot-lighting perspectives beyond the white, male or autistic, which has been the most out-spoken historically and politically. Nonetheless, following Buddha's mate and founder of Daoism Lao Zi, we'll be hyper-alert, and cross-examine '*-isms*—*including* autism, Daoism and neuro-futurism, while also Prizing subjective, lived experience as knowledge.[54]

## FAQ

Let's have a quick-fire round of frequently asked questions.

Q) You haven't explained 'neuro-futurism'—what's that?

A) Ah yes. You might have seen this term before, although this is likely the first time 'neuro-futurism' is in a book. I'd begun mobilising the term 'Neuro-Futurism' in *How to Thrive in 2050.*[55] That's a film I made during the pandemic in 2021. It outlines a vision of a future that doesn't demonise neuro-divergence—and difference in general, but is instead nourished by their creativity. My articulation draws on, as well as departs from the term's varied usages.[56]

Q) OK, and it looks like we're being even more creative with the term in this book?

That's right. We're leaping even further. Instead of only the noun, we'll also re-calibrate 'neuro-futurism' as a verb: '*neuro-futurising*'. This treads on the heels of other action-based, active, activist as well as *hyper*-active—and indeed *hyper*-activist—proposals. They include 'chewing not swallowing', a protest performance art,[57] and neuro-queering, a 'politic, project, or doing'[58] for subverting, defying, disrupting, liberating from both neuro- and hetero-normativity.[59]

We'll also render 'neuro-futurising' in lower case, like what Gloria Jean Watkins has done for her pen-name, bell hooks. This was her feminist strategy to direct focus to her ideas, instead of just herself as an individual.[60] Likewise, our campaign is about the systems and (infra-)structures of society, not identity politics or so-called 'culture wars'.

Q) Why hyphens?

A) Hyphens draw our attention to components of a term, and about how they con-join and go further together. In our case, I want to highlight 'neuro-', 'future', as well as '-rising'. For the same reason, I have added a hyphen to 'Octopussy' in this book for the first time since I began using the term. Rather than to divide a word, my hyphens do the opposite, and show how the sum of a term is *from* as well as *be-come more than* the parts. We're also beginning to re-situate 'leadership' as a socially-constructed *path-way*—meaning process and travel, instead of a fixed/stable/abstract entity—as well as multi-faceted entity—and definitely not an artificially neat or 'pure' hypothesis or theory derived on the arm-chair or desk.

## NEURO-FUTURISING LEADERSHIP

Here's our working definition of leadership:

> **Leadership: A critical and creative process, practice, politic, poetic and path-way of change-, meaning-, and future-making.**
> **Diverse and divergent, decolonised, and neuro-queered, leadership comprises and nurtures artful and a-typical approaches and actions that profit people, planet, play and power-sharing.**

What a chunky, clunky mouth-ful. Which sounds about right. Just as we should not consent to being reduced to a single being,[61] we shouldn't allow 'leadership' to be a simple/simplistic sound-bite. Our under-taking *must* be a party-pooper of the cartoonish constructs of leadership and our Problems with capital P's.

As author Octavia E. Butler (1947–2006) warns, unless we build 'different leadership' by 'people with more courage and vision', we'll 'all go down the toilet'.[62] One month after her declaration about the need for different leadership, Butler kicked the bucket. However, the parables of the neuro-divergent 'mother of Afrofuturism'[63] continue to kick our butts, *hard*.

> *Take the baton from leaders like Butler, hooks and Lao Zi. Don't flush our fortune down the bog. Let's rock the boat. Let's push the boat out. Let's rise to the occasion. Let's make this an awesome—and, as my students will say, 'sick'— adventure. If you dare. And care.*

# CHAPTER 3

# Y: Yell Back, Huff & Puff, Blow the House Down!

*That was our itinerary. And now, let's explore eight possible ways to handle this book.*

## HAND-BOOK

*Neuro-Futurism* is a handy and punchy hand-book. Across **60,000** words, we'll explore 'what', 'how', 'whom with/for/by', 'what if', 'what if we didn't', 'why (not)', and more, towards subverting, defying, disrupting, dismantling and liberating from white-supremacist cis-het-neuro-normative capitalist patriarchal approaches to leadership. It's a provoca-tion—and *not* the last or only word. Practical, portable, petite yet piquant like a political pamphlet, this is our pocket rocket to propel ahead. Our hand-book minds our P's and Q's—there are plenty of p-words and plenty of questions, but we won't be polite. I'm not British.

This book is a mapping of *better* ways of doing, defining and discussing about leadership. I've ordered chapters under the alphabets of A to Z— just not in that order, as you would have noticed. I have re-ordered the English letters, so that this is a customised lexicon. The index and the online edition with hyper-links allow you to craft non-linear (de-)tours to further (dis-)order the book. Furthermore, there are plenty of ~~maps~~ map-pings (noun), which I've been mapping (verb). I use the term mapping

© The Author(s), under exclusive license to Springer Nature Switzerland AG 2024
K. S. Tan, *Neuro-Futurism and Re-Imagining Leadership*, Studies in Mobilities, Literature, and Culture, https://doi.org/10.1007/978-3-031-55377-6_3

interchangeably with 'map-making'. Both are live, alive, on-going process of world-making.[64] My mappings show how entities are inter-connected, and are dynamic, open and in-development. Although un-fixed, my mappings are *pre-fixed* with the term 'monstrous', because we'll cast our tentacles far, deep, wide and wild, to mix and *mis*-match things up. We'll also make 'multiscalar interconnections between movements at microbial, particulate, human, animal, technological and planetary scales, affective atmospheres, social mobility, political movement'.[65] Each mapping often begets further mappings too. There are mappings-within-mappings. Thus, while the book is finite, it's *generative*—encouraging yet other mappings and meaning-making. It is also *generous*, enabling and encouraging creative conflicts, through what I term 'productive antagonisms'.[66]

Can you handle that?

## GUIDE-BOOK

I'm your humble, bumbling guide, who'll share with you the work of exceptional Path-finders not always discussed in leadership contexts. In her concept of standpoint feminist theory, Patricia Hill Collins (b 1948) clarifies that marginalised people can become powerful sites of knowledge not despite, but *because* of what they experience.[67] Academics and employers, if you're struggling, let me help:

> Lived experience *is* knowledge and skillsets. It isn't just 'valid' as knowledge and skillsets, but is a *highly* specialist form of knowledge and skills, over and above your tick-box list of qualifications, certifications, titles and roles.
>
> If you need written words in a serious book to make this legitimate, here you are.
>
> You're welcome.

This book gathers, and seeks to elevate and celebrate, the wit and grit of marginalised body-minds as *leaders* and *leadership*. I will show how they have been advancing knowledge about how power and leadership works (or how power and leadership does *not* work) and, as compellingly, nudge us to where we can *go*.

Spoiler alert: I won't be alive or kicking by 2050. With the venture incomplete, this book is my baton to you. This *A–Z* comprises my notes collated on the move before I die. It's a faster-paced version of philosopher Jean-Jacques Rousseau's *Reveries of a Solitary Walker* which he composed during his walks before he died 250 years ago.[68] But instead of only dwelling about the good/bad/ugly old days, we'll jump into—as well as up and down about—the future. We'll learn from the past constructs of the future and 'failed' projects, develop dystopic and utopian visions, extrapolate from the present (fore-casting), work backwards from a desired scenario (back-casting), and build future scenarios.[69] My provocations aren't just analytical or representational, but performative.[70] It's also positively pungent. To off-set both in-digestion and carbon, I use bullet points, and the book is Print-on-demand.

## Story-Book

Story-telling, like leadership, is about making (up) worlds and transformation, and can help us re-build 'leadership'. But this story-book has *better* characters, plots and creative flair, not the same old (his)tories.

Linda Tuhiwai Smith tells us that each individual's story is 'powerful', and also contributes 'to a collective story' in which everyone 'has a place'.[71] We'll also activate Smith's other tactics of 'researching back' (which follows 'talking back' and 'writing back'). They include: claiming (re-asserting rights), testimonies (sharing oral evidence of 'extremely painful event or series of events'), 'survivance' (celebrating survival), making connections and affirming connectedness (positioning individuals in sets of relationships with other people and with the environment) and envisioning (binding people beyond 'depressing' present-day situations to 'dream a new dream' and 'set a new vision').

I'll include my own stories and testimonies about being in the margins, as well as attempts to migrating out of my place. I'm often out of sync/place with dominant ways of words, space, time, and other body-minds, which others pathologise as 'dyslexia', 'dyspraxia', 'autism' and 'Attention Deficit Hyperactivity Disorder' (ADHD). Do I swallow their bitter pill? Nope.

Whenever I'm not invited to the party, I'll make my own cooler—*hot-ter*—parties. Or, I'll 'pass' as normal, and wear the cartoon of 'model-minority' that my jaundiced epidermis allows, and gate-crash. A bundle of joy at five-foot-one, and told by trolls that I look/sound like an eight-year-old boy fuelled by fart jokes, I'm agile, often slip into crevices and break into spaces I'm otherwise un-welcome.

Furthermore, I'll highlight how I weaponise privilege I have earned, to help en-large spaces for others dis-placed, to ~~talk~~ *yell* back to the Big Boys.

## FLIP-BOOK

This is a flip-book because it's responding to the deficits in knowledge and practice that've made us *flipping* mad.

We'll also flip 'deficits' and 'disorders' into assets. Such subversion and critical appropriation runs with Smith's (re-)claiming. It's also what artists, especially those operating outside of dominant systems, excel in. Since dyspraxia is a 'clumsy child' syndrome and I'm a ham-fisted childish-adult, it's only right to describe neuro-futurising leadership as a clumsy strategy.

Urry would've approved. Futures depend upon 'complex', invisible yet powerful systems, and demand a 'systems' approach.[72] Specifically, Urry calls for 'clumsy'—not elegant or linear—approaches, because when systems fail, they disrupt other systems, and solving 'one problem reveals or creates other problems'. This is especially true with regards to 'wicked problems' or complex global challenges which have multiple causes and complex inter-dependencies between processes. Clumsy approaches also accommodate diverse stakeholders who have radically different interpretations of problems (and solutions) and conditions that are volatile, which applies to us, since this book learns from—and dialogues with—distinct parties.

Furthermore, *Neuro-Futurism* flips over and flogs so-called 'self-help' books. Preachy, pedantic or prescriptive this isn't—feel free to *help yourselves*. The bite-sized Prompts will animate discussions, and are for you to critique, customise and bring to life. That's why the headings are action verbs, and there're references in the final chapter for further investigation.

## SKETCH-BOOK

Rather than only crying or crying foul, we'll transform injustices and injuries into jeers, cheers and gear-changes. UK-Iranian comedian Omid Djalili has been using his platform to call for international condemnation of the Iranian government and its 'regime bots' which have been killing peaceful protesters.[73] This is a powerful term that I will borrow for our project to describe enablers of the powerful systems. I'll also deploy slapstick and puns, as well as shaggy dog stories. In a time of fake-news and cruelty, pinches—no, industrial-sized tanks—of (smelling) salt are essential for any abolitionist and re-construction work. When you read that as recent as 2021, scholars realise that expressing your 'true self' is a 'luxury' that minoritised people can often 'ill afford',[74] 'LMAO' is a logical response.

We'll also draft sketches—Postulations—and step *back* to review the forces behind toxic templates of governance, in order to step *forward* and *up*.

There're also plenty of sketches—drawings, monster-mappings and more (Fig. 3.1). Instead of servicing words, they often rival, contradict or replace them.

## TEXT-BOOK

This is a textbook. It isn't 'text-book' or typical, because our curricula, reading lists, references and compasses aren't decolonised, diversified, neuro-queered. *Neuro-Futurism* will be in libraries, bookshops, toilets and tablets. It should be book-marked, thumbed, fingered, used and abused by students, scholars, sceptics, practitioners, prisoners, policy-makers, the powerful and the power-less.

You might be surprised to learn that I do love text and books. However, normative approaches to writing and reading aren't my mother tongue. Whenever I generate one idea/sentence, I invent **10,000** more alongside that I *must* attend to. I also adore Lao Zi's tactic of playing the crude, child-like fool and vagrant to take the piss out of intellectualism and gentle-manliness.[75]

Still, to be heard in a set-up (pun intended) that fetishises language,[76] you must code-switch and mimic the vernacular. That's why we're *here*, (ab-)using the written word, in a 'high-brow' book published by the wing of a company that generated €3.2 billion in 2019.[77] I'd agreed to a total 'royalty' less than my single day-rate as an artist too.

And nope, I do not work for free, nor do I have 'good-will'. Never, ever ask me or my minoritised peers and students to work for free/out of 'good-will' either.

Since I'm fashionably late to the party, we'll raise roofs and eye-brows. We'll neuro-queer logo-centric and prescriptive norms/forms of language that feign 'objectivity'. We'll join the campaign of hooks' contemporary Audre Lorde (1934–1992)—a poet who was adamant to *not* write theory—to dismantle the master's house with new tools.[78] I see this formidably-embodied by queer, multi-disciplinary Gen-Z creatives.[79] A former student describes their collaborative effort as 're-canonise' the

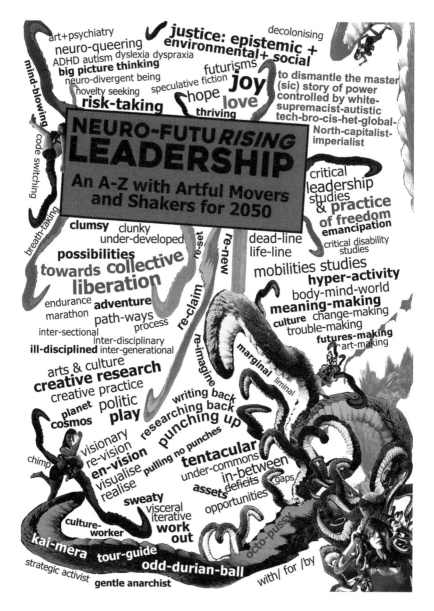

**Fig. 3.1**   More Pungent than the Smelliest Durian. Look! It's a Monster-Mapping!

unique creative energy of their fellow trans-gender, neuro-divergent peers. Nice.

Likewise, *Neuro-Futurism* will huff and puff, blow dusty text-books that canonise violent contents into the dark web or black market, and help bring the house down.

## WORK-BOOK

To make 2050 better than today, there're no magic bullets.[80] The destination isn't even fixed. Being short (of patience) and a regular of Specsavers, I won't—can't—pay attention to everything. Collins—who refers to hooks her 'other mother'—helpfully reminds us that every group's knowledge is partial and unfinished.[81] Grass-roots efforts are necessarily patchy and inconclusive, not least those that aim to flip and queer the norm. As the trans-gender co-founder of the framework of neuro-queering Nick Walker clarifies, 'any effort to establish an "authoritative" definition of neuroqueer' is 'ridiculous', since users 'delight in subverting definitions, concepts, and authority'.[82]

That's where *you* come in. You'll need to help 'do the *work*', as my co-drivers.

We'll step *away* from our comfort zones, and step *forward* and *up*. We won't just stay with the trouble[83] but, like *avant-garde* artists and clumsy ADHD-ers, charge towards danger, and *work through* thorny issues, and *work out* the possibilities of 'leadership'. The term 'heuristic'—enabling others to learn for themselves—is useful here, which is what I will do as your tour guide. Being no *tour de force*, and need *your* in-sight, fore-sight and fortitude too. Through *work sheets and exercises*, we'll kick up a storm.

As an under-developed, under-doggy, octo-pussy monster with ~~two~~ nine left feet and lives, neuro-futurising leadership includes, welcomes and seeks to catalyse Pluralistic—10,000—more Perspectives of leadership.

## PLAY-BOOK

Last but not least, this book is about play.

As ambitious but pragmatic dreamers, we play the game, *insofar as to be able to tweak and transform the system*, to join other dare-devils before us, and to make space for yet others, so that we can collectively re-write the story. We play the system by proposing new rules. To be anti-authoritarian, word-play will further undermine this author's authority. To do this is to go by the play-book of how artists function as leaders. Artists have always transformed the way we think, work, play, are through play, and by re-inventing play-books.

Take one Nam June Paik (1932–2006). By picking up the video camera and using it as a creative medium, Paik didn't just invent an entire artistic genre (video art), or help kick-start a movement (Fluxus, an international community of artists whose wide range of creative experiments focused on the creative process). Nor did he only influence generations of artists and media theorists with his aesthetics and approach to technology (with terms like 'electronic super highway'). Paik was also a media consultant (paid $12,000 in 1974 by Rockefeller Foundation) and policy-maker (writing reports on education, media and more).[84] He was also a thought-leader who embodied the value of mobility and crossing boundaries, literally (as a Korean-American who lived in Korea, Japan, Germany and US) as well as metaphorically (being a multi-hyphenate, as a classical composer-turned visual artist).

So, bunny-holes, cliff-hangers and ellipses will demand *your* intervention. Become my partner(s)-in-crime. Read between the lines, and what isn't written down/in. Join conflicting dots. Fill in the blanks. Customise your toolkit to suit your circumstances and taste-buds. Edit your own ~~endings~~ beginnings. Dismantle my version of neuro-futurising leadership.

Slay the story-teller.

*2050 is looming. We're running out of time. Are you ready?*

# CHAPTER 4

# V: Visualise 2050

*Now that our points of departure are clear, let's apply our long-range vision, to picture far ahead, and imagine our destinations—in the plural form, because there should be multiple possibilities. What could—or* should*—the future look like? Take a look at aspirations that others have shared with me in the eight photographs below (Figs. 4.1, 4.2, 4.3, 4.4, 4.5, 4.6, 4.7, and 4.8*[85]*). If you think this question is pre-mature, I'd actually say that it's nearly too late. But we can* start *now. As the visionary William Edward Burghardt Du Bois says:*

> Now is the accepted time, not tomorrow, not some more convenient season. It is today that our best work can be done and not some future day or future year. It is today that we fit ourselves for the greater usefulness of tomorrow. Today is the seed time, now are the hours of work, and tomorrow comes the harvest and the playtime.[86]

This, here, now, *is* exactly *the time for us to act, states Du Bois. The US sociologist (1868–1963) was the 'Father of modern Pan Africanism'*[87] *because he organised the first Pan-African Congress in 1919 in Paris, which galvanised Black people world-wide that eventually led to the end of colonialism in Africa. So, we need to prepare for our harvest and playtime tomorrow, now.*

© The Author(s), under exclusive license to Springer Nature Switzerland AG 2024
K. S. Tan, *Neuro-Futurism and Re-Imagining Leadership*, Studies in Mobilities, Literature, and Culture, https://doi.org/10.1007/978-3-031-55377-6_4

**Fig. 4.1**   Encourage Questions

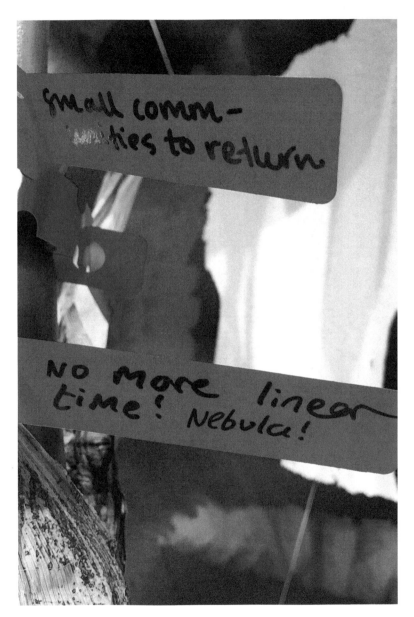

**Fig. 4.2**    Small communities to return; no more linear time! Nebula!

**Fig. 4.3**    Nobody to be hungry

Fig. 4.4   Care about people u don't know

**Fig. 4.5** Difference is normality

**Fig. 4.6**  Come one, come all, have a think, but have a ball!

Fig. 4.7    Neuro-divergent women in leadership

**Fig. 4.8**    Live and always be free and wild

*Reminder: It's not all on me—you must chip in too. After all,* Neuro-Futurism *is a creative collage, an open book. Neuro-divergent processes, which fuel our project, are not-yet-fulfilled developmental processes.*[88] *Our work is also non-linear, like a rhizome, and rhizomatic assemblages are nomadic 'realms that are yet to come'.*[89] *As a mobilities method, neuro-futurising leadership also inherits its 'fluid and decentered modes for knowing the world allegorically, indirectly, perhaps pictorially, sensuously, poetically'.*[90] *What are your visions? Put on your glasses—are they tinted, half-full, half-empty, and/or calibrated to augment our reality? Have a think, but have a ball!*

# CHAPTER 5

# F: Futurise. Up-Rise. Up-End

*By the next generation, will Pussy-cats be appointed Ministers of Dreams and Dreamies, and heal inter-generational injuries via licking and purring, so that the wounded, erased, kidnapped or murdered can rise again,* higher? *To commemorate survival and to up-end the 'depressing' present-day situation, can we whet our appetite for different realities? The following are eight scenarios, but what new dream(ie)s for the future will* you *dream?*

## ARTFUL LEADERSHIP

Twenty-five years on, artfulness will be an essential vital prism and paradigm to think about and do leadership. Palestinian Parkour artful-athletes show the imperialists what 'free-running' means.[91] Systems of organising, thinking and relating as enacted in the poetry and prose by the 'Indigiqueer' are commissioned and operationalised by firms to improve mental health and human–nature relationships.[92] Throat-singers, who're capable of producing multiple-pitches at the same time, replace cut-throat accountants as trustees across organisations, and command the board room to teach others about accountability, using your voice—and active listening. Instead of bulimic cycles of economic precarity, hyper-active props-makers are paid for their down-time and (over-)thinking time.

K. S. Tan, *Neuro-Futurism and Re-Imagining Leadership*, Studies in Mobilities, Literature, and Culture, https://doi.org/10.1007/978-3-031-55377-6_5

Artful leadership develops from, re-mixes and extends exemplars, discourses and movements in the arts and culture. The varied and often overlapping genres since Nam June Paik's prime in the 70s have nourished my conception of artfulness. They include happenings and performance/live art (with the body as creative medium, which Fluxus artists also revelled in), protest and activist art (examining socio-political-cultural power dynamics), participatory art and relational aesthetics (where human relations and their social context are key) socially-engaged art or social art (where humans are a key component of an art work), new genre public art (activist art created outside institutional structures), useful art (art as a process that should impact society as part of everyday life),[93] and more.

Artfulness also follows on the critical groundwork exploring the role of the arts and culture in leading and transforming public discourse by Anne Douglas, an Emeritus Professor in a university in Scotland. Her conceptualisations of 'artistic leadership' (2009[94]), and 'cultural leadership', which the former is a subset of (2013[95]), are exciting. Through careful interviews with contemporary artists, and further anchoring findings with arguments from art history, anthropology, social sciences and more, Douglas proposes the understanding of artists as leaders within and beyond arts and cultural settings. Correlating creativity with innovation, Douglas proposes three path-ways through which artists' 'creative tactics and strategies' keep us 'moving and responsive without being consumed by change': artistic practice, which provides direction by 'asking the right questions'; artists undertaking leadership roles within organisations, and artists participating in civic and public discourses.[96] These discussions were extended in her proposal of a 'more complex and critical approach to cultural leadership'. Set in the aftermath of the financial crash of 2008, Douglas argues that the 'keys out of crisis for cultural leaders' has 'shifted from organisation of governance', to the 'social, ethical, and aesthetic demands of an emerging political era', which 'cultural leaders must themselves play a role in shaping'.[97] Indeed, Douglas' definition of 'leadership' as something with 'many dimensions' including organisation, ethics, social, political, aesthetic, and beyond framings around the hierarchical or economic competitiveness, but encompassing 'concerns for the environment', highlights 'complexities' that she notes are 'not necessarily reflected in other leadership discourses'.[98]

Artfulness embraces Douglas' turbo-charged definition of leadership. Her intervention into gaps in the knowledge and practice of leadership also paves the way for neuro-futurising leadership. What I'm bringing to the table a-new are learnings from critical leadership studies, as well as decolonial and queered critiques of power and knowledge. Championing artistic outputs as well as artfulness, agility, a-typicality and other dimensions that creative workers in the arts and culture possess, artful leadership will impact larger socio-political, civic and public contexts. Instead of the hierarchical or merely managerial, the creative, activist, relational and decolonial will be 'Leadership 101' by 2050.

## THE TOP 1% TURNS BOTTOM-FEEDERS

By 2050, the affluent will have the same value as waste affluence. Beyond their wildest wet-dreams, the 1% become swamps of refugees sent on one-way submarine rides to Rwanda. Climate-deniers banished to sinking islands. Conspiracy theorists fed to skinny polar bears whose icy homes have become soggy swamps. Descendants of slavers provide pedicures to migrants with broken toes from making a dash for long-haul trucks.

People with mid-life crises 'find themselves' not by ascending mountains for Instagrammable photo-shoots that kill their sherpas, but by making sandals for Tarahumara ultra-marathoners in Mexico, who cover distances of 200 miles at a pop like they did in the sixteenth century to out-run/out-wit encroaching Spanish invaders.

Bankers make 'equity', 'interest', 'shares' mean what they say. Public health workers earn more than millionaire 'public servants' in a sunny, shiny tropical island. King William volunteers for Dirty, Demeaning and Dangerous labour. What good-will![99] What an un-lazy Willy! Big Four executives in maximum security jails for taking loo breaks. Amazon bosses strewn alongside opened-parcels on the road whenever they fall sick.

The 'untouchables' have the last laugh.[100] Comedians of Dalit descent rule the world stage as roving states-persons with diplomatic immunity.

And finally, Black Lives Matter.

## COURAGE AND CREATIVITY, NOT TEARS OR FEAR

By 2050, rather than tears or fear, or being down and out, our lives are filled with courage and creativity. The arts and culture are embedded in life,[101] instead of being scape-goated as surplus or luxury. Knitters are hired by WEF, IMFC and other big-lettered-players to nit-pick and re-calibrate society's moral compasses and direct multi-national strategies to battle global crises. Print-makers deliver more compassionate and more accessible road-maps at Davos.[102] Interventions like that of the Artist Placement Group (1960s–1980s), where artists are not outsiders but 'Incidental Persons' working within government, commercial and industrial organisations and introduce new ways of seeing and thinking, will become common-place.[103]

After all, creative approaches—by which I take in an expanded sense, to encompass the arts and culture, everyday creativity, as well as a wide range of terms and their variations including creative/artistic research/practice, practice-led research, practice as research and so on—excel in 'problematising and reflectivity'.[104] Unlike surveys which leadership scholars are addicted to,[105] or other 'traditional' research approaches, creative methods can 'extend the frontiers of research' as a 'generative enquiry that draws on subjective and emergent methodologies', offer 'new ways of modelling and externalising critically-situated knowledge', operating from not just 'explicit and exact knowledge, but also on that of tacit and experiential knowledge', and can generate 'new knowledge or knowing'.[106] Thus, to what we have established about works of art and processes of artfulness as constituents of meaning-making, future-making and change-making, we can add *knowledge*-making. Art and artfulness are knowledge-systems, and neuro-futurising leadership captures the vitality and criticality of the art, artfulness and creativity, in how we do, define and discuss leadership.

In particular, creative mobilities methods are powerful because they're capable of a 'complex engagement' with reality.[107] Jen Southern's *Para-Site-Seeing* (2018–2019) exemplifies the strengths of this approach, being collaborative, trans-disciplinary, anti-colonial, multi-media, multi-scalar and multi-perspectival.[108] It's playful too, as the title also suggests. Co-created with a biomedical scientist-slash-artist, the leading creative mobilities mover-shaker's work mobilises a fictionalised parasite's eye view, to re-lay multiple, complex narratives of a tropical disease that disproportionately affects populations in the global south. By 'encompassing diverse ways of moving through and engaging with changing landscapes, critically analyzing the past', creative mobilities think 'unconventionally' about the 'possibilities of cultivating more just and equitable futures'.[109] Even before the pandemic, Monika Büscher had clarified that, to side-step the imminent 'collapse of humanity', argues that it was 'paramount that 'WE—a sensible number—search for pathways', and arts and creative approaches are key within this.[110] Given the 'systemic shock' of the in-equalities exposed by the pandemic, creativity and courage must drive our path ahead, states the mobilities scholar.[111]

## OCTOPUS TRUMPS THE WHITE ELEPHANTS
## IN THE IVORY TOWER

*Pub quiz: How do you eat an elephant?*

*Good response: One bite at a time, by an octopus.*

By 2050, the octopus wins the battle of the titans, to trump the (white) elephants of elitism, ableism and racism in the ivory tower,[112] and help realise UNESCO's 2050 ambition to repair social injustices and transform the future via prioritising human dignity and cultural diversity, care, reciprocity and solidarity.[113] With care, courage and creativity as key metrics of success for higher education (HE), becoming 'tentacular' becomes a vital learning outcome.

After all, octopuses have blagged, transmogrified and hacked the meaning of life for 296 million years. Having ducked asteroid hits and tectonic shifts that'd slaughtered dinosaurs, it will have no problem teaching HE—which, at only 930 years old, is but a pesky infant—a thing or two about artfulness. 'Curious, embracing novelty, protean in behaviour as well as in body',[114] each tentacle is a mind, problem-solver and sensor. Octopuses have long understood the inter-dependency of the 'head-foot'—which is Greek for 'cephalopod'[115] and, by extension, the body-mind. With their 'high esthetical value' and 'rich behavioral repertoire' that have inspired the arts, spirituality and sciences alike, no wonder cephalopods like the octopus are celebrated as 'outstanding' 'boundary objects (or subjects) connecting seemingly distinct thematic fields'.[116] From B-movies to documentaries on streaming platforms today, octopuses continue to intrigue and inspire us.[117] Given its playfulness (switching off lights), rest-lessness (escaping from aquariums to kill boredom), resourcefulness (camouflaging and shape-shifting) and smart design (bearing half a billion neurons or 'excitable cells' each), the octopus is also a handy emoji for hyper-activity. That it has three hearts further confirms its status as a fitting mascot for a more compassionate educational culture and, by extension, society.

## VISUAL AND MONUMENTALLY DIFFERENT LEADERSHIP

One generation on, leadership is done *differently*, including as a visual practice that celebrates difference. To be clear, by 'visual' and similar terms in this book, I'm not talking about physical eyesight, but about making things *tangible* (not abstract), as well as en-visioning and imagination.

An eloquent expression of what this can look like is captured in *The Human Monument* (since 2019) by Sheffield-based artist Yuen Fong Ling. The 'mobile plinth' is made of, with and by intertwined body-minds of colour assuming ever-changing, temporary formations by supporting and up-lifting—including literally—one another. The artwork-cum-knowledge-system shows that leadership can look different to the pale, male, ossified and white-collar that you see piled up high and erect on stock images and archives. It's also a striking retort to un-movable and un-moving monuments made of concrete, bronze and imperialism that scratch the surface of human potential and knowledge, by failing to include the narratives of the hidden global majority, as well as to persist in scratching, scalding and scraping open wounds of colonised communities by commemorating slavers.

Picturing leadership as a visual practice responds to how, despite being 'more important than is often given credit', visualising leadership had been a 'blind spot' in leadership studies.[118] The 'aesthetic turn' within organisational studies had also emphasised the need to develop ways of knowing that encompass all of the senses, including visual, but the common visual 'fantasy' of a single, 'powerful and usually male' leader who 'saves followers from peril' persisted, affecting how we 'understand and evaluate leadership'.[119]

An assertive turn to the aesthetic will also heed the call to consider leadership not just as a science but an 'arts'—and, in fact, *four* arts. Leadership traverses the philosophical (which asks 'who are we' to explore identity); the visual (which asks 'where are we going' to forge strategic future vision); the martial (asking 'how will we achieve this', to develop smart organisational tactics); and the performing (communicate to followers the above) arts.[120]

A leadership practice that includes and monumentalise difference draws on the work of Michelle Evans, whose credentials include being Founder of the Wilin Centre for Indigenous Arts and Cultural Development in Australia, will also have advanced the leadership as prioritising 'difference', and for 'doing leadership differently'.[121] Countering both the simplistic approaches of dominant leadership approaches to 'diversity', as well as 'essentialistic identity politics' with terms like 'queer leadership', Evans 'calls attention to the power dynamics behind the construction of difference'. Building on theories on post-colonialism and new forms of colonization that occur in globalised environments, Evans focuses on indigenous and post-colonial scholars' understanding of leadership as prioritising 'resistance and refusal from the bottom or the margins of society, rather than from formal positions at the top'.[122]

## NEURO-DIVERGENCE AND MBES BECOME EXTINCT

In the near future, we'll live in a world in rude health. Neuro-Diversity and bio-diversity will become bog-standard. Autistic Greta Thunberg (b 2003) and dyslexic Hong Kong pro-democracy leader Joshua Wong (b 1996), now middle-aged, become CEOs—chief environmental operator and chief equity operator—of nations and the United Nations. Instead of OBE, MBE or CBEs, we award NDEs: anti-empire Neuro-Diversity medals of Excellence.[123]

'Neuro-Divergence' as a concept becomes expanded, as played out in the global Neurodiversity In/And Creative Research Network[124]—and even extinct. Knowledge about human diversity and divergence join up, the same way neuro-divergent processes overlap and aren't discreet. As it stands, the sciences haven't caught up. Neuro-Scientists consider autism, dyscalculia and so on as related spectra of differences in brain physiology and structure, unlike psychiatrists who frame them as 'neuro-developmental disorders', or cognitive psychologists, who stress differences in thinking, processing and sensory issues. In less than three decades, they will not just tango with one another, but work in tandem with those in sociology and disability studies who emphasise socio-economic barriers, and situate human difference as part of a spectrum (Fig. 5.1[125]). By 2050, discourses around 'healthy' versus 'abnormal' brains or minds will be replaced by those around difference as assets. ADHD's big-picture thinking, risk-taking and creative giftedness, as well as dyslexia's problem-solving and divergent-thinking,[126] will have been mapped with features identified as essential for effective leadership in leadership studies.[127] Innovations in the arts and creative research by those who are neuro-divergent become widely-applied.[128] That people with stroke, fibromyalgia and more have also joined the network and claimed to have 'found their tribe', points to the wider implications of neuro-divergence as expanded, and models how an inclusive eco-system can function.

**Fig. 5.1**   Working Hand-In-hand with Other Body-Minds to Move (through) Worlds, Con-Joined by Hope

## WILDER FUTURES

Two and a half decades on, there will be Octo-Pussies galore, to annihilate cock-shaped rockets ejaculated by billionaire tech-bros. These chimeras will hijack the Jupiter Icy Moons Explorer spacecraft, and demand that Homo sapiens update the 2030 Agenda for Sustainability Development,[129] Space in 2050[130] and other impotent agendas.

In other words, by 2050, neuro-futurising leadership will become *more*—not less—*immature*. Our tentacles will sprawl even further, as we continue to cross-fertilise and solidarise with other creative campaigns to re-write the future, and enrich our bid for consent and consensus to build more open forms of 'leadership' that emancipate us from the current. Our off-springs will continue to transmogrify 'leadership' into yet other co-creative neuro-diversity-led (eco-)systems where people and planet prosper via play, poetry, and (com-)passion.

Academic endeavours are great[131] but are, ultimately, *academic*. Neuro-Futurising leadership wants to learn from the truly exhilarating—specifically, artistic and artful futures or futurisms imagined by the marginalised. Efforts like including sino-,[132] trans-,[133] queer diasporic,[134] asylee-[135] and queer cli-fi[136] futures or futurisms yell out the power of story-telling as an anti-colonial process of 'recovery' and a 'struggle for self-determination'.[137] Meanwhile, we'll continue to be wary of efforts that are exclusionary and/or exclusive, such as that of the macho petrol-heads of Italian Futurism in the 1920s.

If 'illuminating the relationship between race and leadership can advance our understanding of how social change leadership happens in practice',[138] I hope that neuro-futurising leadership and the endeavours it fosters will have the energy to do the same.

## RE-WILD PASTS

In our leap in time and imagination, can we up-end *dead*-lines like 2050 into *life*-lines, so that those that've had their lives robbed have new life- and plot-lines, like one Chio Lin Tan?

Born in 1937 in a tropical island, Tan was given (up) by his parents to Malaysians during Japanese rule. When he returned to school, he couldn't read numbers, so he walked out of his Math exam—and education—aged 14. When his adoptive parents died, he made a living by hand-washing neighbours' clothes. Eventually, he crossed the border back to the isle, taught himself to read and write, and became a journalist. He worked wonders with words, but as a migrant worker, was granted only cycles of zero-hour contracts. With an inexpensive hobby of browsing books in a bookshop, he'd chat up the receptionist, who'd also left school prematurely. He worked three jobs to feed the three kids they co-created, who're as flagrantly neuro-divergent. Poor and poorly, she almost threw the toddlers from the tenth floor of their one-bedroom flat. In 2023, Tan is enduring stage 4 bowel cancer and has 24/7 care by a law-graduate Paw from Myanmar, who now inhabits his daughter's bedroom. Questions arise:

- What if ~~Tan didn't fail education~~ the educational system didn't fail Tan? Had he had access to support for his dyscalculia, would he have become a poet or a professor?
- Scholarships granted his kids access to higher education. His daughter was the first scholar for a scheme by Shell, which in 1989 was linked to the execution of writer Kenule Beeson 'Ken' Saro-Wiwa, who'd led non-violent protests against Shell's decades of environmental and health devastation. That she didn't reject the dirty money, and that her entire career and being is a direct result of it, has continued to haunt and taunt her. Without the funding, there was no way I could study in a university, let alone fine art, *abroad*, she convinces herself. Her hypocrisy worsened her internal storm. She hangs on to the advice of Afrofuturist Toni Cade Bambara, who clarifies that the job of culture workers 'who belongs to an oppressed people' is to 'make revolution irresistible'.[139] Understanding 'culture workers' the same way she renders the term 'artists' in the expanded sense to include all workers in the arts and culture, as well as any body-mind-worlds that engages in work to change human culture including and beyond the arts, she strives to pay back and forward by mobilising her luck to support others in their ambitions as an artist-teacher.
- In one art installation for a Circle line subway station,[140] she asks: 'If you can live your life all over again, what would you change? If you could change this question all over again, how would you live your life?'

She dies, like she will, in this book.

*Your turn now. How would you change your question, future, and open (end)ings?*

# CHAPTER 6

# G: Gate-Crash. Change Culture Through Ill-Discipline

*Gate-crash. Grapple with gate-keepers. Get your foot through the door. Smash glass/class labyrinths. Re-frame illness as asset. Grab your seat at the table. Pump your fists. Butt in—axe the blah blah blah.[141] Design better tables. Re-move cock-blocks. Thank former path-finders and lock-pickers. Open further windows of opportunities for others.*

## GATE-CRASHING THE PSYCH-SCIENCES

Being diagnosed with dyslexia, dyspraxia and ADHD in 2015 opened flood-gates. Questions—not answers—inundated my mind: *Isn't everybody different? Why should the medical have the first—or only—word about the body-mind? What can art bring to the party beyond 'mad artist' or superpower tropes?*

To find out, I gate-crashed the world of brain and mind experts in 2017. As the first artist-in-residence at the Social, Genetic and Developmental Psychiatry (SGDP) centre at King's College London, I devised, led and delivered a two-year programme, *We Sat on a Mat, had a Chit Chat, and Made Maps.*[142]

A primary theme was how mind-wandering relates to imagination and illness and, more generally, the cultural and scientific constructs of 'normality' and difference. Generating thoughts unrelated to the external

K. S. Tan, *Neuro-Futurism and Re-Imagining Leadership*, Studies in Mobilities, Literature, and Culture, https://doi.org/10.1007/978-3-031-55377-6_6

environment is a universal human experience. It also underpins creativity, seen not least in Surrealism's celebration of dream-scapes.[143] At the same time, ADHD expert Professor of Psychiatry Philip Asherson argues that *excessive* mind-wandering can impair, and can function as a bio-marker for ADHD.[144]

Switching codes to pass as 'normal' at times and flagrantly 'out' during others, I infiltrated seminars and summits, volunteered as a guinea pig for lab trials, and shadowed Asherson, who was my mentor. *En route*, I processed my learnings and questions through a wide range of outputs, workshops and more.

Key was a tapestry I designed, starring a grotesque octo-pussy. Placed on the floor, this becomes a '#MagicCarpet', which is the nick-name of the project. The carpet 'takes off' and works its 'magic' when others sit on it with me and share how their minds travel and where to. We capture our discussions, disputes and discoveries in mappings. Between 2017 and 2019, #MagicCarpet was experienced by 10,000 people in UK, Europe and Asia, and around 100,000 online through activities, media engagement and more, including an EU-funded film (watched over 64,000 times since).[145]

## BEING ILL AND INTER-DISCIPLINARY

It doesn't matter that #MagicCarpet didn't un-lock mind-blowing mysteries about the grey matter of the hair-less chimp. Neither did it iron-out deep-seated (mis-)understandings between fields. Rather, its *sorcery* is to un-cover a sweet-spot for distinct (gated-)communities to run into—and create sparks with—one another. By irritating the health–illness and art–psychiatry dichotomies, #MagicCarpet triggers new in-sights on difference and inter-species entanglement that can lead to further (un-)learning, questions and actions.

One finding concerns gender. ADHD-ers who identify as female often mask their difference or perform as 'normal',[146] and remain under-researched. As chair for a session at the 5th European Network for Hyperkinetic Disorders Conference in Edinburgh, I invited the 500 researchers and psychiatrists to consider #ADHDart created by/for/with people who self-identify as being both ADHD and women, or #ADHDwomen. Through other platforms like performance-lectures, op-eds, interviews and *open-mics*, I pitted cartoonish neuro-divergent mascots like *Rain Man*, against stories by a young Black woman on how her

Tourette's makes her tic—and *tick*.[147] That pioneering computer scientist Ada Lovelace features side-by-side with the octo-pussy on the tapestry also ensures that women are centre-stage in #MagicCarpet, as both subject and object, and in not just health and neuro-divergence, but also research and creativity (Fig. 6.1[148]). Employing women Black sign language interpreters, disabled migrant students and emerging neuro-scientists as panellists alongside established figures further helped to raise the visibility of women in the intersections of differences.

Indeed, ADHD-ers share in their written feedback that they 'felt like I have finally found my own community', and express 'mahoossive (sic) thanks'.[149] 'Loved it loved it loved it. Felt at home. So Happy!:)'. Those 'who are neuro-typical but don't really fit in the box as well' found #MagicCarpet 'super powerful', too. The tapestry 'screams' for your attention, encouraging 'everyone to step outside their comfort zone'.[150] 'Exciting and innovative', the programme was 'leading the way', and 'breaking new ground'. People 'learned more about the mind [than] what I would have learned in a classroom'.[151]

Back in the classroom at SGDP, #MagicCarpet also succeeded in nudging shifts in how ADHD was understood and taught, which was not insignificant for an institution renowned for innovations in 'fixing' differences. To develop a culture that welcomes productive antagonisms of the art and sciences, I set up 'Art and Science Creative Collisions', and invited a female clinical psychology PhD student to co-lead. Through workshops, inhabitants explored ways to introduce the arts and creativity into their research, or to simply step away from computer screens or laboratories and frolic in paint and glitter. I introduced other exotic species into the Centre too, such as curating a book launch by a psychoanalyst-artist, and guiding a migrant researcher to curate an exhibition exploring trauma, which she subsequently developed for her PhD at Cambridge. Furthermore, I volunteered on several roles, including as personal tutor to students, mentor to staff, and founding member of the Neuro-diversity Staff Peer Network. Researchers became interested in the creative aspects of ADHD, and not just its deficits or as a disorder, 'because of your work with Philip'. For Asherson, #MagicCarpet as 'a leading example of successful collaboration between scientific and cultural sectors'. Its 'innovative integration of art and science' functions as a 'powerful platform for the clinical and scientific community to develop an interesting dialogue' which was 'contributing to both local and national training with healthcare professionals and researchers'.

Fig. 6.1  Riding with Ada Lovelace

What was interesting was how, sat shoe-less on the #MagicCarpet, clinicians felt able to reveal their own mental health challenges and neurodivergence, which had motivated their interest in the field, but which they cannot publicly disclose because of the need to uphold the doctor–patient power dynamic. Of the 500 health policy professionals at the Nesta's People Powered Future Health, several also commended the non-hierarchical and accessible nature of #MagicCarpet, which departs from clinical spaces.

That #MagicCarpet was frequently labelled 'beautiful' distances it from the stigma that often surrounds mental health and psychiatry. 134 people, aged 2 to 85, co-created mappings depicting curious chimaeras, abstract patterns and more. Laboratory processes like electroencephalogram (ECG) and Functional Magnetic Resonance Imaging (FMRI) aside, these widen the visual lexicon of mental restlessness, and make our kinetic imaginations *visible*.

#MagicCarpet also advanced discussions around the role of the arts in knowledge-production. Exploiting art's propensity for ambiguity and play, it showcases how artistic research can shape thinking. This counters the instrumentalisation and subjugation of the creative arts as 'marketing', 'public engagement', 'impact'. The creative arts as something to support/sex-up 'proper' research in the health- or social-sciences is endemic in movements like arts in health, creative health and social prescription, as well as research in general, including in leadership and mobilities. Subverting assumptions of 'illness', and picking and re-mixing disciplines in what I term an 'ill-disciplined' approach,[152] #MagicCarpet scoffs at arguments that mock 'lofty' art as something requiring 'superior cultural intelligence to access', not least because it was put forward by one 'Right Honourable The Lord Howarth of Newport'.[153] Instead, as a body of accessible artistic outcomes with high production values, #MagicCarpet shows how it *builds* cultural intelligence and transgresses the 'high/low' culture binary, having been enjoyed by families at Southbank Centre in London, educational psychologists at SOS Dyslexia Conference in San Marino, and art connoisseurs at the Centre for Contemporary Art in Singapore alike. Like critical medical humanities, #MagicCarpet seeks to '[widen] the sites and scales of "the medical" beyond the primal scene of the clinical encounter', and positions visual arts 'not as in service or in opposition to the clinical and life sciences, but as productively entangled'.[154] Yet, #MagicCarpet goes beyond lip service, by being *artist-led*, countering the dominant approach of researchers contracting artists to glamorise their clinical—pun intended—research. Like artist Deborah

Padfield's intervention into the clinical space with visual tools co-created with patients to describe chronic pain,[155] #MagicCarpet fore-grounds visual practice and subjectivity to enrich conventions that claim 'objectivity' or prioritise text and textbook approaches. It also spotlights ADHD, not autism, which remains the most outspoken and, unsurprisingly, politically-organised, of neuro-divergences.

## ILL-DISCIPLINED CULTURE CHANGE

#MagicCarpet thus presents an inter-disciplinary approach to change- and meaning-making, by over-turning normative constructs of 'illness' could be termed 'ill-disciplined culture-change'.[156] This optimises and displays the creative possibilities of neuro-divergence, going beyond the counter-cultural, critique, advocacy or activism. As a roving carpet and critical device, it fulfils Büscher's call to fore-ground (im)mobilities of bodies that are 'fragile, aged, gendered, racialised'.[157] It also captures the 'fleeting, distributed, multiple, non-causal, sensory, emotional and kinaesthetic' of mind-wandering in this case, 'without holding it still' or destroying its mobile qualities.

Ill-disciplined culture-change aligns with, as well as extends, Anne Douglas' insights[158] around a 'relational' approach to leadership, as well as the need to be strategic—and artful—vis-à-vis organisations and dominant systems that we are necessarily a part of. Far from the performing the 'stereotype' and 'canonisation'—and, I will add, cartoon—of the 'Romantic genius' who is 'tortured, solitary, self-righteous etc', Douglas makes clear that artists need to acknowledge and understand the complexity of systems that we function within. This is not just vis-à-vis the art market system, but larger neo-liberalist systems that we are a part of (such as the economy, since we pay the bills). This shakes the instinct and position that artists may guard, which is that of a completely free-ranging out-sider, beyond contexts or rules. I find framings that teeter toward fundamentalism, essentialism or exceptionalism unhelpful. Likewise, Douglas argues that it isn't enough to be only 'antagonistic' or 'anti-authoritarian', or to only promote 'hostility to state apparatuses', which artistic movements since the 60's have favoured. Instead, artists should develop 'deep knowledge and understanding, not only of the arts, but also of the sphere of civic discourse'. Douglas cites an interviewee who defines leadership as something that demands a close engagement with the specialist languages of policy, and which requires you to understand the underlying conditions within which you are practising. Not purely the aesthetic and material ones, but the political, economic and broadly cultural ones. In other words, it requires you to lift your head up from wherever you might be painting or whatever you're sculpting or whatever you're doing with your highly sophisticated editing system and actually understand the policy world.[159]

What Douglas recommends is an artfulness closer to the dynamics of relational and social practice, with strategies to play and *engage with* the game, in order to play *and shift* the system. For Douglas, the artistic or cultural leader is like that of an 'animator', 'negotiator' and even 'lover', who leads not *despite* but *because* of collaboration and 'making connections'. 'Engagement'—not just opposition—is key, and that entails 'ways of thinking and imagining constructively, as well as critically'. Artists must 'know how to work with organisations (artistic as well as others) as that is where challenging opportunities lie for innovative work', states Douglas. In other words, rather than *against*, anti- or counter-, or only from the margins or outside, this is a positionality that is *with* and *with-in*. Within such set-ups, having 'a vision, team working skills, emotional intelligence, communication skills', which are attributes that artists already excel in, will be key. This relational—and, I will add, relativist, pragmatic, nuanced and *productively* antagonistic—stance demands more wit and grit. As well as play, and fore-play—not unlike dating, or using dating apps.

Just like when using Tinder, Bumble or such-like, parties involved agree to (fore-)play, feeling vulnerable and taking risks. I hadn't expected to grasp the rocket science-level of knowledge that SGDP inhabitants devote lifetimes to. So I didn't. The buzz was in *not* knowing, and exploring exotic frontiers with members of other species, where each wouldn't have ventured alone. 100% of the feedback stated 'Agree' or 'Strongly Agree' to feeling 'challenged in my understanding of how artists and scientists collaborate, and/or my own body and mind and those of others'. The activities were 'positive, intriguing and productive', states one. Another describes #MagicCarpet as a 'generative object, quietly (though in its own way loudly) creating a space that was both safe and adventurous. You and your work really created a unique space, generous and energising'. I've 'achieved something very unusual—a genuinely diverse and progressive format for people to express their thoughts'. When #MagicCarpet won the National Coordinating Centre Public Engagement Culture Change Prize, judges described it as 'challenging and thought provoking, and a really effective way of conveying the positively disruptive energy that engagement can release'.[160]

That's a swipe right alright—tentacular, tantalising, even *tantric*.

## LOVE

#MagicCarpet became my jumping-board to further develop yet other invigorating yet safe(r) spaces to entangle imagination, the psych-sciences and neuro-divergence. Its prime legacy is the Neurodiversity In/& Creative Research Network.[161] Having conceived the network in 2018 to gather the project's followers to further our conversations and actions, I launched it in February 2020, first as a public and open mailing list on a UK academic list-server. The timing was apt as global lockdowns due to the pandemic were soon enforced. By March, 120 people had signed up. Three years on, there are over 420 members, and almost as many related groups that they are affiliated with.

Built on the generative, energising and inclusive nature of ill-disciplined culture change, the network brings to life Linda Tuhiwai Smith's ethos of re-claiming, survivance, affirming connectedness and envisioning through testimonies and story-telling. The Network seeks to disrupt not only able-ist structures of dominant setups, but the often-hidden white-supremacist, colonialist under-currents within neuro-divergent communities. Instead, I am guided by Douglas' notion of being a lover, as well as hooks' dictum of love. A 'beloved community', says hooks, is formed 'not by the eradication of difference but by its affirmation'.[162] We love, not despite our heterogeneity but *because* of it. To assume that a minoritised group is homogenous because it's a-typical to the dominant is to have a cartoonish grasp of difference.

In the same token, the tag-line of the group is explicit in its acknowledgement of the complexity and instability of the terms that constitutes its name, individually as well as the multitude of ways that they can be combined, understood and applied. Rather than a social, academic or support group, the network is framed is around the 'magical and messy entanglements of neuro-diversity, creativity and research'. In fact, the *productive* antagonisms of diverse and divergent interpretations based on members' lived experience, as well as cultural, geo-political and disciplinary backgrounds is the very basis of the network.

The alliance's 'membership' and membership criteria is also not run-of-the-mill. Other than welcoming those who self-identify as neuro-divergent, it admits self-proclaimed allies too. This enables those who're keen to learn to do so in an immersed, authentic and respectful way, and further provide a layer of protection for those aren't ready or able to disclose their neuro-divergence. There are curators, clinicians, CEOs, creatives and critical friends. Practitioners, policy-makers and researchers from the arts as well as psych-, neuro- and social-sciences who are established in extending knowledge that centre neuro-divergence (such as California-based neuro-queering exponent Nick Walker) rub shoulders with those new to their own neuro-divergence. Professors (including Asherson) mingle with emerging creatives and entrepreneurs (such as the founders of Empower to Cook and Genius Within), too. Members share stories, questions and creative expressions directly or indirectly related to (their) neuro-divergence, making the network a unique, shared liminal space for perspectives that don't often run into one another otherwise. Since each individual's story is 'powerful', as Smith states, the 'collective story' that we're contributing to is helping to transform attitudes and advance knowledge and practice around neuro-divergence.

Our live exchanges track the emergence of a hitherto hidden community. The narratives do not just describe existing ideologies; rather, they *create* them. The Network thus counters how neuro-divergent communities have been represented in 'oppressive or negative' ways, if not 'silenced' altogether.[163] Its online origins allows the network to bypass traditional gate-keepers, and enable those ignored in mainstream media a voice, to be examined.[164] As an inclusive platform for knowledge exchange, members ~~tell~~ yell back their own stories, instead of being ventriloquised, commodified or white-washed by others with more social and/or academic capital, not least social scientists and geographers whom, as 'busy-bodies', 'demand to have a say in everything'—as pointed out by one prominent geographer who collaborated with me.

## DIVERSIFYING AND DECOLONISING NEURO-DIVERSITY

The Network's culture avoids the essentialism and exceptionalism—using/abusing difference as a basis for discrimination of others—as well as tribalism and territorialisation which can blight neuro-divergent communities,[165] as demonstrated in the recent high-profile case of trans-phobia.

As also highlighted by multi-hyphenated researcher and Network member Ginny Russell,[166] there are groups that police the 'purity' of members' neuro-divergence (typically autism), while others demand that members have 'official' diagnoses (which disregards how disclosure and access to diagnoses often come with a price, including literally), yet demonise medical perspectives. Then, there are those that gate-keep, self-ghettoise and mimic the mainstream play-book, with apartheid, 'members-only' rulings. The alliance also avoids hierarchies of normativity which are weirdly typical in circles that purport to advance minority rights. These 'rights' often exclude race and class. The most 'accepted' face/story of difference often remains that of the cis-het-white person, which directly or indirectly mutes body-minds and voices that deviate from their diktat or norm.[167] US disability champion Imani Barbarin explains that it is *precisely* within such set-ups that whiteness reigns supreme.[168] This is also why, other than Waterloo and Whitstable, members also hail from Taipei to Jakarta and Kolkata. That was also why I invited a woman of colour—a #MagicCarpet fan and early-career researcher who'd shared how the project had transformed her personal and professional life—to co-lead the Network. I have learnt that those with new-found confidence gained through being in the network are keen to hold on the sense of empowerment, which is understandable. My aim is for not just a system of shared- and distributed leadership—where members' participation, including in decision-making is cultivated—but one where power is much more decentralised, and where the seats will be rotational, so that others can take turns to set new agendas. As someone with thick skin, I am happy to take the hits when/if they happen.

That the Network is an iterative and generative live resource is its forte, with impacts at personal, local, disciplinary, institutional levels and more. I curate workshops and seminars to connect, showcase and share innovations and best practices. Members are, in turn, forging new entanglements, and co-creating further outputs and outcomes. Having rehearsed their ideas at Network sessions, a US neuro-scientist then published a well-received article around augmentative and alternative communication, while a choreographer showcased her 'dysco' at UK's Southbank Centre.[169] Mobilising their new-found confidence, skills and knowledge, members enact ill-disciplined leadership and forge further transformation, including by leading groups like Scottish Neurodiverse Performance Network and Kansas City League of Autistics. Having credited the Network in her commission at UK's Battersea Arts Centre,[170] a professor of drama founded her university's Disability and Neurodiversity Network, nurturing the next generations of ill-disciplined leaders.

As a tentacular *nexus* of local and global connections, the Network models a poly-centric, meta-, super-*galaxy* that empowers body-minds in fractal directions and dimensions, encouraging not just members but members of their respective spheres of influence, who can now advocate for themselves and others, and in the long run, effect culture change.

*Access all areas. Gate-crash and engage from with-in, not just enrage from with-out. As a critical mass of ill-disciplined culture-changers, let's surge forward with better questions, better stories and better leadership.*

# CHAPTER 7

# D: Dys-Play Your Difference

*When asked 'Why don't you eff back to where you're from?', reply by ~~displaying~~ dys-playing your difference (and indifference) as a badge-wearing miss-fit in public. The badges show-and-tell on-lookers what your favourite diagnostic descriptors of ADHD are[171] (Figs. 7.1 and 7.2[172])*

K. S. Tan, *Neuro-Futurism and Re-Imagining Leadership*, Studies in Mobilities, Literature, and Culture, https://doi.org/10.1007/978-3-031-55377-6_7

**Fig. 7.1**    Easily Distracted (by a Handbook on ADHD for Adults)

**Fig. 7.2** Acts without thinking (Platform 9¾); Always on the go (Riding a #MagicCarpet)

*Step outside your home/lane/class/ghetto/margin. Perform your role as a 'model' minority, literally. Don't hide, and show off your thicker, jaundiced skin. Wear your heart(s) and badges on your sleeves. 'Normalise' your 'abnormalities'. Stick up two fingers and ten bunioned toes at by-standers.*

# CHAPTER 8

# U: Un-Learn Tentacularly

*For change to take place, education is key. For bell hooks, education is a future-facing 'practice of freedom'.*[173] *Sure, the academy—like the world it's situated within—'is not paradise'. Still, education 'connects the will to know with the will to become', argues hooks in the tantalisingly titled* Teaching to Transgress. *The classroom 'remains a location of possibility', and learning remains 'a place where paradise can be created'. That's why universities remain a primary site of action and intervention for hooks, and several of our teachers in this* A–Z. *Let's do a deeper dive into a 'tentacular' approach to (un-)learning and teaching in higher education. In what ways can teaching tentacularly transgress current confines, to in-form—and even* trans-form*—higher education, and free 'leadership' into a distributed, relational process that prioritises poetry, play and (com-)passion?*

## BROKEN BOATS AND DOUBLE STORMS

Let's start with the elephants in the ivory tower.

For minoritised inhabitants, the academy is often dystopian.[174] Already a neo-liberalist system that professionalises intellect through metrics and competition,[175] the pandemic became the perfect storm for universities. Yet, instead of heeding the pandemic dictum of 'no one is safe until everybody is safe', many chose to weaponise the crisis to exacerbate austerity or

K. S. Tan, *Neuro-Futurism and Re-Imagining Leadership*, Studies in Mobilities, Literature, and Culture, https://doi.org/10.1007/978-3-031-55377-6_8

're-structuring' measures that un-duly punish Black body-minds. This is captured by the term 'double pandemic',[176] which UK sociologist Jason Arday describes as the 'normalisation of white dominance and anti-Black racism'.[177] The murder of George Floyd catalysed a '"rest-of-the-world" awakening to the lived reality of Black communities', observes Arday, but the global amplification of the Black Lives Matter (BLM) movement has led to 'ongoing backlash at both governmental and institutional level' and cyclical 're-traumatisation and loneliness' of Black lives—hence the title of his paper 'Same Storm, Different Boats'. British-Australian Sara Ahmed pushes the boat (analogy) further out. Non-white women in HE don't just 'end up doing diversity as well as being diversity',[178] she shares. Those who are 'a bit different' or point out institutional sexism and racism are deemed 'causing damage' and 'rocking the boat', like Ahmed herself was.

The seas are rough for non-white body-minds and ideas in the creative arts within higher education (HE). To begin with, the arts and humanities have been in a 'bonfire'[179], scape-goated in favour of Science, Technology, Engineering and Mathematics (STEM) subjects. The subject areas of fine art, theatre creative writing and more have been particularly[180] threatened, with the 'disappearance'[181] and 'erosion'[182] of art schools and fine art education worldwide. This is worsening the historically tense[183] relationship between the art schools/departments and the universities that they're a part of. In the UK alone—as if the government's xenophobic (Brexit), racist (welcoming 'good migrants' from Hong Kong and Ukraine and drowning or imprisoning brown and Black asylum-seekers) and divide-and-rule tactics (increasing migrant surcharges to fund the salaries of teachers and nurses) led by its first brown, billionaire Prime Minister aren't enough—it's also 'cracking down' on 'rip-off' degrees in the creative arts.[184]

But it'd be lazy to only sling mud at bureaucratic philistines. The creative arts has been wearing so proudly its badges of honour of elitism,[185] racism[186] and ableism[187] for so long, it's as if it *prefers* exclusivity, exclusion and extinction, *darling*.

TENTACULAR PEDAGOGY FOR SEA-CHANGE: THREE HEARTS

This is where my octopus rocks into the ivory tower (Fig. 8.1). Tentacular pedagogy is a learning and leadership strategy that re-casts marginalised body-minds and the creative arts in HE from broken boats into rocking, rolling and cracking boat-captains who ~~weather~~ ride the double storm,

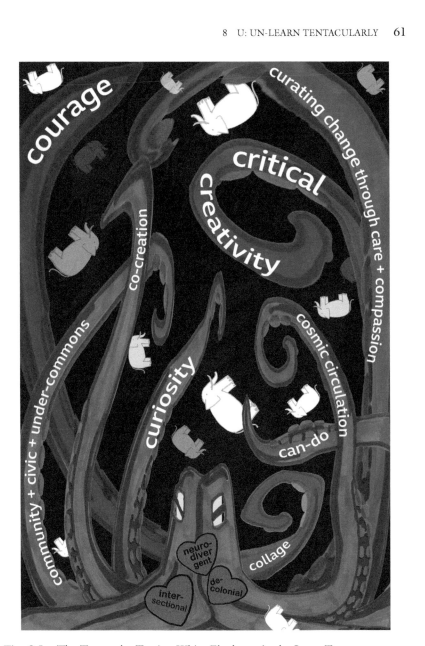

**Fig. 8.1**   The Tentacular Tossing White Elephants in the Ivory Tower

and even help instigate sea-change for HE and beyond. TP is my toilet paper to wipe down the university system's rancid, mammoth droppings. TP also wipes out white elephants and institutional elephantine memories of elitism, ableism and racism. TP has three hearts and nine body-minds, which scoop up some of the running motifs of this book, as well as align with UNESCO's 2050 priorities of care, solidarity and social justice.

## Neuro-divergence

Neuro-divergence, the first heart of TP, remains largely 'invisible' as an issue *and* creative resource in universities.[188] What a missed opportunity given HE's 'omni-crisis.[189] One Leonardo da Vinci would've been drowned in today's system, let alone the 'dog-eat-dog'[190] HE. His mirror-writing—a consequence of his dyslexia[191]—would have been illegible. That's if his ADHD[192] didn't stop him from completing assignments within normative time-frames. If a degree of support—flawed and often *disabling* as they can be—is provided for under-graduate students who're dyslexic, any scaffolding miraculously disappears for post-graduates and staff. Activating research about how creativity, neuro-diversity and leadership inter-relate,[193] TP is for, with and by neuro-divergence, including learners and teachers. Leonardo's compulsion to *dabble*—from generating some 2500 sketches of mechanisms and flight machines that couldn't take off, literally, to creating a painting with a certain smiley lady—would be central to TP. Intellectual promiscuity—instead of 'specialism' or fidelity—and a thick-skin and knack for *failure*—instead of normative notions of 'success'—are skills that *all* learners can benefit from. Not least given the gig-economy and other sea-changes to work as accelerated by the pandemic.

## Decolonisation

TP's next heart is decolonisation. As a function of dominant society, the universities, like prisons, are set up to 'reduce' and 'command' individuals, argue cult scholars Fred Moten and Stefano Harney.[194] Unsurprisingly, Black inhabitants have been the most persecuted. Despite trumpeting intellectual reflexivity, HE actively defends its status quo, and refuses to address its colonial heritage.[195] White fragility makes the British stiff upper lip even firmer, and together conspire to create a deafening institutional silence, although racism in HE has long been firmly-established in scholarship. Despite pledges when called out in summer 2020, it was soon 'business as usual'.[196] By 2023, several UK bodies have even orchestrated steps *back*-wards, trumpeting the need for 'diversity of ideas',[197] openly-mocked Black research leaders,[198] and made standards *less* inclusive.[199] The chances of a Black student getting a good degree is 18.3%[200] lower than that of their white peers—if they survived the aggressions to begin with. 24% of non-white students have experienced racial harassment, and 20% physically attacked—in 2019, not 1919.[201] 'Why isn't my Professor Black?' remains a broken record.[202] That's why Jason Arday is an oddity. The sociologist has discussed the privileges and perils of being doubly-exotic, as the *youngest* Black professor—at the coveted University of Cambridge at that.[203] A Black person who has not just survived but thrived in a hostile system *must* have kin-ship with the octopus, which has lived for 230 million years against all odds. *Is Arday's neuro-divergence—being autistic and with global development delay meant that he was illiterate until aged 18*[204]*—a driver for Arday's* survival and *thrival?*

## *Intersectionality*

TP's third heart honours multi-faceted body-minds like Arday's, in which race, class, gender, and other characteristics 'intersect' and overlap with one another. Sophisticated compasses through which to discuss the spectra of diversity like 'intersectionality'[205] and QTIBIPOC (Queer, Trans and Intersex, Black, Indigenous, People of Colour)[206] are often a mouthful, *because* they're diametrically opposed to cartoonish name-calling like 'BAME' (Black, Asian and Minority Ethnic) that dominant society invents and instrumentalises to reduce, command and cattle-prod others. In centralising approaches historically side-lined, TP also teams up with other minoritised perspectives to address *all* social oppression,[207] towards *collective* liberation. That I've been able to break into and breathe within the hallowed halls of HE and creative arts has been a fluke. TP is my intervention to help ensure that those shut out like my dad will no longer be outliers or bit-actors, but pivotal *action-figures*.

## NINE C'S FOR ROUGH SEAS

TP's three hearts propel its nine arms. Each has a value that begins with the letter 'C', and embed further C's within them, several of which are recurrent themes in neuro-futurising leadership. Let's run through them, in no particular order.

### *Critical Creativity*

TP is a creative research-led leadership approach. It draws on and targets the creative arts, but invites other species and fields to run with, tweak, hack and/or explode into pieces/pixels. TP capitalises on the art school's tradition of autonomous thinking, but tempers its smugness with the 4C's of creativity[208] to include everyday creativity and scientific invention. TP also invites disciplines and fields beyond the creative arts — including leadership studies—as well as communities excluded from HE to make use of it. Picture diverse players, parties and platforms growing tentacles to span and cross-fertilise, to shake neo-classical columns and concrete erections of old and new universities, and co-produce mongrel outputs and outcomes that're more exciting than the sum of the parts. Moten and Harney's 'subversive intellectual' and 'critical academic' is to 'to be in but not of' the university,[209] but also to 'recognize it and be recognized by it'.[210] Clearly, this double-edged strategy demands *artfulness*. No wonder it isn't critical thinking, but *creative* thinking that's considered learning of the highest order.[211]

### *Collage*

TP cultivates novel, meaningful synergies between diverse and/or disconnected body-minds, subjects, disciplines, sectors, classes and cultures. Like the artistic technique of collage, TP is itself an assemblage, mixing and (mis-)matching together 'productive antagonisms', ADHD's big-picture thinking, the Pedagogy of the Oppressed,[212] STEM-to-STEAM[213] movements and more. Drawing on my 'triple-threat' status as an artist, teacher and reflective practitioner,[214] TP also seeks to dis-segregate departments, and holistically con-joins research, knowledge-exchange, enterprise, industry- and public-engagement with widening participation.

## Co-Creation

TP exchanges are multi-directional and anti-hierarchical. To banish the teacher as 'sage on stage', 'teaching' encompasses learning, un-learning and re-learning. Furthermore, following artist-academic-novelist James Elkin's call for creative research to dialogue with other disciplines, as well as HE at large,[215] TP rallies the creative arts to step *out and up*, to pro-actively model leadership within and beyond HE. Diverse learners collaborate at multiple registers, including decision-making, and not just for optics. Through (co-)leading multi-disciplinary, clumsy innovations to un-pick wicked challenges, TP critiques HE's relegation of creative arts as 'public engagement' or 'impact' to sex up 'serious' research. TP thus updates the UK HE mission of the study of art and design, which is to develop 'cognitive abilities related to the aesthetic, ethical and social contexts of human experience' that 'contributes to society, the economy and the environment, both in the present and for the future'.[216]

## Can-Do

TP nurtures resourcefulness and entrepreneurship to lead change within restrictive environments. This draws on the shape-shifting octopus, as well as those who have prospered despite having had their resources exploited, from the Tarahumara runners to Dalit comedians.

## Curiosity

Like octopuses and artists, TP learners are curious. Openness, risk-taking[217] and humility (which artists don't always possess) are integral in curiosity, as is being 'ill-disciplined'—meaning playful and inter-disciplinary—which can counter the university's project of turning 'insurgents into state agents.'[218]

## Community + Civic + (Under-)Commons

Curiosity and humility also drive TP's quest to make creative arts less insular, and more leaky, by way of growing tentacles to collaborate with and learn from other species and disciplines. This includes communities and learnings that are hard to reach the elephants of HE erase from their memory, canon and pearly gates. TP asks universities to not just dump the word 'civic' in their mission statements, but fulfil UNESCO's call for education as a 'public endeavour and a common good' by 2050.[219] As seen in #MagicCarpet, TP communities include not only students, but also peers, professors, professionals and proletarians, within and outside creative arts and the university system, in defiance of stiff silos that 'non-traditional' body-minds are pigeon-holed into. In nurturing anti-hierarchical, cross-generational, trans-disciplinary learning communities, TP adheres to hooks' call for the value of celebrating difference in communities that are 'beloved'. It further heeds hooks' call for 'communities of resistance' for democratic educators.[220] This chimes with Harney and Moten's famous 'Undercommons', namely 'maroon communities of composition teachers, mentorless graduate students, adjunct Marxist historians, out or queer management professors, state college ethnic studies departments, closed-down film programs, visa-expired Yemeni student newspaper editors, historically Black college sociologists, and feminist engineers'.[221]

## *(Cosmic) Circulation*

Just as neuro-diversity is a subset of bio-diversity,[222] TP seeks to 'give back' to society, nature and the Cosmos, prioritising zero waste in natural and human resources. Iterative and generative, TP enacts 'Look, Think, Act'[223] to incite and 'sustain reform in teaching/learning ecologies'. To enrich the 3R's of writing, arithmetic, reading, TP also up-cycles frameworks like 'Create, Circulate, Connect, Collaborate'[224] and rhizomatic learning.[225] It further acknowledges 'tentacular thinking',[226] but rejects both its arachnid and colonialist stances. Instead, I run with anti-colonial iterations that weaponise 'unruly tentacles'[227] as a 'new kind of party' to celebrate 'multiplicity in knowledge production', critique[228] 'contemporary neo-liberal academia which ossifies, fixes, and freezes feminist flows'. In activating 'troublesome unlearning' to confront learners' 'own privilege and situated knowledges',[229] TP amplifies that declaration that 'the party is over' for 'middle-aged, male, colonialist, violent knowledge'. It cosmically rejects the 'hierarchy of oppression'[230] and 'white supremacy in heels' and its 'defensiveness', 'racial slurs and doxing'.[231]

## *Curating Change Through Care and Compassion*

TP reminds us that 'curating' originated in care and healing.[232] The octopus' three hearts and its versatility inform TP as a leadership and learning model that's compassionate yet visionary. I seek to embody such a change-maker in what/how I teach/learn. Being an outsider gate-crashing into spaces previously shut to others like myself, I use my privilege to open new doors for yet others, and making learners leaders and (my) co-leaders.

### Courage

Teaching alone lacks the capacity for transformative change, but an embodied, 'teaching through the skin' can re-direct the 'knowledge object as future project' to envision alternative futures, argue Harney and Moten.[233] This is not for the faint-hearted. To be with-in yet critically-distant, your skin must grow thicker than the elephant's hide.

## A MASTERS TO KNOCK THE MASTER STORY OF 'LEADERSHIP'

TP underpins a Creative Arts Leadership (CAL) Masters (MA) programme that I was recruited to design as Programme Leader for a university in the north-west of UK.[234] My working definition of 'creative arts leadership' encompasses creative approaches to leadership, framing leadership as a creative practice, which has embedded within it assets of the creative arts. To counter the danger of the 'single story' of how leadership is taught, I curated the MA to celebrate different, more courageous and visionary 'leadership', with/for/by those from disadvantaged backgrounds to gen-erate personal, organisational, and/or social change. To address the cul-tural-ethnic homogeneity and falling international recruitment in the arts, I struck deals with the triple-accredited Business School. I fought to suc-cessfully raise the MA's budget to embed inclusive learning support. Through consultation with over 100 groups and individuals whose approaches fit my understanding of CAL, I seized gaps as opportunities. Synthesising scholarly with marketing data amid and in response to the double-pandemic, I married ambition with pragmatism.

Three years on, and after multiple panels, defence and re-writes, the MA was approved. Entangling imagination with business acumen, sustain-ability and decolonisation, it aims to equip and empower learners to explore and embody its possibilities of CAL, and was the first MA in the Faculty of Arts and Humanities to collaborate with the Business School. The multi-limbed elephant-cum-humanoid-slash-god Ganesha must have tossed out the rusty/dusty white elephants, and wielded his magic, as patron of arts and sciences, letters and learning, *as well as* deva of intellect and wisdom, and the god of beginnings. Modules include 'Curating

Change', a 'master-class that seeks to dismantle the masters' narrative on leadership' by centring neuro-diversity, kindness and LGBTQIA+ rights within leadership discourses—likely the world's only postgraduate leadership programme to do so. Other modules, like 'Business as Unusual' (on Personal and Global Leadership) and 'Social, Ethical & Environmental Enterprise for Leaders', complemented options offered by Sociology, History and Politics. Students refine their own learning and leadership through a 'Synthesis Project'. Through 'reverse mentoring', students engage with Personal Tutors and exchange skills and knowledges through their lived experiences.

The MA was praised for its captivating titles, as well as 'transdisciplinary', 'ambitious and progressive' contents. Its multiple 'areas of excellent practice' makes it a 'happy, hopeful, powerful, and impactful programme', while its ethos of 'learning from students' is 'progressive', presenting 'an opportunity to be something the university shouts about'. An industry leader agreed to co-teach, praising the MA for being 'bold' and 'unique'. It 'prepares students to think differently and to be quite creative. Importantly, Kai has also made it relevant to people from all backgrounds. You're taking creativity and the creative excellence in the art school, but blending it with that business know-how, rigour and business excellence.' Audio-visual assets I'd commissioned (Fig. 8.2[235]) brought the MA's ambitions to life, with a film reaching 350,000 hits.[236] With its heart(s) of neuro-divergence, decolonisation and intersectionality, and driven by Critical Creativity, Community, Co-Creation, Collage, Can-Do, (Cosmic) Circulation, Curiosity, Curating Change and Courage, could such a HE course become a location of possibility to co-create paradises? I can't wait for the MA to run in 2023 to find out.

PLAYING THE GAME TO TWEAK AND TRANSFORM THE GAME AND SYSTEM

Tentacular Pedagogy joins up my learnings and findings as a university teacher, consultant and developer for the past 25 years, and helps me to rally others for the next 25. Making futures is inseparable from making art and making change—as well as making knowledge, as hooks and Harney and Moten advise. Many in the business of teaching—and especially teaching the creative arts—do what we do, despite set-backs, because we believe that the creative arts, education, HE and the creative arts in HE, *can* be a force for good.[237] We tell ourselves that these remain productive path-ways

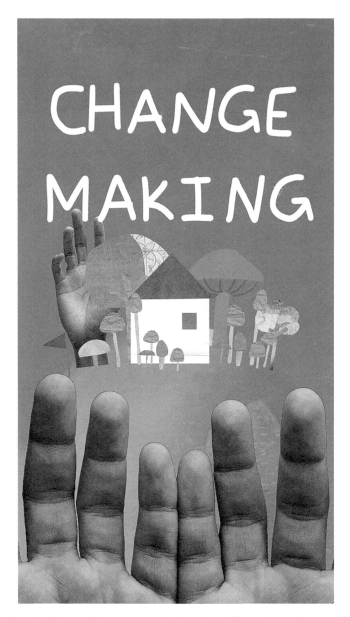

**Fig. 8.2**   A Different Masters House Built with Different Tool-kits

to do the work, and that change takes time. That's why we work with students, who will lead the following generations to ask better questions, and instigate protests and revolutions, even if they continue to get crushed. With multiple arms and centres, TP is my strategy 'to be in but not of' the university. Slipping through crevices to solidarise with underdogs and insurgents, TP seeks to de-stabilise harmful power structures, and build better futures.

*Teach transgressively. Learn and lead tentacular-ly. Ride the double storm, to drive sea-change within and beyond the university, to re-form better universes.*

# CHAPTER 9

# H: Make Head-Ways Hyper-Tactically

*To be 'in but not of' hostile systems, make your boundaries clear. Forget point-less power poses[238]—it's time to be hyper-tactical. Call the shots. Make head-ways. Thrive. Here's a summary of, plus web-links and QR codes for (Fig. 9.3), a triple-threat of my own protocols that outline the minimal require-ments of my work within systems* that render me odd *that I consider odd. Two of the three documents are work-in-progress, as I update them frequently. Referencing and extending guide-lines by other marginalised body-mind-worlds, the documents are specific to my circumstances. I invite the neuro-divergent and/or marginalised to apply and/or adapt them to fit your own personal and professional contexts.*

## ACCESSING KAI

This first document that you can customise for your arsenal is entitled 'Accessing Kai'. This is on my primary website www.kaisyngtan.com/art-ful.[239] This document ~~is my access requirements is my request for reasonable adjustments~~ outlines the terms and conditions that clients, commissioners and institutions must provide to *gain access to* myself. This includes remov-ing un-reasonable, harmful barriers in terms of neuro-divergence, disabil-ity, race and more that are in place. Firm and no-nonsense, but also making clear that the list is non-exhaustive or fixed (since circumstances change),

© The Author(s), under exclusive license to Springer Nature Switzerland AG 2024
K. S. Tan, *Neuro-Futurism and Re-Imagining Leadership*, Studies in Mobilities, Literature, and Culture, https://doi.org/10.1007/978-3-031-55377-6_9

the document is a one-stop place grounded in legal, practical, medical and scientific-data that dominant systems often demand. There are further links to explain ways to pronounce my exotic name, examples of good practice, payment guidelines, as well as links to legal frameworks, and additional tool-kits and references by others (Fig. 9.1).

This tool-kit provides individuals and collectives with a template to author, articulate and advocate for themselves. You can formalise your minimal standards to work in the form of friendly 'tips',[240] or as professional 'riders' (conditions or provisos common in theatre and performance[241]), or explicit clauses within contracts and so on. Such articulations are useful if employers or commissioners (repeatedly) ask you to explain your differences. Since dominant culture fetishes the written word, let's use written words that smell neutral and formal and can speak for you when spoken words trip you, and/or when you cannot separate the act of vocalising from your true being. Its affirmative tone avoids further stigmatisation that 'access riders' and 'disability passports' may unwittingly cause, and help ensure that the needs of the minoritised body-mind aren't (dis-) regarded as 'special' or 'surplus'.

The toolkit has been widely adapted and disseminated, and applauded as 'life-changing' and 'sector-leading' by both neuro-divergent and 'mainstream' individuals and organisations.

Just as how 'one does not need to be neuro-divergent and/or LGBTQ+' to engage with neuro-queering,[242] and how a social justice prism in mobilities should elevate 'understanding of what constitutes access, and barriers' for all, I want those who're 'standard', and therefore set or inform standards of dominant systems, to embed my guidelines into those 'standards'.

Don't forget to give full credit to this work, unless you wish to star in my other live document, 'How to Be a Polite Oppressor (Top Hits)'.

You're welcome.

## ANTI-RACISM PRODUCTIVE ANTAGONISMS

Next up is an article, entitled 'Towards and Anti-Racist PhD: Anti-Racism Productive Antagonisms'.[243] This is a set of practical steps to reduce ~~unconscious~~ race-based bias in a university process,

It was published in a special edition of a journal on the decolonisation of arts education edited by the US decolonial expert in design, Elizabeth (Dori) Tunstall, and is now open-access with no pay-wall. I've outlined behaviours for the PhD candidate, supervisor and external examiner during the viva voce examination. Applications can be made beyond HE, as I

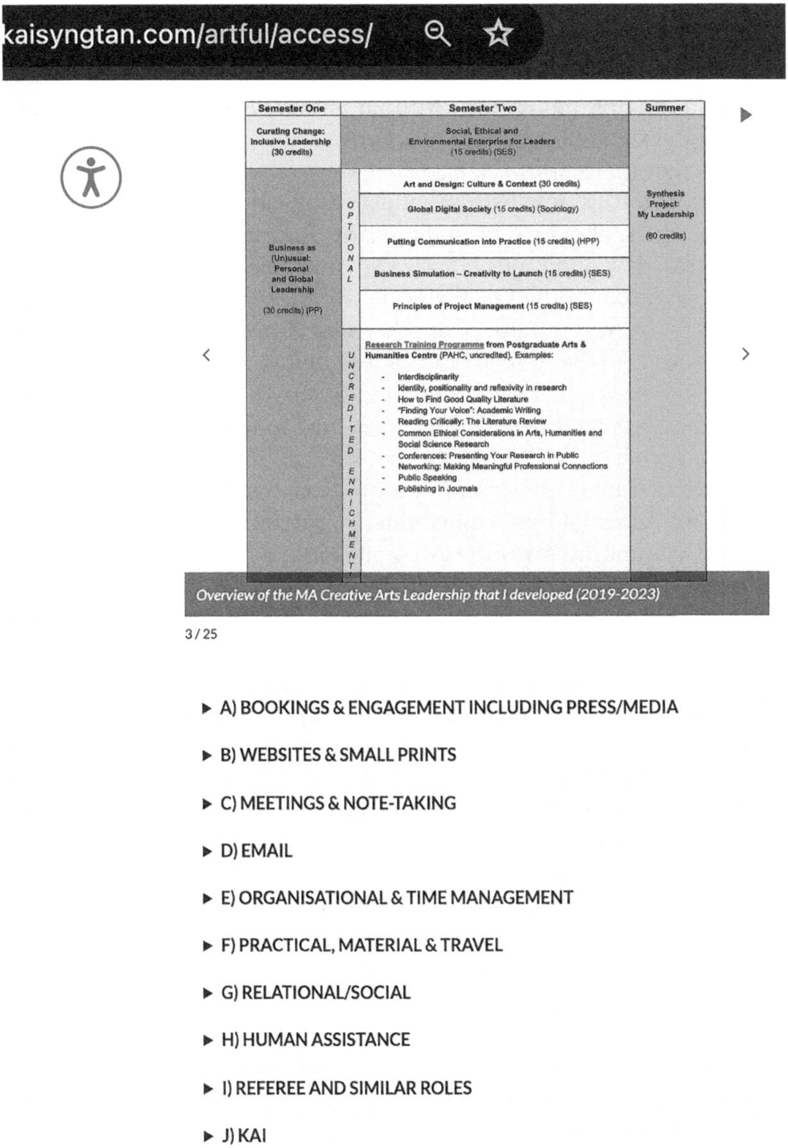

kaisyngtan.com/artful/access/

| Semester One | Semester Two | Summer |
|---|---|---|
| Curating Change: Inclusive Leadership (30 credits) | Social, Ethical and Environmental Enterprise for Leaders (15 credits) (SES) | Synthesis Project: My Leadership (60 credits) |
| Business as (Un)usual: Personal and Global Leadership (30 credits) (PP) | Art and Design: Culture & Context (30 credits) | |
| | Global Digital Society (15 credits) (Sociology) | |
| | Putting Communication into Practice (15 credits) (HPP) | |
| | Business Simulation – Creativity to Launch (15 credits) (SES) | |
| | Principles of Project Management (15 credits) (SES) | |

OPTIONAL UNCREDITED ENRICHMENT

Research Training Programme from Postgraduate Arts & Humanities Centre (PAHC, uncredited). Examples:

- Interdisciplinarity
- Identity, positionality and reflexivity in research
- How to Find Good Quality Literature
- "Finding Your Voice": Academic Writing
- Reading Critically: The Literature Review
- Common Ethical Considerations in Arts, Humanities and Social Science Research
- Conferences: Presenting Your Research in Public
- Networking: Making Meaningful Professional Connections
- Public Speaking
- Publishing in Journals

*Overview of the MA Creative Arts Leadership that I developed (2019-2023)*

3 / 25

▶ A) BOOKINGS & ENGAGEMENT INCLUDING PRESS/MEDIA

▶ B) WEBSITES & SMALL PRINTS

▶ C) MEETINGS & NOTE-TAKING

▶ D) EMAIL

▶ E) ORGANISATIONAL & TIME MANAGEMENT

▶ F) PRACTICAL, MATERIAL & TRAVEL

▶ G) RELATIONAL/SOCIAL

▶ H) HUMAN ASSISTANCE

▶ I) REFEREE AND SIMILAR ROLES

▶ J) KAI

**Fig. 9.1**   Accessing Kai

did for a masterclass for an all-white board of music organisation. The toolkit has also since been credited on listings by the Association for Art History and Clore Leadership programme. The recommendations can latch onto existing frameworks without any need to shift standard, or to go through extended processes of approval.

You've got no excuses.

My effort travels on a path-way opened by radical movers, shakers and culture workers, like the outstanding 'Anti-Racism Touring Rider', which was co-created by numerous UK theatre companies and generously-shared with 'everyone committed to change in the arts sector, irrespective of scale or remit'.[244] In Autumn 2023, another *tour de force* for the advancement of EDI is seen in the publication of a definitive guidance on advancing trans-inclusion, which was an outcome of surveying over 130 museums and heritage organisations.[245] I'm also excited to find out about the 'Anti-Racist Partnership Agreement' in the form of a visual contract that the Scotland-based neuro-divergent and queer lawyer-turned-artist Jack Tan has led on. Accessible yet embedding a profound understanding of the legal and cultural, this work was commissioned by a university, and co-developed with minoritised individuals and collectives through workshops over a period of time, and will be trailed and tested. Such a care-ful approach is a typical mode of operation of Tan's. Moving away from rendering relationships as 'punitive' and 'adversarial', Tan's visual cards focus on the relational. They draw on 'native, migrant or indigenous ways of doing partnership' which focus on stories, beliefs and values. By referencing 'pre-colonial and the global majority traditions of creating more-than-verbal legal documents', and embedding examples from the Incan 'Quipus', which were auditing or book-keeping records in the form of knotted cords, to Inuit 'song duels', Tan aims to 'move us to a beyond-colonial legal relationality'.[246]

What a gorgeous *gift* to us all.

## A BELOVED, BEYOND-COLONIAL RELATIONALITY

The third, on https://rb.gy/ujeuea, is all about love.[247]

My live document of guidelines towards inclusivity in meetings, workshops and so on is inspired by many excellent guidelines shared by minoritised communities during and since the double pandemic. I made sure that 'Islamophobia' and 'transphobia' were explicitly named as unwelcome, which were sometimes missing in other guidelines. Members of the Neurodiversity In/& Creative Research Network can co-edit it. The document sets up a framework to enable cross-fertilisations of diverse body-mind-worlds in a productively antagonistic way, to a 'beyond-colonial relationality'. Importantly, it foregrounds intersectionality and ways to avoid perpetuating often-hidden power dynamics and privileges (Fig. 9.2). It adheres to the three hearts and nine C's of Tentacular Pedagogy, and adds another C: **Consent**. Countering surveillance or voyeuristic gaze (such as since summer 2020 when global majority body-minds were systematically asked to re-count—and re-live—their trauma for the benefit of others' 'learning'), consent—rather than coercion and command—guides these guidelines.

I've shared these best practices with a Fortune 25 company (leading to their development of more inclusive workplace practices) and a Venice Film Festival award-winning VR gaming company (after rebuking them for exploiting the goodwill of neuro-divergent subjects for free advice). My tentacles even reached a senior staff of a Ministry of Defence, which wants to recruit neuro-divergent spies.

Could the a-typical James Bonds and Octo-Pussies hijack the mission of Ministries of Defence and avert wars?

In terms of next steps, I wish to by-pass platforms hosted by Big Tech, and migrate this onto alternative, open-access platforms. I'm also keen to embed learnings from exciting movers and shakers, such as the magnificent 'jellification process'[248] of Anjelica 'Jelly' Robinson. 'Miss Jelly', as she calls herself, runs a mobile hairdressing salon in the form of a van called 'Peace and Love Studios', in Houston, Texas, USA. She specialises in working with children who find 'traditional' salons challenging, including autistic children. 'All wiggle worms welcome!' she declares on her website. Her Instagram documents how she painstakingly works ~~around~~ *with* her clients, listening and collaborating directly with them in kind and powerful ways, sometimes dis-obeying the instructions of their informants (parents or carers). Miss Jelly has drawn on her own lived experience as a Black woman who'd overcome her own adversities to carve out a unique and indispensable role. The magic of 'jellification'—a relational, *love-led* exchange cultivated over time through reward, encouragement and the celebration of micro-wins—results in joy by parties involved. And fabulous hair.

All that said, come the day when hyper-tactics are extinct, because they've become 'standard', and spaces become ~~safe(r) more respectful accessible~~ joyous. As Harney and Moten clarify regarding the 'object' of abolition:

docs.google.com

**Neurodiversity In/& Creative Research Network**

**Community Guidelines for inclusivity**

Co-created live document. Last updated by Kai Syng Tan, August 2023

*The Neurodiversity In/And Creative Research Network is a growing, global alliance of 400+ neurodivergent innovators and allies. We encourage members' contribution and feedback to help us to make our space more inclusive for all. We have consulted guidelines co-created by other communities to share the following list of points. Adhering to the community agreements is a collective responsibility and everyone is individually responsible for checking their own behaviour. The list is not exhaustive, and this document is live. We welcome your feedback to improve these guidelines and to make our community safer. Email Kai kai@kaisyngtan.com*

1. **This is an inclusive space.** Ableism, Xenophobia, Homophobia, Racism, Sexism, Transphobia, Islamophobia, Anti-Semitism, Prejudice based on variations in our cognitive and communicative and behavioural setups, ability, Asylum status, Class, Ethnicity, Gender, Gender presentation, Nationality, Religion and/or any other forms of discriminatory language and/or behaviour is NOT welcome here.
2. **Power dynamics exist here in this space. Be aware of the space you take up. Be mindful of your privileges, assumptions and prejudices and allow space for *all* voices to participate. Be mindful of intersectionality, as well as to not fall into oppression olympics.**
3. **Respect everyone's identity and background, including pronouns and names.** Do not assume anyone's gender identity, sexual preference, survivor status, economic or immigration status, background, health, etc.
4. **Respect everyone's physical and emotional boundaries.** Check in before discussing topics that may be triggering (e.g. sexual abuse, racism, physical violence or encounters with police).
5. **Respect that there are varying opinions, beliefs, experiences and privileges as well as different ways of learning and interacting.**
6. **Do not judge, look down on or enter into competition with others.**
7. **Be responsible for your own actions and the language you use;** be aware that your actions and language have an effect on others, despite what your intentions may be.
8. **This is a safe space to test thoughts and ideas.** It's a space to maybe say things we've not said before. A space where we are not being judged, whilst trying not to judge ourselves. A space to be kind to ourselves and each other. A space for active listening - where we try to acknowledge and respond to things people have said, before changing the subject. Reminder: Challenge the idea, not the person.
9. **Take collective and individual responsibility for creating a safer space for everyone.**
10. **Work together to foster a spirit of mutual respect:** Listen to the wisdom everyone has to share.
11. **Be kind with your words.** Give generously to allow everyone time and space to speak and share their thoughts and ideas.
12. **Ask questions before assuming.** The best way to understand the choices, actions, or intentions of one another is by asking. 'Respect the person; challenge the behaviour.'
13. The rules still apply if you are under the influence of drugs and alcohol.
14. …..

**Fig. 9.2**   Cross-Fertilisations for a beyond-colonial relationality

Not so much the abolition of prisons but the abolition of a society that could have prisons, that could have slavery, that could have the wage, and therefore not abolition as the elimination of anything but abolition as the founding of a new society.[249]

## ACCESSING THE HYPER-TACTICS

Here are the three QR codes that you can scan to access the respective documents (Fig. 9.3).

## NEURO-FUTURISING LEADERSHIP

Let's re-assess our campaign and re-work our definition of 'leadership':

**Leadership: A beyond-colonial poly-centric and promiscuous politic, poetic, path-way and of change-, meaning-, knowledge-, and future-making.**

To think about and do leadership in this way is to neuro-futurise leadership. Neuro-futurising leadership draws on and shows (off) the value of neurodivergence, as well as body-mind-worlds that 'deviate' from the dominant. It dismantles the master's (sic) dangerous story of leadership, as an application of innovative, non-standard ways of processing, surviving and thriving in the world. Strategies include hacking normative systems, problem-solving with limited resources, 'big picture' thinking, risk-taking, joining up hidden dots, and making novel connections with new, squiggly tentacles.

Thus, instead of the individual, managerial or hierarchical, leadership encompasses the relational, organisational, socio-political, collective, ethical, aesthetic, environmental and more. Instead of providing answers, leadership is about asking better questions. Instead of quick-fixes and being fixed, leadership is mobile, multi-scalar, multi-dimensional, clumsy and always in the process of becoming.

With not one but three hearts, leadership is governed by love. Leadership en-tails learning, un-learning and re-learning. With nine head-feet, leadership celebrates 9C's: Critical Creativity; Co-Creation; Collage; Can-do; Curiosity; Community + (under-)Commons; (Cosmic) Circulation; Curating Change through Care; and Courage.

Leaders come from all walks, including ill-disciplined culture-workers, creative-activists, civic-animators, under-dogs, odd-balls, wiggle-worms and octo-pussies.

We're hyper-tactical, crafting and co-creating better strategies, stories, (infra-)structures and systems. It's about playing the game insofar

**Fig. 9.3**  QR codes for (left to right): 'Accessing Kai', 'Anti-Racism Productive Antagonisms', and 'A Beloved, Beyond-Colonial Relationality'

as to em-power us to tweak and transform the system, in order to profit people (of all walks and ilk), planet, play, and power-sharing, and to abolish prisons.

Diverse and divergent, de-colonised and neuro-queered, leadership comprises and nurtures artful, agile and a-typical approaches and actions.

Leadership is sweaty, embodied and visceral. Re-designing tables, flipping arm-chairs, constructing new monuments of workers, gate-crashing and re-writing canons demand wit, grit, guts, tears and toil.

And hope.

Long story short, leadership is a love-led Practice of Freedom.

*There's still a long way to go. Let's crack on.*

# CHAPTER 10

# E: Energise. Gently Anarchise

*To enquire into, energise and extend the possibilities of leadership, let's get hands on and get our hands dirty. Follow Lao Zi's 'dao', which captures both the literal and figurative meanings of the word 'way'. In a single stroke (or a few strokes), the pictogram of 'dao' con-joins the feet/action/practice with head/thinking/reflection, body, mind and place, road with method, course with discourse* (Figs. 10.1 and 10.2).

> *Run from place to place. Think on and with your feet. Embody the 'head-foot', like the cephalopod. Be a 'gently anarchist'.*[250] *Like a child, dis-trust words, the intellect and adults. Let your imagination run riot.*

---

The images are developed from those in: Tan. *Physical and Poetic Running.*

K. S. Tan, *Neuro-Futurism and Re-Imagining Leadership*, Studies in Mobilities, Literature, and Culture, https://doi.org/10.1007/978-3-031-55377-6_10

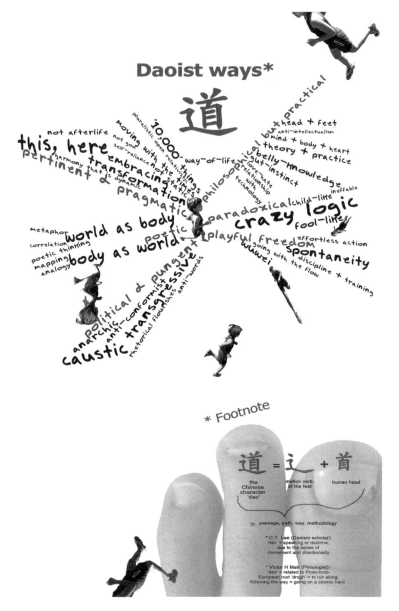

**Fig. 10.1** Daoist Head-Ways and Foot-Notes

# Iterative course-discourse

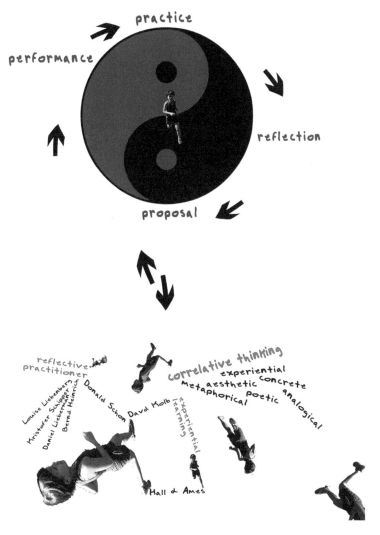

**Fig. 10.2**   Iterative Course-Discourse

CHAPTER 11

# R: Run New, Sweaty (Dis-)Courses

*Since leadership and (dis-)course both entail endurance, running and think-*
*ing, what could the child(-ren) of leadership and endurance running pro-*
*duce? Let's find out through a run-down of my '(Re-)Boot (Re-)Lay/Play*
*Running Camp'. Warning: It's no walk in the park. Let's get your* ~~hands~~
*feet dirty.*[251]

## WHAT ARE THE DRILLS, THRILLS AND CHILLS?

*What:* Run to the hills if you want a workshop that's run-of-the-mill.

*Where:* Our Camp occurs at your local e-waste dump, or any economy
treated like rubbish by the Global North, like Agbogbloshie in Ghana,
which has the world's largest mountain of electronic waste.

*Whom with/for/by:* The Re-Boot (Re-)Lay/Play Camp is a master-class
led by local artists and children. The kids call the dump home and office,
or have parents who are zero-hours workers of Big Tech and related firms
and cottage-industries. Our Camp is essential training for investors, entrepreneurs, engineers, law-makers, stock-holders and academics of/in technology and related fields. The more power you have, the higher premium
you pay, which will be distributed to the kids' families.

*How:* Here, three is the magic number. There's a relay of three 'legs'.
which can be repeated 3, 30 or 300 times across the camp, for 3, 30 or
300 breaths/days/generations. The rounds are:

*Leg I:*

- The masters mix and mis-match participants into small groups, for runs of 3, 30 or 300 minutes each time.
- Here's the catch: participants are tethered hand-in-hand, heartbeat-to-heartbeat, in groups of 3 or more members (example: Elon-Musk-child-composer). The more body-minds tethered, the more difficult it is to move, let alone move at speed and in sync, much less *run*.
- Catch 2 (*or 22*): Runners respond to the question, '**What is my dream for fairer AI for 2050**'? Each person shares their own definition of 'fairer' is subjective. No interruption allowed. Participants must hold the (s)pace for one another.
- Throughout, the child/artist will keep time and ask questions to clarify or provoke, and lead the direction—literally and otherwise—of the run.
- When time's up, participants go to the drawing board—literally and metaphorically—to draw *on* their discussions, to draw *up* three action points related to principles (moral/political/poetic), policies (company/national) or programmes (computer/educational) for fairer AI in the future, on cards made of re-cyclable materials.
- There will also be a short rest for participants to digest learnings, wipe off sweat, tears and fears. Those ill from the toxic fumes from the rubbish will receive first-aid treatment.

*Leg II:*

- Participants are re-mixed. New sets of tethered runners forage three most 'valuable' items from the rubbish mountain. How you define 'value'—monetary, laborious, moral—will be discussed and agreed upon. What you select and keep is negotiated. Again, the child/artist will chair the discourse.
- Following the run, the runners examine the trophies collected, from which they are to develop into a head-dress or foot-wear together, which will become a memento for the next generation about how rubbish ours have been.
- The group with the heaviest leftover by weight loses. Punishment: Repeat of Round II while wearing the sculptures created *and* carrying the leftover rubbish, and addressing the question '**What's the**

**weight—moral and more—of our rubbish?**' The definition of 'morality' will be discussed and agreed upon.

*Leg III:*

- 3 hours/days/months/years on, participants re-unite at the same e-waste dump. We get back to our original groupings with the same masters. Again, the child/artist, now older, will chair the discussion.
- Tethered and wearing our sculptures, participants re-visit the question, 'What is my dream for a fairer AI for 2050'?. We'll also review the cards made previously, and assess how the dump has changed. In addition, we'll evaluate how our personal and professional behaviours, thinking and actions have un-folded since, and how that matches or not our ambitions and/or principles/policies/programmes.
- Injuries—physical and otherwise—may be incurred because the e-waste mountain will have overflown and become more difficult to navigate, and the wearable items deteriorated with time. First aid treatment will be provided for the physical injuries. Runners attend to co-runners' other injuries and emotional labour.
- The relay ends in a collective ice-bath, during which participants ask: '**What's *my* next step towards a fairer AI for 2050?**'

## WHAT'S THE WORK-SHOP WORKING OUT?

Cross-generational, generative and iterative, the (Re-)Boot (Re-)Lay/Play Running Camp is a sweaty work-*shop* to work-*out* what a fairer AI-led future could/should look like.

The camp is my proposal for Big Tech's call for a 'sabbatical' from AI, which they declare in an open letter is a 'threat to humanity'.[252]

How dare you, Timnit Gebru responds. Aren't these tech-moguls the culprit and threat? The Ethiopia-born computer scientist explains that the small group of people with total power have been exploiting workers at the bottom of the tech food chain.[253]

Gebru's Distributed AI Research (DAIR) is her reply to the inequity of the information ecosystem. As a 'space for independent, community-rooted AI research, free from Big Tech's pervasive influence',[254] DAIR also silences armchair pontifications by academics enjoying an 'AI summer'. Gebru knows. She was fired from Google as co-lead of its Ethical AI team—and her story echoes those by other minoritised body-minds kicked about/out by the 1% firms, which are likely only 1% of many more tragic stories that remain hidden/ignored/erased.[255]

Running with the Fortune's World's 50 Greatest Leader—whose child-like voice belies her courage that fires what a minoritised whistle-blower describes as 'slingshots' at Silicon Valley's 'Goliath'[256]—the camp is my sling-shot to hit back at the Big Bullies, via running, *artfully*.

## WHAT'S RUNNING ARTFULLY TO DO WITH LEADERSHIP?

Running artfully can animate discourse about running and leadership. it's also an energising change-making strategy.

To begin with, the essence of leadership—travelling, endurance and guidance—is embodied in the why and how humans run, which is nothing short of *artful*.[257] Since *Homo erectus* began running two million years ago to hunt antelopes, their descendants, the *Homo sapiens*, haven't stopped running. We're tailor-made in body-mind to endure running long distances, equipped with ligaments specific for trotting, sweat pores and pain-killing hormones. Apart from being able to recognise and remember the 6-hour treks, we're also fuelled by long-range vision to take the first steps in the first place.

This intoxicating cock-tail of grit, wit, salt and hope has kept humans running. Running booms have been reported whenever things get rough, including during the Great Depression, post 911 and as an accessible exercise during the Covid-19 lockdowns.[258] Beyond physical and mental health, running also promotes social mobility (think foot messengers in the pre-Amazon days, whose reliability enabled them to access restricted domains, and East African villagers who run away from poverty to win marathons), and even proximity to higher planes (think 'marathon monks' in Kyoto, and why long slow distance is seductively-abbreviated as 'LSD').

Clearly, running is a vehicle for not just as a mode of transportation but *transformation*.

## WHAT'S RUNNING ARTFULLY AS A LEADERSHIP STRATEGY TO DO WITH THE ARTS?

Running as a transformative process is captured by our arts and culture too.

From mythological action figures (Greece's 500 BC Pheidippides) to songs (Velvet Underground's *Run Run Run*) films (any number of apocalyptic Zombie films), it's clear that running is pivotal for survival and *thriving.*

Running has an affinity with the written word. There are no fewer than 81 idiomatic phrases like 'run amok' in the English. Running is also a run-ning motif across fiction and non-fiction canons alike. The usual suspects like *The Loneliness of the Long Distance Runner* by the apt-ly named Alan Sillitoe or *What I Talk About When I Talk About Running* by Haruki Murakami aside, there's *Raymond's Run* (1971) by a friend of Octavia Butler, author-filmmaker-teacher Toni Cade Bambara (1939–1995).[259] The short story stars a young heroine Squeaky, whose fighting-talk goes:

> And if things get too rough, I run. And as anybody can tell you, I'm the fastest thing on two feet. I never walk if I can trot [...] I'm ready to fight, cause like I said I don't feature a whole lot of chit-chat, I much prefer to just knock you down right from the jump and save everybody a lotta pre-cious time.

Squeaky isn't just a talented distance runner. She is Black, and is a carer for her disabled brother Raymond. Running is her sling-shot and two fingers—plus ten toes—to the un-caring, un-moving/un-moved white-supremacist establishment. Squeaky's story speaks loudly about how run-ning *artfully* is about shaking things up, moving forward, and leading new (dis-)courses of action.

## How Can Running Artfully Transform the (Dis-)Course of Running?

When I began to collide running with art, I found myself informing—and helping to *re-form*—how running has been understood.

As a kid locked in poverty on a land-starved island-city-state, I'd run about in the neighbourhood, and run after school busses. But when teach-ers and adults shouted 'Stop running! Walk! It's for your own safety!', I began to loathe running, adults, adulthood, and school.

In 2009, I ran away from home for good. I re-learnt to run, as a cheaper way to spend my energy. By 2013, I'd wobbled across 10,000 miles and 7 marathons, and written-up (or down) a 100,000-word thesis around what I'd termed 'trans-running', under-scoring running's transgressive and transversal possibilities. To counter the joy-lessness of the ivory tower, I took my seminars outdoors with 'running-discourse'.[260] To placate Chairs whose sedentariness and shortage of joyful hormones made them un-fit arm-chair critics, I devised 'speed-play-drift'. To mock 'dick-lit' written by academics who humble-brag about their heroic runs and run-ins with wolves/'primitives' in 'wild' sites to conquer nature/own demons/others or advance the frontiers of civilisation and knowledge, I introduced 'body as a sight/site of protest' as a sweaty, feminist personal-political strategy to counter bound-feet—historical and metaphorical—that immobilised.[261] To reject the competitive and ableist aspects of running, I re-configured the runner's high as a creative thinking strategy. To chide how those with seats at the table pretend that words are neutral, truth-bearing vehicles,[262] I punctuated my writing with running-related idioms. To protest the physical act of writing, I starred as 'Kaidie'—Kai dies, *geddit?*—in a 1000-day run, which ends in her death once she locates the Meaning of Life. I interacted with 1.3 million visitors to my blog. Responding to what sci-fi author William Gibson termed as the 'consensual hallucination' of the internet,[263] I high-lighted how the 'digital' pointed to fingers and toes too, not just computers, and activated the hyphen to dove-tail binaries like the body-mind, virtual-physical, and more (Fig. 11.1[264]), which has since further joined forces with my ribbons, tentacles and more.

Once I grew sick of conferences by talkers-walkers without bite or brio, and tired of holding my breath for running-focused ones, I began to run my own activities.[265] Curating and conversing with people from all walks, we scrutinised running beyond the natural or sport sciences. Through the transdisciplinary RUN! RUN! RUN! Biennale (#r3fest, 2014–2018),[266] I introduced over 100 projects, papers, propositions, from more than 50 academic, cultural, as well as third sector organisations like the Sri Chimnoy Centre (which relates running with mediation). By 2016, I'd begun to crumble the knowledge monopoly held by fit—meaning athletic, *not* attractive—geographers whom I'd termed MAMIRA (middle-aged men in running shorts in academia, after the infamous middle-aged male cyclists in Lycra or MAMMIL). I'd nearly walked out of the BBC studios when one MAMIRA and fellow guest on a radio programme proudly shared his 'fantasy' about being an 'outsider' while running.[267] He had also used his many high-profile platforms to criticise 'new-comers' who were 'diluting' running by being slow or sloppy. To yell back, I rallied more such im-pure inter-lopers. My party-poopers included Welsh theatre-maker Eddie Ladd, Mexican psychologist-slash-digital-humanities scholar Elisa Hererra Altamirano, and Free to Run, a group for female runners in conflict zones like Afghanistan. We discussed how migrant, aged,

**Fig. 11.1** Monster-Mapping Trans-Running

neuro-divergent and disabled body-minds activate running as motif, metaphor, medium and method.[268] By 2018, multiple PhDs, papers and artworks were also born, with methods like 'joghraphy', 'running adrift', 'continuum bodycity' and 'landscapism', and figures like the 'artistlete' shared. #r3fest 'alumni' went on to birth yet other efforts, like the RUN! RUN! RUN! International Body for Running and the Running Cultures Research Group.[269]

Meanwhile, my solo explorations made head-ways too. *Anti-adult Run*[270] premiered in Kuopio, Finland. Capitalising on how '*anti*' refers to 'against' in the English, and, beautifully, 'gift' in the Finnish languages, this was an intervention developed with local children (aged 7–14), whom I put in charge of leading master-classes to teach adults (top age: 84) the *gifts* of giggling and unadulterated fun through running, tripping and making a fool of ourselves in public. *Anti-adult Run* expresses Lao Zi's advice to be child-like, in order to defy the hypocrisy of grown-ups, and echoes how Bambara's young protagonist Squeaky calls out on the 'fraudulent postulates of an anxiety-stricken white supremacist culture' through a 'community-specific, self-confident, passionate, high-energy, vernacular language of resistance'.[271] Against reproduction for 10,000 reasons, I was/am allergic to children, but the mini-masters' forth-rightness—so unlike the confusing ways of adults—tripped me.

Then, there was *Hand-in-Hand*. Here, body-minds are tethered together by a red ribbon, and share their dreams for the future while running together. Responding to the deep fissures of divide in the UK as expressed by the referendum vote to leave Europe (2016), and inspired by how blind runners collaborate with sighted guides, *Hand-in-Hand* is an exercise in empathy, trust and solidarity. I'd designed the ribbon after reading about how migrants in a Welsh facility had to wear red wrist-bands to gain access to food. Multiple iterations have since been explored, including with nurses in Manchester, children in Grenoble, as well as people seeking asylum in London.

When the pandemic struck, I gathered artists to co-found the Running Artfully Network.[272] RAN (*geddit?*) champions art-inspired running and running-inspired art to explore health, climate and social justice. To strengthen its pipe-line, RAN's core curatorial team includes a Gen Z-er, and we distributed bursaries to minoritised efforts, including Run the World, a theatre-cum-health initiative for migrant women.

## HOW CAN RUNNING ARTFULLY TRANSFORM
## THE (DIS-)COURSE OF LEADERSHIP?

Collectively, these endeavours have updated 'running studies' from a dis-course centred around professional athletic bodies when first proposed by a geographer, into a critical and creative practice-related discourse that ~~cuts~~ *connects* across disciplines. My solo and curatorial efforts have made me 'the person who has done the most', and the *de facto* lead of a more creative, inclusive leg of running studies.[273] This could be termed 'running artfully studies'. How #r3fest precipitated RAN, and how both are engendering exponential impacts, affirm the leadership value of running artfully, and shows how it can animate how we study 'leadership'.

This is timely. I'd begun using the term 'running artfully' in 2018, after mobilities scholar Monika Büscher termed my efforts as such[274] in a hand-written letter to me, where she also shared that she'd picked up running. Before that, Büscher'd already warned that, to survive a 'ruined utopia', creative approaches to mobilities can 'enable new response-abilities', a term she coins to cluster experiments.[275] To raise our game, we must thus up our pace. Running artfully—where artists are leaders of (dis-)courses through art that uses running and/or running that incorporates running—can be a step forward. 'Good art must sweat', declares[276] Dutch-Moroccan author-marathoner Abdelkader Benali, and running 'makes the heart skip', claims Chinese-French artist-athlete Zejun Yao,[277] both #r3fest and RAN alumni. Applying Chinese-Daoist body-mind-place poetics, running artfully subverts passive or Cartesian set-ups, and runs up-stream against mobilities' (macho) fixation with auto-mobility. Surely sweat, grit and heart-beats outwit cars in involving 'complex social, spatial and cul-tural interrelations', and can create 'dreamscapes' that 'rearrange socialities'[278]?

Just ask Kaidie.

Running artfully as a leadership discourse can also drive home messages about human-environment precarity. When a RAN artist ran along River Thames, I'd highlighted how the 240 km course will be shorter soon, when our rivers dry up.[279] Such an effort comes hot on the heels of that like the 7200 km relay from Scotland to Egypt *Running Out of Time* dur-ing UN climate change conference COP 27, as well as pays homage to the tradition of durational performance, like US-Vietnamese-Japanese artist Jun Nguyen Hastushiba's ongoing run since 2011 equivalent to the diam-eter of the earth. For those who'd forgotten that 3% of greenhouse emissions is by IT, running artfully can connect our digital-carbon foot-prints too.

To foster different leadership and leg-acies, I stepped aside from RAN in 2023. Those with sturdier knees are carrying (on) with the relay (baton) and exploring new horizons. I've helped to name the RAN workshop *Running Towards a Sustainable Future, and not Running Away from a House on Fire.*[280] I'm heartened to see new stories and (dis-)courses. Just as we've gotten sick of stunts by privileged body-minds like Extinction Rebellion, we're getting fed-up with macho, navel-gazing approaches to endurance-running, and are instead exploring ways to make spaces more accessible for diverse body-minds.

## HOW CAN RUNNING ARTFULLY HELP BUILD NEW HOUSES?

Which brings us back to our (Re-)Boot (Re-)Lay/Play Running Camp.

Up-cycling both *#antiadultrun* and *Hand-in-Hand* to engage with climate- and tech-justice, my message was not just about *not* running away from our house that's on fire, as per Thunberg's plea. My 'house' also references that of Audre Lorde's. I argued that fire-fighting or only think-ing about 'sustainability' aren't enough. Instead, we must be more active, pro-active, intra-active and *hyper*-active, to co-create *better* houses—*sans* walls, ceilings, labyrinths, gates or prisons, but mobile, modular, fluid, with tentacles. Running artfully can be part of that *new* tools to build such new houses.

In particular, running artfully heartily can offer exciting path-ways to discuss more productive ways to shake and wake us up from the non-consensual hallucination. This is urgent, because today 'hallucination' encompasses how AI cooks up 'flat out lies' and mis-information.[281] Still, even as AI magics artworks and threaten artists' livelihoods, AI can't sweat. Like the Tin Man in *Wizard of Oz*, AI has no heart either.

Unlike DAIR or Squeaky.

Speaking truth to power, Squeaky is 'the only one talking in this ventriloquist-dummy routine', despite—or *because*—she's a child. Like the pre-adolescent, the story of Raymond's Run seems not-yet-formed, and seem 'on-the-way-to-somewhere' texts, although 'Bambara's children arguably have essential lessons to teach their elders, if they listen well'.[282] As Bambara herself states, such characters are 'tough but compassionate', and 'triumphant in [their] survival[283]'. Squeaky is our mascot for running artfully as a leadership approach.

To the question *'what does leadership smell and taste like'?*, Squeaky would likely yell back, in her more-than-verbal community-specific, self-confident, passionate, high-energy, vernacular language of resistance:

*Salty. Sweaty. Gritty. Gutsy. Bloody. Bloody brilliant.*

*Trot, don't walk. Primal yet far-sighted, responsive and grounded, yet with heads in the skies,* running artfully can *(re-)hydrate (dis-)courses. Let's run riot!*

# CHAPTER 12

# W: Wake & Shake off Smoke-Screens

*'Stay woke', said Blues musician Lead Belly aka* Huddie William Ledbetter, *when commenting on 'Scottsboro Boys'.*[284] *His 1938 protest song describes the 1931 case of nine Black teenagers in Scottsboro, Arkansas who were accused of raping two white women (Figs. 12.1 and 12.2*[285]*). 'Stay woke', echo the killer whales, who're indignant that, nearly a hundred years on, nothing has changed.*

*Roused from being beached at an e-waste dump, the killer whales rise up, shaking their fists, biting back, protesting, wailing: 'Stop the killing. Don't consent to the hallucination. Wake and shake off the smoke-screens. Can't technology augment humanity? Won't you see with your heart?'*

© The Author(s), under exclusive license to Springer Nature
Switzerland AG 2024
K. S. Tan, *Neuro-Futurism and Re-Imagining Leadership,*
Studies in Mobilities, Literature, and Culture,
https://doi.org/10.1007/978-3-031-55377-6_12

**Fig. 12.1**    Augment Reality. Stay Woke

**Fig. 12.2**   Make Your Heart Sore-Soar

# CHAPTER 13

# Z: Zing & Sting Leadership

*Since leadership sucks, can neuro-queering, mobilities, justice and artfulness lend a hand (or tentacles), to add zing, sting and spring into its steps? Let's scuttle across—and make novel links between—fields that don't usually collide with leadership studies, and pit themes and methods against one other, to reveal (under-)common grounds, gaps and opportunities. I'll introduce new terms by dove-tailing terms together, too, like how Germans tape-worm theirs together. My entries are in the form of a mini A–Z. A few alphabets are clustered together, and/or have more than one entry each, although I'll present the alphabets in the normative order. You're welcome. My kindness is to incentivise you to fill in certain entries. Show me and show off what you've learnt so far, as we're mid-way through our adventure.*

## A, S: AUTHENTICITY; *SUCCESSION* (AND SUCCESSORS)

Since Sun Zi's *The Art of War* and Plato's *Republic* over 2500 years ago, as many schools of theories, methods, styles, (dis-)courses of 'leadership' have emerged, across disciplines from anthropology, management and behavioural science to (pop-)psychology and more. From *King Lear* to its successor, the TV series *Succession,* it's also clear that humans are obsessed

© The Author(s), under exclusive license to Springer Nature Switzerland AG 2024
K. S. Tan, *Neuro-Futurism and Re-Imagining Leadership*, Studies in Mobilities, Literature, and Culture, https://doi.org/10.1007/978-3-031-55377-6_13

with the drama and politicking that comes with Machiavellian figures. This obsession is rivalled by that of leadership scholars regarding question-naires and surveys, which could explain why they have largely ignored the wealth of materials in fiction.

While the more interesting scholars attest that the party for macho, violent modes of leadership is over, and have proposed alternatives that claim to be more authentic, transformational or both, the regime bots of intellectually-imperialist ways—the Master/hero/Great Man ruling over slave/subordinates/followers championed by the pro-slavery and pro-eugenics (like University College London poster-boy Thomas Galton)—still linger.

The competition for power in leadership studies makes the plot thicker than that of *Lear* and *Succession* combined. Take Authentic Leadership, which purports that the solution to the troubled world and 'loss of faith in previous forms of leadership' is to be true to one self.[286] Another con-tender to the throne goes one up by calling itself Authentic *Transformational* Leadership, and mud-slings others like Transformational Leadership as 'counterfeit', swearing by Western moral and ethical values and processes.[287]

*How authentic, transformational or ethical can discussions be, if they remain Euro-centric, ignore fiction, and/or fail to explore beyond archetypes like Lear? Shouldn't attention be paid to problematise the nature of the 'true self', particularly vis-à-vis minoritised body-minds[288]?*

## B, L: BUTT-LICKING

*Complete the following:*
Butt-licking,          like          brown-nosing,          refers to ....................................... ...... .. Especially since Summer 2020, those who're keen to position themselves as 'allies' curry-favour minori-tised movers and shakers, who can swat them off by ... ... .................... .................... ............

## C, W: Critical-Historical Approaches; World-(re-)Building

Critical-historical approaches like Critical Leadership Studies (CLS) inter-rogate traditional frameworks like leader–follower binary/dualism, by exposing the 'dark sides' of the cult of the individual leader, and exploring leadership within informal organisations and more.[289] Anarchist groups, for instance, eschew leaders and hierarchies, and instead emphasise collective meaning-making by 'a range of leadership actors'.[290] These groups are 'prefigurative', in that in seeking to abolish some or all forms of hierarchy in society, they also model how an alternative democracy can work in the future society. They're 'building a new world in the shell of the old'.

*What if CLS joins forces with other critical-historical approaches that also* build new worlds in the shell of the old, *like mobilities and neuro-queering? What about what might be termed 'critical leadership practices' happening at grass-roots level by those who are 'different' and 'see things differently' (Fig. 13.1[292])?*

## E: Equity, Emancipation, Excuses and Exercises to Heal

If #BlackLivesMatter (anti-racism)—plus #MeToo #TimesUp (anti-misogyny), as well as #WeShallNotBeMoved (anti-ableism)—haven't made it clear that equity must be prioritised in leadership, there's Brexit and economic and environmental crises, which the World Economic Forum has attributed to the 'failure of leadership'.[292] Nonetheless, leadership studies is far from emancipated from its shackles, continuing to marginalise radical thought-leaders like bell hooks, including her powerful insights on the margins and change-making.

*On the left margin below, you'll find a handful of what the poet has said about the margin as space for radical transformation.[293] Next, read the entries 'M' and 'J' for mobilities studies and justice. On the right side, discuss the resistance of leadership studies and mobilities justice to transformation and the pleasure and power of knowing.*

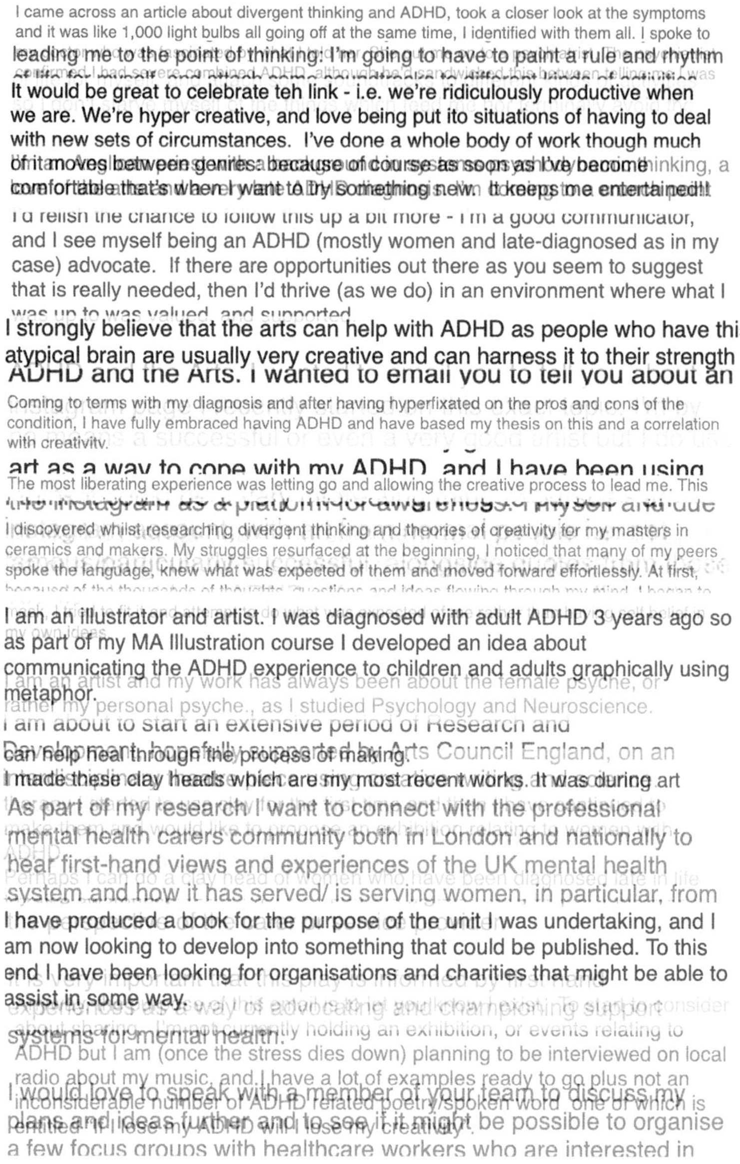

I came across an article about divergent thinking and ADHD, took a closer look at the symptoms and it was like 1,000 light bulbs all going off at the same time, I identified with them all. I spoke to leading me to the point of thinking: I'm going to have to paint a rule and rhythm

It would be great to celebrate teh link - i.e. we're ridiculously productive when we are. We're hyper creative, and love being put ito situations of having to deal with new sets of circumstances.  I've done a whole body of work though much of it moves between genres. because of course as soon as I've become thinking, a comfortable that's when I want to try something new.  to keeps me entertained!

I'd relish the chance to follow this up a bit more - I'm a good communicator, and I see myself being an ADHD (mostly women and late-diagnosed as in my case) advocate.  If there are opportunities out there as you seem to suggest that is really needed, then I'd thrive (as we do) in an environment where what I was up to was valued, and supported

I strongly believe that the arts can help with ADHD as people who have this atypical brain are usually very creative and can harness it to their strength ADHD and the Arts.  I wanted to email you to tell you about an

Coming to terms with my diagnosis and after having hyperfixated on the pros and cons of the condition, I have fully embraced having ADHD and have based my thesis on this and a correlation with creativity.

art as a way to cope with my ADHD, and I have been using The most liberating experience was letting go and allowing the creative process to lead me. This

I discovered whilst researching divergent thinking and theories of creativity for my masters in ceramics and makers. My struggles resurfaced at the beginning, I noticed that many of my peers spoke the language, knew what was expected of them and moved forward effortlessly. At first,

I am an illustrator and artist.  I was diagnosed with adult ADHD 3 years ago so as part of my MA Illustration course I developed an idea about communicating the ADHD experience to children and adults graphically using metaphor.

I am about to start an extensive period of Research and

can help heal through the process of making Arts Council England, on an I made these clay heads which are my most recent works. It was during art As part of my research I want to connect with the professional mental health carers community both in London and nationally to hear first-hand views and experiences of the UK mental health system and how it has served/ is serving women, in particular, from I have produced a book for the purpose of the unit I was undertaking, and I am now looking to develop into something that could be published. To this end I have been looking for organisations and charities that might be able to assist in some way.

systems for mental health. holding an exhibition, or events relating to ADHD but I am (once the stress dies down) planning to be interviewed on local radio about my music, and I have a lot of examples ready to go plus not an I would love to speak with a member of your team to discuss my plans and ideas further and to see if it might be possible to organise a few focus groups with healthcare workers who are interested in

**Fig. 13.1**    Critical Leadership Practice and World-(Re-)Building

| *hooks on the margin* | *Excuses for leadership studies* | *Excuses for mobilities justice* |
| --- | --- | --- |
| 'Within complex and ever shifting realms of power relations do we position ourselves on the side of colonising mentality?' 'Or do we continue to stand in political resistance with the oppressed, ready to offer our ways of seeing and theorising, of making culture towards that revolutionary effort which seeks to create space where there is unlimited access to the pleasure and power of knowing, where transformation is possible?' 'This choice […] shapes and determines our response to existing cultural practice and our capacity to envision new, alternative, oppositional aesthetic acts'. | | |

## F, Y: FLIP-FLOPPING/YIN-YANG-ING

Stories in leadership remain 'largely told from the perspective of straight, white men' who 'assume that straight, white manness is the norm'.[294] When a man expresses his 'true self', it'll be 'acceptable—even laudable', while expressing one's 'true self' or 'authenticity' is a 'luxury' that the minoritised can 'often ill afford'.[295]

This entry gathers a few inter-related code-switching strategies that the minoritised body-mind can swiftly 'flip-flop' between when moving within complex and ever-shifting realms of power relations. Methods including those inspired by autism research[296] and octopuses. In agilely 'Yin-Yang-ing' between different identities, you send confusing signals and grey existing boundaries. By cunningly calibrating attention (own, others') and expectations (own, others') when you're hyper-visible, invisible *and/or both*, you can dodge being pigeon-holed, and stay *un-fixed* in location/situation/identities, be un-fixable, and divert others' un-due fixation on you. *Drawing on your lived experience, fill in the blanks:*

| Strategy | Definition |
| --- | --- |
| Compensating | Behavioural modifications to 'blend in' or appear neuro-typical (dressing like others; suppressing repetitive behaviours, or avoiding taxing social events). |
| Passing | Blending in enabled by compensation. |
| Thick-skinning | Capitalising on the inability to read social cues well to gain immunity from bullying and trolling. |
| Camouflaging | Disguising to avoid detection. |

(*continued*)

(continued)

| Strategy | Definition |
|---|---|
| Foot-in-mouthing | .... ...... ........ |
| Masking/copy-catting | Suppression of traits that make you different by regulating those behaviours (like hiding controversial opinions) and increasing behaviours thought to be desirable, including by copying others (like smiling or laughing at what appears to be a joke). |
| Wearing wolf/sheep-clothing | ... ... ...... .................... ........................ ...... |

## G: Goat (Escaped)

*Complete the following:*
Instead of being a scape-goat, an **escaped goating** is a leadership strategy that involves ...... ........ ... ........ ........ and relates to GOAT (Greatest of All Time) by ........... ............. ................. ...... ..........

## H, M: Hyper-activity; Mobilities

*Since all disciplines have blind-spots, could hyper-activity, leadership and mobilities work together to reveal new insights about the power dynamics of difference? To think outside the pill-box, use the notes below to put forward a case.*

- **Hyper-activity and difference:** Hyper-activity is the eponymous 'H' in ADHD or Attention Deficit Hyper-activity Disorder. Its restlessness as a concept and practice presents exciting possibilities.[297] Classified as a 'mental disorder' since 1968, features associated with hyper-activity include running about, being 'on the go' as if 'driven by motor', 'butting into' conversations. When not spoken ill of, mocked or dismissed, associated with crime, bad parenting or Big Pharma, ADHD is often hidden from public discourse and imagination altogether.[298] Affecting over 3% adults worldwide, undiagnosed ADHD costs the UK billions of pounds annually, causing or exacerbating anxiety, depression and more, which are, in turn, contributing to the ongoing global mental health crisis.
- **ADHD and leadership:** Features like 'risk-taking', 'courage', 'extraordinary creativity and energy', 'out-of-the-box thinking', 'knowledge-craving', 'above-average openness to experience' and

'giftedness' are other hardly-discussed features of ADHD.[299] These overlap with descriptors around innovation and leadership, and reinforce the hypothesis on how distractibility and hyper-activity were vital for early human's survival.[300] Today, ADHD in action is seen in comedy (UK-Indian comedian Joshua Bethania), sport (Olympian Simone Biles) and more.

- **Hyper-activity and mobilities:** Hyper-activity and mobilities should be birds of a feather that flock together—in theory. That mobilities studies is 'expanded and energetic',[301] and concerned with not just people and goods but *ideas,* parallel hyper-activity's cease-lessness of mental activity. As a multi-faceted enquiry with an affinity for butting into different topics, mobilities mirrors hyper-activity's agility, curiosity and tentacular nature, too. In particular, creative mobilities' propensity for 'resolute experimentation', 'complexity' and 'promiscuity'[302] seems to be a swipe right to both hyper-activity and leadership. *Doesn't mobilities research seem to both exemplify and foster hyper-activity—or is it the other way around?*

- **Moving forward together?** *Can the framework of leadership as a process be the sweet spot where fruitful entanglements between hyper-activity, mobilities, and leadership occur?* Leadership as a process investigates the 'wider picture' of leadership, i.e., the 'integrated system' of complex, ongoing, overlapping inter-connected series of places and technologies events, systems, stories and spaces[303]—which can include hyper-activity and mobilities. The big-picture approach echoes the ADHD'ers big-picture thinking too. Furthermore, instead of discrete entities, or an obsession in individuals, traits or behaviours, leadership as a process focuses on 'movement, flow, interaction and collective activity', plus language and sound. These features are usually neglected in leadership studies and, as descriptors, they also fit mobilities research. This emerging approach to leadership advances the understanding of 'leadership's collective and open-ended character'—so too, will its enmeshing and integration with ADHD and mobilities research.

## I, X: INFLUENCER/INFLUENZA, X-FACTOR

*Complete the following statements.*

Studying what makes influenzas tick—their 'X-factor' to make them highly-contagious as viral infections—can shed light about how we understand influence and the performance of power, by … … … … …

# J: JUSTICE?

Despite sharing socio-constructivist roots with CLS, 'leadership' seems ignored in mobilities research. Instead, perhaps similar to how future studies had been 'rejected' in the social sciences,[304] as well as how mobilities is resisted in literary studies and, by extension, the arts and humanities,[305] leadership seems derided as a neo-liberalist construct. After all, mobilities was founded as a 'critique of capitalism', and concerns 'social justice, social change and social futures', argues mobilities' co-founder Mimi Sheller.[306]

Its noble intentions aside, mobilities remain fraught with 'unevenness' and 'inequities'. That was why Sheller came up with 'mobility justice', which spot-lights 'spatial restrictions on the mobility of wheelchair-users, or the limited mobility of racialized minorities under police regimes of white supremacy, or the constrained mobility of women under patriarchal systems of violent domination, or of sexual minorities under heteronormative regimes', and more.

And despite mobilities' affinity for turns—spatial, relational, material and more—mobilities have ignored the 'neuro-turn' in the 1990s, as well as the current neuro-diversity bandwagon.

*If mobilities research is 'a new way of approaching social research, social theory, and social agency',[307] isn't it time to respond to invitations to explore neurodiversity and neurodivergence as a creative mobilities discourse[308]? Wouldn't the failure to do so risk 'presuming neurotypicality',[309] and perpetuating—not reducing—injustices within mobilities research? If a-typical cognitive modes occur in one in every seven humans, and over 1.4 billion humans will be neurodivergent by 2050, wouldn't any attempt to investigate (im)mobilities remain incomplete, without the discussion of neurodivergence?*

*If bell hooks' musings on margins can't shift the minds of our righteous mobilities scholars, surely the muscular manoeuvres of Fred Moten on fugitivity and settler-colonialism, would? Summer 2020—when one racialised minority was murdered at the knees of white supremacist police—has long gone, and so has Autumn 2023—when 14,800 were murdered in Gaza after extended periods of constrained mobility under patriarchal systems of violent domination, but where's the engagement with abolitionist and emancipatory work by minoritised movers and shakers?*

*Have I, as a clumsy reader, mis-understood its goals of 'social justice, social change and social futures'?*

*What are the excuses of mobilities research?*

## K: KINDNESS

In our conversations about leadership, Darren Henley tells me that kindness is key.[310] That it's woolly is precisely why it matters, he shares.

In March 2020—just weeks after lockdown was enforced in the UK—the Chief Executive Officer of Arts Council England rolled out schemes to dispense £330 billion of emergency funding for artists and organisations. He grounded his action with the United Nations' call for 'kindness, generosity, empathy, and solidarity' in times of crisis.[311]

## N, Q: NEURO-QUEERING

Kindness, generosity, empathy and solidarity underpin the foundations of 'neuroqueering',[312] which also critiques the minority-on-minority violence that I've been raising in the book.

Drawing on crip, queer and critical race theories, the term was developed by an online community of autistic people in the 1990s. It recognises how supposedly 'inclusive' frameworks often privilege 'curative narratives' and 'prioritise certain bodyminds' over others, and instead seeks to engage with 'a diversity of bodyminds' to explore how 'whiteness, able-bodiedness/able-mindedness, compulsory hetero-sexuality and cis-ism coalesce through each other'. Neuro-Queering thus 'opens up identity by recognizing the malleability and fluidity' of diverse body minds.

Malleability and fluidity also under-pin leadership from a neuro-queer prism. When I asked Nick Walker what a 'leader' is, she describes them as a 'facilitator' who is in the 'continuous process of emergence and self-actualisation.[313]

*Can 'neuro-queering leadership' be characterised as a continuous process of emergence and self-actualisation by queering both hetero- and neuro-normativity, and by recognising and facilitating the malleability and fluidity of diverse body-minds?*

## P, O: OPPRESSION; POWER, OPPOSITIONAL (AESTHETIC ACTS)

*What's power—and specifically, French philosopher Michel Foucault's approach to power—got to do with leadership studies?*

Plenty, say leadership scholar Brigid Carroll and others,[314] who explain that the idea and practice of power is a 'key way to understand leadership as a position, as an act and as an academic subject'. Drawing on Foucault's argument on how power and knowledge is both contextual (shaped by the society we are in) and historical (the 'truths' which are held in place by the educational, media and economic institutions we are in at that moment and in that place), they adopt a 'critical-historical' lens to investigate how certain ideas about leadership have become dominant, and the strategies used to promote these claims, and expand on his notions like disciplinary power and self-policing (where the powerful exercise so much control that others are manipulated into minimising their action and autonomy due to fear of being watched or punished).

*Consider Foucault's power in discourses on power. What are the dark sides of his dominance within leadership studies and beyond? What are new, oppositional aesthetic acts to resist his oppressive influence? Do so by conducting further research on hooks' admiration for and critique of Foucault. Another approach is to work through how mobilities research tracks the 'power of discourses, practices, and infrastructures of mobility' through the 'relation between local and global "power-geometries"'.*[315]

## R: RESISTANCE

The Chinese word for leader—领袖'*ling xiu*'—literally means 'collar and sleeves', but Hong Gong Ping, a migrant from South China to a southern island on an equator, preferred sleeve-less singlets, shorts and flip-flops. As an illiterate orphan, Hong turned the corner himself by getting educated through peeping into windows of schools. When he saw kids running about in the village instead of receiving education, he rolled up his sleeves to turn his corner-shop, which also functioned as a food-bank for the poor, into a classroom. His anti-Japan efforts during the Occupation made him go on the run. Being a hair-less chimp that's jaundiced too, his effort to grow a 'beard' amounted to nothing more than whiskers, but his masking worked, and soon after the war his daughter, whom I'm a daughter of, was born. Today, the education philosophy of the school includes 'critical thinking skills, creativity, empathy, and a sense of social responsibility'.[316]

## U, D: Under-Dogging

*Complete the following:*
This is a more-than-human leadership strategy in response
to ........................ and draws on ...........................
when.......... ........... Warning: ................................. .................

## V, T: Vis (High); Trouble-Making

*What can we learn from wearers of high-vis jackets, who're often blue-collar*
*workers least visible in society? I'll share an entry from my own journal.*
'It's *exhausting* to make social art as an anti-social hair-less chimp. To
sabotage my melt-downs, I'd get outside of my self/flat, and work as a
volunteer, often wearing my high-vis jacket that I wear when cycling.
Serving Christmas dinner to home-less people helped to postpone my
break-down until Spring. As a marshal for the World Naked Bike Ride, I
directed traffic—no mean feat for a non-driver with two left feet. Being a
London Ambassador during the 2012 Olympics, I passed as a local to
guide other lost souls to their destinations, while spiralling downwards
inside. *En route*, I'd run into other high-vis wearers who are the *authentic*
leaders instigating *transformation*—without bravado or fan-fare. As a
National Health Service (NHS) responder at vaccination centres during
Covid, the first person who said hello to me was Rose Godkin, a former
NHS burns nurse for 50 years. A legend in local volunteering, Godkin
calls herself a "trouble-maker"—"but why would I want to be anything
else?"'[317]

## Z: Zelensky's War Against Z

*Moving on from Lear and other classical leadership stories and approaches,*
*and synthesising what we've learnt so far, analyse Volodymyr Zelensky's ongo-*
*ing war against Russia's invasion, which has the shorthand of the symbol 'Z'.*
*You may discuss his:*

- ...artistic portrayal of President in the TV series *Servant of the People*
  (2015–2019) versus his 'strong-man' nemesis Vladimir Putin;
- ...art direction (wearing a green jumper evocative of the military;
  scripted speeches evoking Shakespeare and Europe; weaponisation
  of slogans and selfies).

- ...artfulness (transforming the tragedy of war into opportunity to advance campaign to join Nato and strengthen military prowess; swiftness in firing prominent players for mis-speaking).

*Black fugitive movers and shakers have guided us to ensure that neuro-futurising leadership teams up with other minoritised perspectives to address all social oppression. How could Zelensky form coalitions with other oppressed people in Congo, Myanmar or Sudan?*

# CHAPTER 14

# M: Monster-Map. Move Mountains, Moons & Mars

*To build a new world in the shell of the old, make your own mappings, tentacularly, spectacularly,* monstrously.

### SPRING 2023, SOUTHWEST COAST, UNITED KINGDOM

Following 5 hours of train, tube and bus rides. I reach the port-city of Southampton. I'm looking for a new flat to call home—my 9th in my 18 years on this isle, which follows 7 different visas, 2 resignations from permanent academic positions, and 12 house moves.

No luck.

Storm Noa hits, and men and boys hit on me as I pass by them. I hit back. I wake up the octo-pussy inked on my body. My octo-pussy whips up Kung-fu poses, transforms its tentacles into blades that spray peas at the offenders, then helicopters me into a building.

*Found Cities, Lost Objects: Women in the City* is on display. This exhibition encourages viewers to 'discover the city through the eyes of female artists', states artist-curator Lubaina Himid.[318] She adds:

*'Maps are instruments of power. [...] The science of cartography allowed colonisers to navigate space in order to appropriate it, to exploit resources. [...] Cities are places to make history, make money and have the ability to*

© The Author(s), under exclusive license to Springer Nature Switzerland AG 2024
K. S. Tan, *Neuro-Futurism and Re-Imagining Leadership*, Studies in Mobilities, Literature, and Culture, https://doi.org/10.1007/978-3-031-55377-6_14

113

*predict the future [but] naming streets, squares and parks can also reflect a symbolic domination.*[319]

Cities can be 'constraining or disabling', adds the migrant-turned-leader of UK's under-discussed Black Art movement in the 1980s. This show 'challenges the status quo' by displaying maps that are painted, printed, pixellated, embodied, burnt, sculptured and more, to re-claim 'lost lives and lost objects'. By re-viewing 'our own relationships with the city', viewers 'gain a greater sense of self'.

I run into one Phyllis Pearsall. After being mis-led by an out-dated map, the Londoner decides to develop her own. Being a non-driver, Pearsall would wake up at 5 a.m. daily, to walk a total of over 3000 miles to index 23,000 street names across the capital. In 1936, she publishes her first *Geographers' A-Z Atlas to London*. This became a 'staple of Londoners' glove compartments and handbags for decades', states Himid. Although Google now direct our travels and lives, mapping transformed Pearsall 'from bedsitter to household name'.[320] Himid calls her 'one of the most successful business-people of the twentieth century'. Pearsall describes herself as an artist.

The storm stops. I leave the City Art Gallery. As I wander, I wonder:

*Aren't leadership and mapping two peas in a pod? Aren't both embodied feats of travelling, endurance, guidance and meaning-making? As relational processes connecting diverse actors, places and objects, what can each teach the other?*

## 2500 Years Ago, China

*'Through our body, we may contemplate the body. Through our family, we may contemplate the family. Through our hamlet, we may contemplate the hamlet. Through our state, we may contemplate the state. Through our world, we may contemplate the world. How do I know the world is so? By this here!'—Lao Zi 500 BCE*[321]

In the Chinese politic and path-way of Daoism, mappings are instruments of empowerment. The words and ways of its founder Lao Zi show how the body-mind is inextricably linked to the world—hence body-mind-world.[322] This is millennia before Descartes or disability studies made any initial baby-babbles.

Body-mind-world captures how the body-mind is a mapping of the world. As an ever-changing entity with myriad, the world comprises 'ten thousand' elements. While this echoes the 'rhythms and temporalities that create spaces in constant movement and change'[323] of mobilities studies' conception of realty, Daoism goes way further, with 'correlative-' or 'poetic-thinking', where metaphors and visual imageries rule. The dynamic, creative force of the cosmos—the '*dao*'—is pictured, including literally, as running through the body via a network of energy channels, pulses and moving fluids. Instead of resisting change, humans should 'go with the flow'.

At the same time, the world is also a mapping of the body-mind. Diagrams depict body parts as analogous with the natural and human-made world. Lungs, noses and souls are expressed as mountains, moons, passage-ways and cities, which, in turn, denote the seasons, state, stars and more. Past-present are also bonded, as the spleen ties us to our heritage and fore-bears. Hair-less chimps are encouraged to traverse these land-scapes in order to *locate* ourselves.

In short, rather than something that is sinful or vapid, the body-mind is an emergent site of knowledge, agency and transformation. The well-known *yin-yang* diagram typifies the poetry of this relational, reciprocal body-mind-world system.

No wonder the *dao* has mileage and has permeated many facets of Chinese culture. This ranges from medicine, arts, martial arts, food, geo-mancy and geopolitics, to self-cultivation and environmentalism—which are also all *correlated* and mapped together. Evidently, this body-mind-world paradigm has long squared complex conundrums. This includes contemporary short-termist political hot potatoes like how environmental sustainability correlates with health, mental health, costs of living, social justice and more. All this, more than 2500 years prior to the Western band-wagon to conceptualise inter-species and inter-planetary relations to avert environmental catastrophe (actor–network/non-representational/more-than-human theory, anyone?).

But the joke's been on me.

Sure. I've made it clear that no -*ism* is fool-proof. Cultural chauvinism is cartoonish and boring. It doesn't take Monsieur Foucault to tell us that historical framings had historical issues too. Nonetheless, colonialism has form when it comes to raping, retrofitting and re-branding. Linda Tuhiwai Smith, hooks and many have clarified how knowledge gained through colonisation has been used, in turn, to colonise our mind.[324] There are countless examples of how indigenous practices are white-washed and demonised, then re-marketed as 'radical' Western ideas and ideals, and subsequently weaponised to mock and gas-light the cultures that it had looted from.[325]

How rich. And I was the fool.

Since social mobility in my home-town (sic) means impersonating the ways of its former rulers, I'd pooh-poohed my Daoist roots as superstition. It was after re-turning to England in 2009, when I lost my footing, that I re-discovered Daoism, and running, and re-covered.

Is it a coincidence that Daoism was born of crisis? Lao Zi conceived of the *dao* while on the road as a vagrant, having walked out of his role as a civil servant in protest at the corrupt government then. That's why he urges adults to remain 'like a child' who's 'restless', 'homeless', 'insatiable' 'ignorant and stupid' 'foolish and crude'.

No wonder Daoism is correlated with 'anarchism', including by Audrey Tang when discussing her leadership strategy during the pandemic.[326] The Silicon Valley executive-turned Digital Minister is nothing if not anarchistic, as the first trans-gender person in office in Taiwan, which is a nation resisting China's colonial rule. Artist Jack Tan also evokes Daoist cosmologies in his work, such as in his creative interventions at rural and natural sites.[327]

*Wouldn't it be timely to frame Daoist mappings in leadership terms, to collage the internal-external, personal-political, micro-macro for our fraught moment? How could mappings function as a form of guide to cultivate the self, nurture the community and cosmos, move mountains, and rise above storms and crises* (Fig. 14.1[328])?

## SINCE THE 2000S, GLOBAL NORTH

Laura Lo Presti's 'migratory mapping' could shed some light.[329]

Created in response to the 'dehumanising' discourses surrounding the anti-migrant crisis, and drawing on mobilities, (counter-)cartography, migration and more, the cultural geographer's proposal brings together 'technology, politics, culture, emotions and non-human elements that shape the discussions, emotions, and actions surrounding the migrant crisis', including how maps themselves 'migrate' and move.

Instead of 'maps', which are closed, stable and static,[330] mappings are synonymous with 'wayfinding', and migratory mappings explore maps as

**Fig. 14.1** Mapping/Storming

'conceptual, imaginative and methodological' tools, and reveals their 'cognitive, affective and emotional faces'. As 'situated and embodied' practices of mobility, mappings address processes that lead to the 'production, circulation and consumption of a map', and capture 'kinetic landscapes and human mobilities' beyond the frame.

Concerned with the processes, practices and performances,[331] migratory mappings are 'autonomous objects' and 'open and mobile processes' that operate in a 'wider ecology that involves and positions bodies, dense surfaces and movements', and are constantly revised by users who 'browse, touch on, feel and redesign them',[332] particularly on digital platforms. Migratory mappings include and synthesise diverse materials, and mobile methods like walking interviews, GPS records and more. As a mode of 'visualising mobility and mobilising visualisations,[333]' digital formats provide a 'relational, mutable and nearly real-time navigational performance' which can 'move and refresh with the user'.[334] Users are active actors, engaging in a 'visuo-spatial act' that's embodied, creative, kinetic, haptic, and even visceral.

As a 'messy'—and I'll add *monstrous*—method, Presti's migratory mapping collates a 'symphony' of movements requiring 'performative, sensory and post-humanist grammars'. Elements include visual scripts, 'images, and objects that connect migrants in their imagined destinations and return', and 'digital connectors used for orientation and connection during migration', which, in turn, combine and behave differently according to different actors.

In other words, rather than mirroring reality, a migratory mapping is an 'affectional companion', 'lifeline navigational tool', and 'endless engine of emotion and movement' that's autonomous, while *also* embroiled in other movements of information, experiences and more. Through its capacity to step in and out of its various roles, migratory mappings make visible the 'ambivalent condition of im/mobility experienced by subjects who are forced to the margins of the politics of movement'.

Presti's rich proposition clarifies why the visual matters, and echoes discussions raised by Erin Manning. I am intrigued by some of what the philosopher-dancer has said, although I need to dig further about her positionality and intentionality. Manning states that visual outputs 'heed indigenous and black and neurodiverse and queer forms of knowing'.[335] This is interesting because it connects visual knowledge with power, and further extends a tentacle to neuro-queering. It's just as well that, by the nineteenth century, dyslexia was described as 'word-blindness' and visuo-spatial thinking.[336] Manning's conceptualisation of diagrams also fit that of mappings, for, diagrams resists the 'neurotypicality of knowledge production', and can 'connect to how else we can unknow, unown the language of the order-word as it has been passed down' by neuro-typical generations. Manning describes the diagram as 'wild', 'messy' and anarchistic, and argues that it is a form of 'orientation for the creation of new modes of existence'. A diagram 'write(s) sideways into the academy', and as a 'mode of survival' for 'life-living', it can 'move the diagram of power/knowledge'. All these descriptors seem to resonate with Presti's migratory mappings, as well as how we have been formulating mappings in general so far.

*Can migratory mapping move the diagram of power/knowledge and re-direct discussions, emotions and actions surrounding the migrant crisis, such as the leadership crisis? Since there's no agreed definition of 'crisis leadership',[337] can we consider not just how leaders respond to organisational difficulties, but confront the symphony—or cacophony—of external forces and crises that organisations dance with(in)?*

## FOR 60 MILLENNIA, AUSTRALIA

*'Colonialism wasn't just about collection. It was also about re-arrangement, re-presentation and re-distribution.'—Linda Tuhiwai Smith 2012*[338]

When invited to deliver a master-class in Canberra in 2006, I asked a mate about the highlights of the capital of Australia. 'Power, politics and pornography' came the reply.

These three P-s are played out in Larrakia artist-activist Gullawun Daniel Roque Lee's work *The Final Hearing of the Kenbi Land Claim of 1995*, at the National Museum of Australia.[339]

Although described as a 'sculpture', the work is a mapping of diverse actors and elements, including an aeroplane, which flies next to our resident monster-mascot: the octopus.

This is hardly surprising. Octopuses have amused the arts for millennia, as its muse. A cameo appearance is seen as early as 1300–1200 BCE on a Minoan jar.[340] Symbolising the 'weird', 'unknown and unidentifiable', octopuses' 'monstrous excess of suckers and limbs' achieve a 'particular intimacy with the human', declares the ocean-themed exhibition *Aquatopia*.[341] If perfect 360 degree-eyesight and no blind-spots[342] aren't impressive enough, did you know that octopuses can 'see' light with their tentacles[343] through darkness, and even use the visual information to determine the location of its own body?[344] Lao Zi, Himid and Presti would have approved of this artful and embodied body-mind-world geo-locative mode of *thrival*.[345]

What's pornographic, however, is how work relegated outside of the Western canon like Lee's is shrouded with blind-spots. Although Aboriginal culture dates back 60,000 years, this and other works featuring tentacles by Aboriginal communities—as well as Aboriginal knowledge at large— remain largely un-known and un-identifiable beyond the communities and specialist fields.

It gets odder.

In fact, Aboriginal visual outputs are 'forms of knowledge that express cultural intellect', explains Liz Belanjee Cameron.[346] We deny their status as knowledge-systems when we labelling them 'mere' 'art', which, as we have shown, is deprioritised in the hierarchy of knowledge. And by prefixing 'aboriginal' to 'art', we've been ghettoising them twice over, and devaluing 'thousands of years of generational knowledge systems, where visual information has been respected, appreciated and valued', states the scholar-artist. In fact, Lee's work doesn't just highlight 'significant sites, sacred sites and dreaming tracks'.[347] The 96-cm-tall object is Lee's retort to the vulgar violence on the Larrakia people, reclaiming lives, objects and stories lost, including ongoing efforts to retrieve their territories on Kenbi—hence the title.

I didn't know any of this.

I'm ashamed.

I've got a long, long way to go to de-colonise and detox my own body-mind-world.

## SINCE DAY DOT AND BEYOND THIS, HERE

*Altogether now—could we think about 'monster-mapping' as a beyond-colonial, relational crisis leadership strategy?*

Mapping together what we've run through in this chapter, I propose monster-mapping as a method of way-finding and re-direction during and beyond crisis. Both a noun and verb, monster-mapping is a body-mind-world '*dao*' that's embodied, kinetic, haptic, decolonised and relational. To monster-map is to make visible the im/mobility experienced by those forced to the margins. Its monstrous excess of suckers and limbs re-claim lost stories and objects, and dance with the un-known. Nourished by indigenous knowledge-systems, monster-mappings enable the migrant, neuro-divergent and indigenous to re-gain a greater sense of self.

Monster-mapping also maps together the myriad forms of mapping and concepts that I've been creating since day zero, as a neuro-divergent artist-migrant living life on the run. Octavia Butler had a 'big pink notebook' in which she made herself 'a universe in it', to become any-body and to be 'anywhere but here, any time but now, with any people but these'.[348] Similarly, my sling-shot to reality was pen and paper, which was what I had instead of toys.

I monster-mapped to direct alternative scenarios, using text and making marks that silenced the scoldings, beatings and punishments en-forced by adults. My constant shouting matches with my folks rendered me un-filial and 牙尖嘴利 *'yajian zuili'*, meaning 'sharp-toothed' and quick-witted. To 'we'll give you up for adoption and disown you' and 'why don't you use that mouth of yours to become a lawyer', I'd scream back 'I didn't ask to be *here, did I?*', with hot angry tears. This invited more punishment, so I invented my own escape routes on paper. Making my internal wanderings visible also enabled me to run away from taunts from posh English-speaking class-mates about being odd, and battle with cabin fever in the land-scarce, economic tiger-miracle of a shiny tropical island that I was stuck in. Teachers mocked my size, laughed at my uneven bowl-cut by my mother, made me wash the school toilet as punishment, and force-fed Western textbooks that I was expected to regurgitate. So, for two years, I stopped eating, sleeping and speaking, to produce map after map to un-pick, re-mix, chew on and work things out for myself. This was how I grasped the values of the visual in learning,[349] and the body as creative medium. This also kick-started my life-long habit of waking up in the dead of the night to defy normative, linear approaches to time, and to re-group, compensate, and hyper-focus. It's during these moments that I'd spot, from the comfort of my window, fellow bottom-feeders who're also un-wittingly a-wake, who're making their way to or from work, such as cleaning up society's shit in night-clubs and offices.

To break the cycle for good, I flew the nest again. The rest-lessness and teenage angst were never out-grown, but my world and world-view aug-mented. My mappings became *monstrous*, greedily traversing from 16mm film and hyper-text to performance, tapestry and oil. I made my body a sweaty site-sight of motion, commotion and intervention. I under-took tours and detours via running, swimming, drowning, skipping, rolling and more. I invented entire cities like one 'Nondon' for Kaidie to search of 'a/the meaning of Life' in 1000 days, to make my own history and my own future (Fig. 14.2[350]). I then mobilised hyphens to (cor-)relate distinct

Fig. 14.2    Kai Dies

elements to activate in-between, liminal spaces, and tape-wormed terms like 'island-hopping'. The hyphens were eventually let lose, and became tentacles.

Here we are.

Monster-mapping is my instrument of power. Its malleability and mobility makes it a lifeline and navigational tool for me to work through personal and political crises. After all, 'living differently is not living in another place but living in the same place and making in the mind a different map', states an artist in Anne Douglas' report.[351] Dis-placing myself into different worlds allow me to re-process, re-order and re-define my place. Visualising mobility and mobilising visualisations, monster-mapping is my conceptual, imaginative and methodological Swiss-army knife. The processes of (re-)mixing and (mis-)matching are so joyous and intoxicating, *à la* the runner's high, that the journeying become pleasurable, mesmerising ends in themselves that I never want to end. To monster-map is to play boundlessly with knowledge-formations, synthesise yet also split objects, mess up the micro-macro-meta, visit curious bunny holes, rehearse and perform conflicting provisional conclusions. As a *mega*-monster-mapping of monster-mappings, this A–Z participates in an endless engine of emotion and movement, and can influence external cacophonies of flows too, to write sideways into the academy and move the diagram of power and knowledge.

*Fire poisonous peas at forces that dehumanise and demonise difference. Map collectively, cosmically. Map monstrously, magnificently, to shift diagrams of power and knowledge. Map, to not hide in the mountains, but to move mountains, moons and Mars. Map, not to reject the world, but to ~~live in~~ make your place in this world, and to open up new spaces for yourself and others.*

# CHAPTER 15

# C: Clock-Block: Drive Your Own Destiny

*Since leadership studies should learn from the arts, such as a 'novel, a paint-ing, or a religious text',[352] let's study what speculative fiction—especially by those working in resistance from the margins of society—can reveal.*

## SPEECH SOUNDS

What if a pandemic robs you not just of smell or taste, but speech, sound and meaning?

This is the shocking premise of *Speech Sounds* (1983) by Octavia E. Butler (1947–2006).[353] Like Bambara's, Butler's words are precise and pungent, and traverse themes of mobilities, imagination, care, children, gender and disability. Yet Butler pushes us further in this piece of specula-tive fiction. The protagonist of *Speech Sounds* isn't a person, but a 'new virus, a new pollutant, radiation, divine retribution' that has wiped out the population of Los Angeles.

> 'The illness was stroke-swift in the way it cut people down and strokelike in some of its effects. [...] Language was always lost or severely impaired. It was never regained. Often there was also paralysis, intellectual impairment, death.'

© The Author(s), under exclusive license to Springer Nature Switzerland AG 2024
K. S. Tan, *Neuro-Futurism and Re-Imagining Leadership*,
Studies in Mobilities, Literature, and Culture,
https://doi.org/10.1007/978-3-031-55377-6_15

Across merely 5621 words, the story un-folds swiftly, like a silent film played at 16 frames per second, and spliced together with jump cuts and ellipses. Gestures and 'hand games of intimidation' aside, characters use 'squeaks', 'whimpers', 'grunts' and 'bared teeth' to mime their emotions and intentions. Driven by 'frustration, confusion, and anger', miscommunication, fights and murderous thoughts and actions were thus commonplace. Our heroine uses a pin shaped like wheat to approximate her name 'Rye'. Having lost her spouse, kids and the capacity to express, Rye is beset with 'loneliness and hopelessness'. She hits the road to find her remaining relatives in the city of Pasadena.

Rye's road trip echoes the 'elusive and trackless' mourning of 'love and loss'[354]—plus a generous dash of disgust. She's 'sick to her stomach' with 'hatred, frustration, and jealousy', plus 'grief and anger'. She keeps feeling that 'she would vomit' and when 'she did vomit', Rye's dis-content chokes herself. Having worked as a teacher before calamity struck, Rye's job was to nurture and transform body-minds, including those of the next generation of change-makers. Besides, being a teacher of *history*, Rye is a curator not just of her own, but also of humanity's intellectual and cultural pasts and futures. Rye's nausea is thus personal, as well as political and collective:

> **'She had lost reading and writing. That was her most serious impairment and her most painful. She had taught history at UCLA. She had done freelance writing. Now she could not even read her own manuscripts. She had a houseful of books that she could neither read nor bring herself to use as fuel. And she had a memory that would not bring back to her much of what she had read before.'**

Rye boards a bus. When a fight breaks out, she alights to hitch-hike with a driver. Alas, she 'found and lost the man so quickly'. Across stroke-swift sequences, we see Rye engaging with the younger man in a dance of danger, jealousy (her 'deep, bitter hatred' of his ability to read maps), threatened rape, pleasure and protection (consensual copulation with a condom), followed by three deaths (his, after failing to stop a man from fatally stabbing a woman who also shoots Rye's lover, and whom Rye then kills). Just when we find Rye kneeling, 'alone—with three corpses', Butler magics up two children—who're capable of speech. Rye wonders aloud:

> **'Fluent speech! Had the woman died because she could talk and had taught her children to talk? Had she been killed by a husband's festering**

anger or by a stranger's jealous rage? And the children … they must have been born after the silence. Had the disease run its course, then? Or were these children simply immune? Certainly they had had time to fall sick and silent. Rye's mind leaped ahead. What if children of three or fewer years were safe and able to learn language? What if all they needed were teachers? Teachers and protectors.'

Rye has made it clear that she doesn't want children 'who would grow up to be hair-less chimps' (Fig. 15.1[355]). Nonetheless, these kids have shaken—and awaken—Rye up. She thought she had 'no reason to live', but now recalls her role as a teacher—'a good one'—and *protector*. Since 'the illness let these children alone, she could keep them alive'. Rye places the kids in the car, takes to the driving seat, suddenly recovers her ability to drive, and, as unexpectedly, *vocalises*:

> '"I'm Valerie Rye," she said, savoring the words. "It's all right for you to talk to me".'

With this tingling cliff-hanger, *Speech Sounds* ends.

### THINKING ALOUD & DIFFERENTLY ABOUT LEADERSHIP & NEURO-DIVERGENCE

It's only right for us to discuss creative-, meaning-, change- and future-making in and around *Speech Sounds*. Butler is crowned 'Oracle'[356] because her stories are prescient of our moment, and her X-ray vision see through the brutality—and beauty—of hair-less chimps, as well as helping us envisage how things can become.

As critical disability scholar Sami Schalk explains, speculative fiction 'defamiliarises' or artfully displaces the reader, to make our 'unconscious preconceptions about (dis) ability, race, and gender more readily apparent', challenging us to 'think outside of the accepted definitions of these categories'.[357] In *Speech Sounds*, Butler uses the pandemic to discuss these inequities and the failure of the system which are un-folding today through both the Covid-19 pandemic and environmental calamity. 'The illness had played with them', states Butler. The virus censures human's exceptionalism, with hair-less chimps becoming animal-like and without 'rationality, agency, autonomy of self-consciousness'.[358] Despite donning a police uniform and baton, Rye's lover dies, so that 'law and order were nothing—not

**Fig. 15.1** A Chimp (next to a Sloth)

even words any longer'. Mirroring the non-fictional world, the 'least impaired people' have an 'attitude of superiority' and merely 'stand back' and 'let those with less control scream and jump around'. Patriarchy and gender-based violence—which also rose during lockdown[359]—are rehearsed here: the murderer is the woman's spouse and, although the illness has 'killed more men' and male survivors being 'more severely impaired', Rye's lover remains literate, traumatising Rye with 'anger, frustration, hopelessness, insane jealousy'.

Since this is a speculative and fictitious construct, tables can be turned—*and then some*—as they have for Rye. As Schalk argues, the 'nonnormative nature of the representation of (dis)ability, race, and gender' demands 'similarly nonnormative methods of reading and interpretation'. As I am of a non-normative body-mind, I'd like to expand on Butler's points about access (or lack thereof) to words or voice, in the contexts of framing of leadership in terms of difference, i.e., 'different leadership' that has 'courage and vision' (Butler), as well as doing leadership differently and spot-lighting differences (Evans[360]). The difference I'd like to focus on is neuro-divergence.

Clarification: It's important to note that both Schalk and Butler have stated that disability or race shouldn't be the only atlases to read Butler's work. To do so is to, in Schalk's words, 'reduce and ignore not only the complexity of the work, but also the complexity of oppression'.[361] From the beginning of neuro-futurising leadership, I've also warned against reducing and pathologising difference. 'Diagnosing' *marginalised* people—*posthumously*—would be *infinitely* criminal!

Nonetheless, Schalk also clarifies that Black women's speculative fiction 'theorizes new possibilities and meanings of the bodymind by focusing on representations of diverse bodyminds in the future'.[362] Instead of 'ableist assumptions about a technologically created, disability-free future', works like Butler's emphasise the 'importance of context to understanding a person's experience of disability and the possibility of pleasure from/through disability'. Moreover, although Butler's dyslexia was public, Schalk agrees that it hasn't been sufficiently discussed.[363] In addition, *neuro-futurising* leadership critically-appropriates what dominant culture assigns as 'impairments' into forte.

Thus, we'll be flipping things upside down—and turning tables in spectacular ways.

## Turning 'no Access' into Assets

Let's look at those without access to words in *Speech Sounds*, I'd like us to consider those failed by educational systems, plus those who are dyslexic and/or illiterate, as well as those who fit both descriptions. Butler describes herself as 'a bit dyslexic' and 'slow' in reading, leading to her struggling in school.[364] She'd also been vocal about those in power 'taking money away from every cause' and 'making it harder for people to get an education'.[365] When Butler called for 'different leadership' by 'people with more courage and vision', she was likely including 'teachers and protectors' like Rye, who are custodians of not just erased memories ('books that she could neither read nor bring herself to use as fuel'), but makers of future memories (children who're 'able to learn language').

What about those without access to voice? I'm thinking of the underclass engaged in 3D work. Butler describes her mother, a cleaner, having to 'go through back doors' and enduring 'those humiliations'. Butler's writing amplifies those silenced, to make readers 'feel the history: the pain and fear that black people have had to live through in order to endure'.[366]

Furthermore, Butler was sparse with her speech. Her writing is 'lean and to the point'.[367] In her essay *Positive Obsession*, Butler recalls being described as 'backward' and 'quiet' as a child, and even called herself 'stupid, clumsy, and socially hopeless', and stated how 'shyness is shit'.[368] These descriptors find parallels in medical literature on neuro-divergent processes. So-called neuro-developmental processes often co-occur, too. Hence, if Butler was dyslexic, she was likely also autistic, which features traits like social awkwardness, selective mutism (like Thunberg and Arday), and heightened sensory perception, including increased auditory perceptual capacity.[369] Butler states that she would 'learn better through listening than through reading […] I hear every word and that way I can remember it'.[370] Autism is also associated with hyper-focus, which is signalled in the title and contents of her essay *Positive Obsession*, on her love for writing since child-hood. Then, there's dyspraxia, where clumsiness, as well as driving automobiles are typical obstacles. Butler has stated that 'dyslexia hasn't really prevented me from doing anything I've wanted to do, except drive'.[371] Given her talent for mind-wandering, she was likely to be with ADHD too.

The pleasure in this discussion is Butler's *artfulness* in re-purposing these 'deficits' as assets for herself and Rye. Rye's odyssey mirrors the author's, but also illustrates the transformative power of art. Through writing, Butler's 'own universe' took her 'anywhere but here, any time but now, with any people but these',[372] yelling back at the white-supremacist cis-het-neuro-normative capitalist patriarchy. Butler's manipulation of time recalls 'crip time' in disability studies, which concerns disabled body-minds' subjective approach to time,[373] as well as 'chronopolitical time' in Afrofuturism, which re-orients history and re-constructs 'counter- or alternative futures' that prioritise 'Afrodiasporic subjectivity'.[374]

It's just as well as both time and listening are understood to be fundamental to leadership. Butler's approach clarifies that 'many important processes and behaviours related to leadership', like 'sense-making that is grounded in the past' and 'attempts to act on the present so as to change the future', and that it's *time* to prioritise time in leadership studies.[375] *Speech Sounds* also highlights how listening with empathy is critical to re-writing our future. This aligns with how active-emphatic listening is highlighted as an essential leadership feature.[376] We must stop 'fixing the silenced', and instead hear what we 'need to hear' in order to 'fix the system'.[377] *Speech Sounds* connects sense-making between the past (Rye's as a teacher; pre-speech human), and future (Rye's students; the kids; post-pandemic) by emphatically listening to the silenced (Rye; Butler) and listening as transformative (Rye listening to the children when they spoke, which silenced her suicidal thoughts).

## Buses as Vehicles to Transform Fates & (Dis-)Courses

Buses play a part too in terms of access, listening and fixing the system, in both *Speech Sounds* and Butler's life when writing her story.

When a friend was dying of cancer, Butler took a bus weekly to visit and read passages from her work-in-progress. When a fight broke out during a ride one day, Butler felt trapped:

> *'I sat where I was, more depressed than ever, hating the whole hopeless, stupid business and wondering whether the human species would ever grow up enough to learn to communicate without using fists of one kind or another.*[378]

Since buses feature in mobilities justice and creativity,[379] it should not be a leap to consider their role in a mobile, creative and different mode of leadership. After all, the bus was the site to catalyse change when Rosa

Parks refused to give up her seats for white passengers in Alabama in 1955. Her insistent immobility sit on the shoulders of a line of Black women who defied segregation by similarly standing on their grounds and sitting on their butts in modes of public transport since 1854.[380]

It was also on a public bus where Butler created the line, 'There was trouble aboard the Washington Boulevard bus'. This is a turning point for both Butler and Rye, as this statement jump-starts *Speech Sounds*. Instead of 'putting her gun in her mouth', Rye walks out of her doldrums and hits the road via a bus.

Mobilities research tells us that works of science fiction can 'offer a different kind of truth or "transknowledges"',[381] but beyond cycling in HG Wells' work, or self-flying vehicles in other SF worlds, Butler's bus—as well as speculative fiction by marginalised authors—reveal portals to not only disrupt assumptions about how body-minds move in an alternative reality, but also expose the limitations of dominant knowledge production constructions. Could these hitherto silenced insights re-direct discourse about our future and leadership, and help change the course of and augment our collective knowledge destiny?

In a world of 'quarantine, social distancing, and market instabilities', Sheller also reminds us that 'we will need even more critical mobility perspectives and innovative applied research to find any kind of footing for sustainable human futures'.[382] As a creative practice-led endeavour, doesn't *Speech Sounds* heed Sheller's call? In fact, it exemplifies a robust creative response to the gaps Sheller has identified within mobilities justice,[383] namely fostering differing perspectives and styles of contributing to knowledge, from the micro to macro, and synthesising heterogenous types of data and approaches. *Speech Sounds* also efficiently communicates complex findings to wider audiences and has the capacity to influence policy, social movements and politics and help find appropriate solutions to real-world issues. It even answers the question of 'What is the future and how can we reach alternative mobility futures'?, too. As Butler states:

> *'When I began writing science fiction, when I began reading, heck, I wasn't in any of this stuff I read. The only black people you found were occasional characters or characters who were so feeble-witted that they couldn't manage anything, anyway. I wrote myself in, since I'm me and I'm here and I'm writing.'*[384]

It isn't a leap to re-place 'science fiction' in the quote with mobilities research. Or leadership studies.

Have our ears been pricked up yet? What other excuses have we got?

## NOT GOING DOWN THE TOILET

Rye, who is anything but feeble-witted, wouldn't be patronised with excuses. She's the dogged under-dog, perhaps an older sister of another fear-some fictitious female, Squeaky. Instead of running, Butler has endowed Rye with the ability to drive, which does so triumphantly in *Speech Sounds*' grand finale, in a car that carries other people's children.

All of this speaks to and extends Anne Douglas' discussion about wheels and vehicles as metaphors in cultural leadership.[385] We can think of an organisation or institution as a 'vehicle' or 'vessel', and the task of keeping wheels turning as a 'mechanical process' and a 'complex operation', which 'requires particular managerial skills'. This is 'distinct from the role of the leader', whose role it is to look 'beyond the vehicle to "find direction"', and 'responds to the demands of the landscape to achieve that direction', and to do so not just within or on behalf of an organisation. The landscape, which is 'made up of aesthetic, social, political and economic realities', is 'shifting and uncertain'. A leader can 'design, construct or remake vehicles—organisations and institutions—accordingly'. Not only that, as someone who 'takes responsibility' and 'engages with external forces; who resists, steers, or accelerates', the leader 'shifts perspective on that landscape' to 'reshape it'.

Rye made use of a bus to find her own direction, responded to swiftly shifting and uncertain contexts by hitching a car. She didn't re-construct a vehicle, but re-shaped her world and that of other people's children and, by extension, that of all our children, when she took on the responsibility to take behind the wheels by driving a car and resisting external forces. That the story ends tantalisingly wide-open also evokes the unspoken pact between Butler and her ailing friend—who both knew that the latter wouldn't 'live to read [Butler's story] in its completed form'—as well as Butler's explanation of her affinity with science fiction—'because it was so wide open', with 'no walls to hem you in'. When Rye breaks the fourth wall and tells the reader that '"it's all right for you to talk to me"', Butler is inviting us to write the sequel(s), to draw new road-maps ahead. Even with a voice 'hoarse from disuse', Rye's lover cries 'Da, da, da!', as if echoing the artists in the 1920s who referred to themselves as 'Dada' as they tried to re-build the world from the ruins of the first world war.

How Butler drives the destinies of Rye, the children, as well as her own has opened path-ways for generations of off-springs since. Butler's work exposes how 'able-mindedness and able-bodiedness are socially constructed and upheld through racial and gendered norms', and outlines 'new social possibilities', states Schalk.[386] Likewise, speculative fiction by the neuro-divergent (like Nick Walker's graphic novel series *Weird Luck*) and QTIBIPOC (including a UK artist 'fictional activism' which re-centres marginalised stories and characters from dominant cinema[387]) can also highlight leadership's productive antagonisms with difference, neuro-divergence, mobilities and the creative arts and humanities.

*Speech Sounds*—as well as the stories behind it, and the 10,000 stories it's fostering by different leaders about different, courageous leadership— are collectively up-ending fate and up-lifting our hope, to ensure that we don't all go down the bog. Although born 'in weariness, depression, and sorrow', by the time Butler finished writing *Speech Sounds*, 'my hope had come back. It always seems to do that.'[388] As teachers, protectors and other-mothers, both Rye and Butler are coaxing readers to birth yet other emancipatory approaches.

*Stop fixing the silenced. Hear what we need to hear, in order to fix the systems. It's all right for us to talk about better stories of mobilities and leadership. Clock-block. Cock-block. Transform your sorrow into hope. Re-orient history. Re-construct counter- or alternative futures of a mobile approach to leadership. Replace feeble-witted characters, scenarios, endings, knowledge, with different, courageous drivers of new destinies. Write yourself in.*

# CHAPTER 16

# L: Lunge Forward in Your Battle-Cat!

*Finally, a (dys-)service animal that's also an AI-powered wearable! Put on your battle-ship-leader-ship-cosmic-battle-cat-cat-suit* (Fig. 16.1[389])
  *Become stronger than He-Man and other Masters of the Universe! Swifter than Don Quixote on his ass! Cleverer than Alice's grinning Cheshire cat! Mightier than Ganesha and other multi-limbed gods! Lock horns with white elephants and petrol-guzzling four-wheelers! Run down busses before they throw you under them! Surf the double-bat-shit-storm! Lunge forward in your Battle-Cat!*

© The Author(s), under exclusive license to Springer Nature
Switzerland AG 2024
K. S. Tan, *Neuro-Futurism and Re-Imagining Leadership*,
Studies in Mobilities, Literature, and Culture,
https://doi.org/10.1007/978-3-031-55377-6_16

135

Fig. 16.1    Your Battle-Ship-Leader-Ship-Cosmic-Battle-Cat-Cat-Suit

CHAPTER 17

# Q: Have Quickies with Other Species

*The dating app Tinder is out-dated. Alongside co-runners for the LSDs or long slow distances ahead, you need to* speed*-date, including with those who aren't* your *(stereo-)type, to find new sole-soul-mates. Drawing on my allergy to boredom and extensive field-work, I've created Hinder,[390] where you swipe right to members of other species to envision better, alternative, futures together. Here are three quality quickies, and, for contrast, three woe-ful wed-locks, all presented as scripts for you to enact.*

### QUALITY QUICKIES

#### With Beth[391] (Gen Z-er)

*Ext. Beth's Garden, Manchester UK—Day*
BETH and OCTO-PUSSY are seated, facing each other. ORION, two, is playing nearby.

**OCTO-PUSSY**
You're a young art teacher. Do you think of the future? How does that connect with your past?

© The Author(s), under exclusive license to Springer Nature Switzerland AG 2024
K. S. Tan, *Neuro-Futurism and Re-Imagining Leadership*, Studies in Mobilities, Literature, and Culture, https://doi.org/10.1007/978-3-031-55377-6_17

**BETH**

I do think about the future. I was 21 when I gave birth to my son Orion. My mum is Jamaican and my father was born in Germany. I teach students with special educational needs. I want to make the arts curriculum more diverse and differentiated and to talk about significant issues around us, because we can use art to broach those difficult subjects.

**OCTO-PUSSY**

Art and teaching art as hammers, not mirrors. How do you see the next generation?

**BETH**

I do see a difference between myself and my students. They are a lot more aware of LGBTQIA+ people and things that marginalised groups face. It takes a lot to un-learn internalised prejudices. I'm grateful that the next generation are able to go through that unlearning process sooner than our generation was, and that the ones preceding were. There are wider conversations to be had about the intersections of race, class and gender and sexuality. It's only through fostering these difficult conversations that we can enact change.

**OCTO-PUSSY**

But old fogies can't just sit back and let the kids do the heavy-lifting.

**BETH**

Exactly. If someone uses homophobic, transphobic language, challenge it. If someone uses racist language, challenge it. Making the world a better place is a series of acts of kindness to ourselves, to others and to our planet. I can't be anything other than hopeful. I want to be optimistic. I hope that the best of the things can happen.

## *With Cock-Roach (320 Million Years Old)*

**OCTO-PUSSY**

I get the point of Kafka-esque bugs and cool eco-systems modelled by world-saving fungi—I'm myself an evolved iteration of something from a misogynist spy-thriller from yester-year. But I've never cared about cockroaches until a dyslexic business and community leader cites you as a role model.[392] So, seduce me.

## COCK-ROACH

Sure. I've been around since the Jurassic Period, outlasting even your octopus, and survived the mass extinction that annihilated many species.

## OCTO-PUSSY

I'm not ageist but you're too old for me.

## COCK-ROACH

Wait—there're 4600 species of us! What are you looking for?

## OCTO-PUSSY

Not much, just someone to change the world with. Too soon? Or too late?

## COCK-ROACH

Better late than never. I'll be your perfect side-kick. From ice-cold places and deserts to nuclear radiation attacks, we have survived—and will likely continue to thrive.

## OCTO-PUSSY

Impressive. Humble too. And inquisitive. Let me tell you what I love, which is what hooks says about love. The 'moment we choose to love we begin to move against domination, against oppression. The moment we choose to love we begin to move towards freedom, to act in ways that liberate ourselves and others.'[393] Thoughts?

## COCK-ROACH

Why do women love talking about love?

## OCTO-PUSSY

Old school. Charming. Come on then, give me quality dad jokes on tap.

## COCK-ROACH

I can wing it anywhere. Ta-dah!

## OCTO-PUSSY

Hilarious. Is that why're you creepy, hiding in dark and filthy spaces?

**COCK-ROACH**

That means that I'm not scared to get down and dirty—*especially* with you.

**OCTO-PUSSY**

Hot. You need to tickle my mind more. hooks tickles mine. In her vision of 'new, alternative, oppositional aesthetic acts', she defines leaders as individuals who are accountable to 'the group', who show love and compassion through their actions, and are able to engage in successful dialogue.[394] Does that ring a bell?

**COCK-ROACH**

Taco bell?

**OCTO-PUSSY**

FFS.

**COCK-ROACH**

Wait! I've got another dad joke. I excel in team *app-roach*—geddit?

**OCTO-PUSSY**

G*d knows why I'm single by choice.

**COCK-ROACH**

It gets better. I eat anything, and even live for weeks without my head—can you beat that?

**RE-STRATEGISER**

Stop beating around the bush. Show me your team-work and eating capabilities.

## With Bob[395] (Baby-Boomer)

*Int. Bob's Studio / Octo-Pussy's Living—Split Online Screen—Day*

**OCTO-PUSSY:**
I love your 'slogan art' declaring 'There is Still Art, There is Still Hope', 'Make All Schools Art Schools' and 'Art Makes People Powerful'. Your recent proposition of artists as 'key workers', on par with health workers, is brilliant too. So, what does the term 'artfulness' mean to you? I've been thinking about artfulness as a strategy. This responses to how the Covid-19 virus is described as being 'crafty', as it hijacks your body to jump off to other bodies.

**BOB:**
I love the idea of artfulness and people having to think in different ways and come up with solutions and plans. Making art is a way of keeping that human instinct for individual thought alive. Also we are promoting that idea that we've got to exercise our sense of free speech just as much as we've got to exercise our bodies. Because when you are making art, you are sort of in this space. It's like before Christmas or before Diwali or Eid. You're kind of preparing for tomorrow.

**OCTO-PUSSY:**
… It's a sense of anticipation and something coming into being…

**BOB:**
Exactly. You're making these things, which you hope to show. Like when you're making films. It forces us into a world of optimism. I think the idea that you come up with your own ideas is very important for democracy and human rights. Covid made me revisit the very first art book that I bought: *On Modern Art* by Paul Klee. He talks about this idea of the life force. He has a metaphor of a tree. You've got the octopus, but he has a tree. The body of the tree is in a way that of the artist. It has roots which research things and see things. And then the artworks are the tentacles, the branches.

**OCTO-PUSSY:**
What a powerful imagery.

**BOB:**
Great idea, this idea of the life force. And actually there's something…

**OCTO-PUSSY:**
… life giving about it…

**BOB:**
Yes. And I might catch this idea that art or experimental music will crush the virus. It's not a total joke. It's about driving forward with new ideas. And if you're coming up with stuff in your studio, you're thinking about the future. It does force you to be optimistic.

## WOE-FUL WED-LOCKS

### With Disabled Feminists (Leeds)

*Int. Windowless Arts College. July 2014. Day One*

**SELF-PROCLAIMED 'DISABLED WORKING-CLASS FEMINIST' LINE-MANAGER**
Let's welcome our first ever foreign, non-white person. Everyone, Kai's way older than she looks, although the role says 'junior', pays half of her former salary, and she turned down an invitation to be a professor back home.

**KAI**
Cheers, I moisturise.

*Two Months Later*

**LINE-MANAGER**
Did you have anything to do with Tom's divorce? You've been close to him.

**KAI**
Who's Tom? I've been away co-leading a £4.8million project in Asia, and infiltrating the American Association of Geographers' meeting in Chicago. I'm not humble-bragging because you've used my work for your application reports to become a university, remember?

**DISABILITY TUTOR-CUM-CRONY**
Isn't it great that Leeds brings you down to earth? We northerners don't get our heads too big.

*Multiple Variations on This Theme Later*

**KAI**
What's going on? Why are these sisters harassing me?

**HUMAN RESOURCES DIRECTOR-CUM-CRONY**
Relax! It's just banter innit. This is how UK culture is. Loosen up!

*Following 2.5 Years*

**SENIOR PEOPLE-CUM-CRONIES**
Your promotion application was disqualified because we don't think you're ready. We've awarded professorship to someone half your age with 1% of your track record.

**KAI**
But I was the first person here to become reviewer for a research council. I've been putting the institution's name in new territories by winning a national commission too.

**EVERYONE (CHORUS)**
Since you're doing so well, your request for reasonable adjustments is dismissed.

**AD-HOC DISCIPLINARY PANEL**
After thorough investigation that we didn't tell you about, we're issuing a warning and subjecting you to disciplinary action for being ambitious.

*June 2017*

**KAI**
You've used my work to win awards and become a university in the past three years. I've lost 5kgs this month. I'm done. I'm going back to London.

## With UK Arts and Cultural Sector

*Int. Windowless Art World*

**HOPE-FUL CHEER-LEADER**
We know that leadership in arts and culture, like the sector itself, have both been broken for a while. Despite mountains of reports, recourses and courses since the 1990s,[396] why are we still here?

## GATE-KEEPERS
Good question.

## DIS-ENFRANCHISED QTIBIPOC WORKERS & AUTHENTIC ALLIES
Just look at the titles of two recent articles: *We Need Collectivity against Structural and Institutional Racism in the Cultural Sector* and *Bullying Bosses, Broken Boards, and a Crisis of Accountability*. The former puts forward a powerful case against the 'destructive nature of individualism championed by arts institutions', and demands radical action beyond performativity.[397] The latter catalogues 'racial, gender and age discrimination to sexual harassment, class prejudice and side-lining' in the sector plus fraud and financial mismanagement, to bullying, victimisation and coercion'.[398]

## PERFORMATIVE ALLIES
Our names are Persephone/Katherine/Ollie/Asparagus. We are nepobabies who studied arts management/art history at Courtauld/St Andrews and worked for free as an intern at posh museums through our god-papa's connections. While Black people have to worry about getting killed, we worry about getting promoted before we're ready.[399] We will end up assuming leadership positions because of our hard work (long live meritocracy!). Leadership is not our problem.

## WOKERS/WORKERS
It literally is. Anne Douglas' groundwork on artistic and cultural leadership has paved the way for other discussions, such as on disabled dance leadership.[400] Strangely, the arts and cultural world have snubbed these and imaginative forms of organising, thinking and making from its own creative inhabitants. Instead, it's obeyed the play-books of business models and schools. What missed opportunities!

## IMPERIALISM REGIME BOTS (INTERRUPTING)
… Shame. Let me sip my oat-milked flat white for my self-care. Bye!

## STILL-HOPEFUL CHEER-LEADERS
Don't be a flat white. We'll talk your language—money. The global 'cultural bloodbaths' from funding cuts and 'great exoduses', especially by minoritised practitioners, are bringing the industry to its knees.[401] Isn't this the oppor-

tunity to show how innovation through diversity *pays?* Have you read a recent book from an inclusive design perspective that calls for 'new cultures of leadership' to address 'human hurt and exclusion'.[402]

### ZOMBIES OF IMPERIALISM

If the system ain't broke *broke*, why fix it? We need to fix how niche and risky your work is instead.

### THOSE IN FOR THE LONG RUN & STRATEGISING WHICH BATTLES TO FIGHT

Here's an idea:[403] How about paying creatives to become change consultants for non-arts contexts? Wouldn't that be a win–win for both the economically-precarious artists and companies unable to turn things around with sky-rocketing costs as well as Covid hangover?

Artists have always crafted novel ways of organising, making, change-making and, as Bob and Roberta Smith also state, future-making, by giving form to imaginations of scenarios that confuse, amuse and bemuse. While gamers may be talented in scenario-planning, artists make meaning by providing form, coherence and direction to unknowns. In particular, insights by neuro-divergent artists can expose the limitations—and possibilities—of whom/what/where we are and can be. Doesn't Octavia Butler take us for a psycho-geographical ride in her devastating *Speech Sounds?*

### ZOMBIES' NON-WHITE POUND-SHOP IMITATORS

Calm down darlings. Get real.

### MARATHONERS WITH LONG-RANGE VISION

As the Arts Council England CEO argues, 'creativity boosts our economy', 'empowers our communities, enhances our education system and enriches our everyday lives'.[404] As a driver of innovation, creativity is the 'catalyst that will enable the next generation to invent tomorrow'. It's a shame that your art history curricula didn't cover the likes of Nam June Paik.

### THE HALLUCINATED

You need to move on.

### OPTIMIST

I'll share recent examples then. Like Jess Thom, aka Touretteshero. Her artfulness of doesn't just include innovative interventions in comedy, theatre and mainstream TV, but also equipped her to successfully transform UK's

Battersea Arts Centre the world's first relaxed arts space, where people can fidget as part of enjoying plays. There's also the game-changing crowdfunding platform Kickstarter, which was kickstarted by artist Perry Chen. And, without the Slade Action Group's occupation of the School and concerted series of actions in 2021, would its first ever Black Director, Nigerian-born British artist Mary Evans, have been appointed in 2023[405]?

## THE UN-WOKES

Who are they again? Have we told you about our love for Slade Professor and 'towering genius' Lucien Freud's paintings of his students-cum-girlfriends[406]?

### With Disabled Feminists (London)*

*Skip if you feel a *déjà vu* as a previous section.

### Int. Windowless Disability Arts World

#### OCTO-PUSSY
Come sit on my #MagicCarpet with psychiatrists!

#### DISABLED DISABILITY ARTS DOYENNES
You ungrateful turn-coat. How dare you sleep with the enemy! They'll try to fix you! Let *us* fix you instead. I'll tidy up your messy CV/career/life, for only £999 an hour.

#### OCTO-PUSSY
Messy? How come MOMA New York, Guangzhou Triennale and 900 other commissioners never complained?

#### BENEVOLENT PRODUCER/ACCESS WORKER HIRED TO WRITE MY BID
Stop fibbing or mis-remembering—you sound like an 8-year old boy. BTW we've run out of time to write your funding application.

#### OCTO-PUSSY
Aren't you paid for thirty hours, not three? We're 60 minutes from the deadline!

## SELF-PROCLAIMED NEURO-DIVERSITY ALLY
You can't count, remember? Are you having a melt-down? Let me rescue you. My higher emergency rates will be £999999.999999999999 per hour.

## ONE ACE ARTS COUNCIL
Your bid sucks. Again.

## OCTO-PUSSY
But it's my third failed application with 'professional' bid-writers.

## ACE
You poor disabled artist. We'll pay for more support-workers for you.

## OCTO-PUSSY
I'm poor because, unlike the writers, I'm not paid to work on my own funding bid. Didn't you know that my efforts to put proposals together is more than that of Hercules, Sisyphus and Ganesha combined? Wait, is this a scam?

## ACE
Blame yourself for being different, but thank you for oxygenating entire cottage industries of 'disability arts support workers' and making our diversity stats look healthy. We've also made our application system a 'nightmare' by design[407] because waging this continued war on artists is an ace business for us.

## ARTFUL PROBLEM-SOLVER
Here's an ace business idea. Like how Viagra was invented to solve heart problems but created erect cocks and became a blockbuster hit for floppy men instead, how about we re-package Grantium as a quickie diagnostics tool for those who can't bear the 5-year National Health Services wait for referral for ADHD or dyslexia diagnoses? I'll name my proposal #savetheNHS—*the Hell-Hole*[408] *Leg.* Thoughts?

## WHITE TEAM MEMBER WHO REFER TO THEMSELVES AS NOT JUST ALLIES BUT 'ACCOMPLICES'
Cool! Now can you give me a bonus?

## CONFUSED
You're in charge of my spread-sheets. Can't you see that I've been paying myself below the living wage to work on #MagicCarpet since walking out of a permanent role in Leeds?

## DISABLED FEMINISTS

You have a day-job? You work in organisations? What a sell-out! Unlike us radical culture workers sponsored by trust funds and rich spouses. Nothing about us without us! Down with ableism! Illness and neuro-divergence are superpowers! Our disability is a free pass to make us white-supremacist, classist, anti-trans, anti-science. Don't you dare be sacrilegious about the social model of disability!

## DISABLED FEMINIST SOCIAL SCIENTISTS
## ENTITLED TO BUTT IN EVERYWHERE

Let us coin big terms, write clever books and explain how art works. We'll even make/curate social art, rob art fellowships/funds, plus write long emails to complain about your unethical and un-rigorous ways.[409]

## WHITE SUPREMACISTS IN HEELS

We'll even woman-splain Western feminism to you, and become your spokesperson to simplify your *actual* intentions to the world about 'us' on high horses versus 'them' evil big Pharma-controlled medical sciences.

## OCTO-PUSSY

I'm so sorry that you have become female versions of your
fathers, brothers and bosses. Bye.

## WHITE SUPREMACISTS IN HEELS

Wait, can you pose for our Insta? Your good-will in another un-paid role and tanned skin tone in our background will make ours dazzle.

# NEURO-FUTURISING LEADERSHIP

Speaking of dates, it's time to up-date our definition of leadership.

**Leadership: A beyond-colonial, more-than-verbal, kinetic poly-centric and promiscuous politic, poetic, path-way of way-finding, re-direction, and change-, sense-, meaning-, trouble-, knowledge-, and future-making.**

**To think about and do leadership in this way is to neuro-futurise leadership. Neuro-Futurising leadership draws on and shows (off) the value of neuro-divergence, as well as body-mind-worlds that 'deviate' from the dominant. It dismantles the master's (sic) dangerous story of leadership, as an application of innovative, non-standard ways of pro-**

cessing, surviving and thriving in the world, such as hacking normative systems, problem-solving with limited resources, big-picture thinking, risk-taking, joining up hidden dots, and making novel connections. Thus, instead of the individual, managerial or hierarchical, leadership encompasses the relational, organisational, socio-political, collective, ethical, aesthetic, environmental and more. Instead of providing answers, leadership is about asking better questions. Instead of quick-fixes and being fixed, leadership is mobile, malleable, multi-scalar, multi-dimensional, clumsy and always in the process of becoming.

Leadership is sharp, bared teeth and monstrous excess of suckers and limbs. With not one but three hearts, leadership is governed by love. Leadership en-tails tentacular learning, un-learning and re-learning. With nine head-feet, leadership celebrates 9C's: Critical Creativity; Co-Creation; Collage; Can-do, Curiosity; Community + (under-) Commons; (Cosmic) Circulation; Curating Change through Care (and Com-passion); and Courage.

Leaders come from all walks. We are Deviant, Defiant Dare-Devils. We're ill-disciplined culture-workers, creative-activists, civic-animators, chimeras, octo-pussies, dogged under-dogs, hair-less chimps, odd-balls, wiggle-worms, and cock-roaches. We work hand-in-hand, heart-beat-to-heart-beat, and holding (s)paces for one another as critical friends.

We're crafting and co-creating and fostering better strategies, stories, (infra-)structures, systems, and yet other new, alternative, oppositional aesthetic acts. We move hyper-tactically, to play the game insofar as to em-power us to tweak and transform the system, in order to profit people (of all walks and ilk), planet, play, and power-sharing, and to abolish prisons. We generate unlimited access to the pleasure and power of knowing, to transform external cacophonies of flows, write side-ways, and move mountains of power and knowledge, moons and mars.

Diverse and divergent, de-colonised, and neuro-queered, leadership comprises and nurtures artful, agile and a-typical approaches and actions. Leadership is sweaty, embodied and visceral. Running artfully, yelling back, clock-blocking, boat-rocking, monster-mapping, re-designing tables, flipping arm-chairs, constructing new monuments, gate-crashing, pivoting, futurising and up-rising, speed-dating, gently-anarchising, lunging forward, dys-playing your difference, and re-writing canons demand wit, grit, guts, tears and toil.

And hope.

Long story short, leadership is a love-led Practice of Freedom.

*Dump woe-ful wed-locks. Have quickies with other species. Set a timer for 3 or 30 minutes, 3 or 30 weeks. Let sparks fly. Spar back and forth. Collide creatively and antagonise productively. Jolted out of your comfort zone in a time of polarity and time-poverty, you'll emerge with an after-glow of optimism. If it sucks, fret not, for, the date will soon be over.*

# CHAPTER 18

# B: Boom Boom! Be the Bees Knees

*It's time to discuss the turds and the bees. Let's bee-gin with bees.*

### BEES

Bees *move* the world. If bees stop flying/working, hair-less chimps and many other body-mind-worlds will cease eating/living. Almost 90% of wild plants, 75% of crops, and every third mouthful of human food relies on pollinators like bees.[410] Large, hairy and round, bumble (or humble) bees posses a loud hum and live under-ground, unlike honey bees which live above, and produce more honey.

The latter's colonies have sophisticated social structures. Thousands of stinged female worker bees buzz about, cooperating in child-care, home-building and feeding. The one-stinged queen bee in each colony is responsible for laying eggs. Resolutely single, she's serviced by a harem of drone bees. Sting-free but time-rich, these males' single mission in life is to operate their sexual organ—*if* the queen fancies them. No wonder the drones are nicknamed 'lazy Willi' in a 1912 paper, and are often considered as 'flying sperm', although (male) biologists insist that they're vital to the eco-system.[411]

Bees have inspired leadership concepts like 'distributed leadership' (shared decision-making), 'hive mentality' (group-think) and 'queen bee

© The Author(s), under exclusive license to Springer Nature Switzerland AG 2024
K. S. Tan, *Neuro-Futurism and Re-Imagining Leadership*, Studies in Mobilities, Literature, and Culture, https://doi.org/10.1007/978-3-031-55377-6_18

syndrome'.[412] The latter is likely invented by lazy Willies to describe 'bossy' and 'ballsy' females that they cannot fornicate with.

## KNEES

To move on earth, knees are key. Most four-legged animals have two knees and two elbows, although elephants have four forward-facing knees. In hair-less chimps, knees are the largest joint, and one most easily injured.

Knees can also be abused to immobilise, as well as used to mobilise. In February 2020, Ahmaud Arbery used his for running, and was gunned down for 'trespassing' in a white neighbourhood. Three months later, four police officers knelt on the neck of another Black man for 9 minutes and 29 seconds. This led to the resurgence of the Black Lives Matter (BLM) movement. Founded six summers prior by Patrisse Cullors, Alicia Garza, and Ayo Tometi, BLM was a response to another police murder, of another Black body-mind, teenager Trayvon Martin.

Taking the knee, which was started by footballer Colin Kaepernick in 2016 when he knelt on one knee during the American national anthem in protest of Black oppression, became wide-spread in Summer 2020.

Still, as we know, cycles of systemic maiming and murder of Black body-mind-worlds haven't ceased.[413]

## BEES (WORKER)

The worker bee has been a highly-visible image in UK's Manchester for over 150 years. Apart from the city's official coat of arms, it dons murals, shop, and even the skin of residents as tattoos.

The symbol recalls the north-western city's hive of activity during the Industrial Revolution, where workers were dubbed 'busy bees'. Like how the letter 'Z' has been used to focus and direct support for Russia's invasion of Ukraine, the symbol of the worker bee helps to galvanise a sense of collectivism in Manchester. This is not just vis-à-vis its socio-economic rival of the capital of London, but politically and culturally regionally, played out for instance in the 'roses rivalry' in the 30-year war between its county of Lancashire and Yorkshire in the 1400s, and transpired since into community, local and regional leagues of rugby, football and more.[414] Since a terrorist attack during a pop concert in 2016, the bee has 'taken on a life of its own',[415] and come to represent a sense of unity.[416] It's even inspired a local chain of ultra-hip and woke 'co-working' spaces named

'Colony'. When I asked how this relates to UK's imperialist past, they asked me to 'move on already', as if it was their call.

Proud they are, of the worker bee city's history of civil disobedience. At St Peter's Square alone, there's been Peterloo (when the British troops charged into 60,000 protesters demanding parliamentary reforms in 1819), Pankhurst (painter-turned-Suffragist Sylvia, whose statue stands is a landmark in the square), and BLM protests in 2020. The city was also a hub of cultural upheaval in 1970s, birthing Punk bands like Joy Division and Buzzcocks.

## Bees (Fever, Buzz-Cock-and-Bull-Stories)

My four years in Manchester was buzzy. I worked feverishly, and forged alliances with others keen to do the work. I'd also acquired both Covid and hay-fever. If Manchester is encapsulated by Peterloo-Pankhurst-Protest-Poetry-Punk, I can tape-worm other P-words to summarise my stay: 'Postgraduate Programme-Pan African Congress celebration-Pub Quiz', amid the double Pandemic. Let's whizz through them.

### *Postgraduate Programme*

I was hired as a specialist to develop a Masters (MA) course. 6 months in, Covid hit. This thwarted the MA's progress. Universities had to pivot—while staff were left second-guessing managements' moves. It didn't help that the department I was in was divided, having been only recently-birthed with the shutdown of a theatre school after union battles and layoffs.

Exploiting my status as a newcomer and boundary-spanner, I initiated a virtual forum for the co-creation of sustainable approaches. I also sought to use my body-mind to exemplify and explore the possibilities of 'creative leadership'.

Though termed the 'Common Room'. I'd have preferred *Under-Commons Room*, to centralise Harney and Moten's productively antagonistic stance. I curated workshops around anti-racism, curricula decolonisation and more, highlighting the value of 'equity' over equality, and how, without 'inclusion', 'equity, diversity and inclusion' (EDI) was a buzz-word. Since anti-oppression is everybody's responsibility, I invited white colleagues to co-chair. I introduced community guide-lines, shared resources, and invited alumni to share historical wrong-doings.

As a result, the Acting programme created anti-racism policies, initiated a mentoring scheme by Black alumni, and increased its offer from 3% to 35% for global majority students that year. Another Common Room 'alumni' initiated 14 hours of EDI training for the Faculty's doctoral programme, ensuring that inclusivity is prioritised by emerging academics. As a head of School and programme leader subsequently, the co-chairs further operationalised decolonial approaches.

### Pan-African Congress Celebrations

The momentum of the Common Room led to my co-leadership of a regional festival to show how Black Lives Matter, *quite a bit.*

A UK-Nigerian Professor of Architecture and a highly-respected author of a book on Enoch Powell led discussions with regional academic, cultural and community bodies to organise activities to mark the 75th anniversary of the Pan-African Congress, which was held in 1945. Despite its impact on global history in nationhood and post-colonial diplomatic relations, which had gathered future African leaders on a site where the university stands, traces—physical and otherwise—had become virtually erased.[417]

The lock-down, as well as increased workload and maternity leave, stalled progress. Capitalising on the cartoon of the non-threatening 'model-minority' and poster-girl for difference that I can pass for, I stepped forward to help move things forward by gaining access to people and spaces blocked to others. Between August and October, it was a whirlwindy buzz of strategising, persuading, exhaustion and exhilaration. It was a team effort.[418] My tasks include naming the unassuming the Professor of Architecture 'Curator', who, in turn, named me 'Co-Curator'. I conjoined efforts with an over-arching theme and hashtag #PAC75.[419] I doubled the budget of our grant application to include student engagement, media documentation and sign language interpretation. I commissioned minoritised students and alumni to create audio-visual assets (Fig. 18.1[420]). Through the UK government's Access to Work scheme, I recruited and trained a Research Assistant to enhance workflow.

*Viewing the Past and Looking to the Future* became a successful 4-day festival of 18 performances, seminars and more, in collaboration with 11 partnering institutions, including the Manchester Poetry Library. Marking Black History Month in October, this amplified diverse leadership and intersectional cultural engagement. Immediate, exponential and

**Fig. 18.1**   Pan-Africanism-BLM

long-lasting impacts were achieved, and valuable resources and path-ways developed. Black students chaired sessions with poet Lemn Sissay[421] and other elders, thus evoking the leadership of the Congress attendees. My tentacles collaged various wings across institutions, to consolidate assets. #PAC75 reached 18.2 million people worldwide, including a BBC Radio 4 programme and bespoke video channel.[422] This was equivalent of £168,000 in advertising costs, and advanced the university's EDI, community and internationalisation agendas. We also donated £500 to the W.E.B. Du Bois Museum Foundation, which honours the work of Du Bois. Apart from a plaque, there's now a permanent installation commemorating the Congress. My instigation of a tri-university legal document to share resources has stream-lined bureaucracy, and paved the way for future collaboration. Materials continue to be used by various universities, including two postgraduate courses 'Remaking Modern British History' and 'Documentary Production' and even in Africa. Says a University of Ghana academic:

'I was particularly excited to see [...] African (Diaspora) and students generally, participating actively in the event and celebrating their ancestors and promoting "blackness" [...]. The resources would be particularly useful for my teaching and especially for its historic contents and great Pan African thinkers.'

#PAC75 was truly pan-African and looked to the future. We were buzzing. *Were we on the verge of a break-through? Could this joy—not just safety from cycles of violence—be the new norm?*

## Pub Quiz

Short response: No. Longer response: The momentum and quality of impact of both PAC75 and the Common Room opened path-ways to intimated and animated further changes. But with every step forward, there were several back, in the following three years.

*Q) I have time. So what were the steps forward?*

A) Being invited to taking on formal departmental, faculty and university EDI leadership roles. Using paths un-locked to commemorate other minoritised efforts, like curating the university's first LGBTQIA+ History Month Festival. Establishing a cross-institutional 59-member race equity group. Modelling how art and culture can generate fruitful spaces for teaching-learning, knowledge-exchange, professional training and public engagement to celebrate ally-ship, intersectionality and the leadership of Black students and staff. Enabling tentacular learning across disciplinary and hierarchical divides. Running interventions like the Anti-Racism Reading Group, enabling students to earn credits, acquiring and studying works of fiction and poetry by non-white movers-shakers, and decolonising reading lists. Supporting initiatives like a student–staff anti-racism task-force in the Business School. Advising on senior recruitment panels. Invited by Provost to co-strategise the university's future mission, and successfully advocating for 'creativity' and 'inclusivity' to be institutionalised in the university's 2030 mission. The E&D Department renamed 'EDI', and 'E' replaced by 'equity'. EDI as a standing item at meetings. University reports using Common Room, PAC75 and REAP.

*Q) Why so sour then, sour-puss?*

A) University reports using Common Room, PAC75, REAP and more. Efforts uncredited or stolen. No equitable work-loading for labour. Zero funding. Prompting the popular quiz: 'Did Kai become Senior Lecturer because she's not white?' Being exhausted. Being 'too collegial' for promotion. Recruitment of and promotions for the identikit of pale, stale and male. Efforts to advance race studies shut down. Termed 'aggressive', 'activist', 'rebel' by brown regime-bots and 'allies' who'd put up black squares during BLM. Failed 7-month fight for a trans-student dead-named and mis-gendered by staff, acting as what I call a 'body-blocker' to stand *in* and stand *up* for her and maintain her anonymity, amid denials of wrong-doing, accusations of 'over-sensitivity', weaponising of data protection laws to stall progress etc. 8-month delay for payment of honoraria for artists contracted. Constant requirement to prove how disabled I am, making case after case for a support worker with funding I have earned, seven of whom were bashed through the system with unstable contracts. The exodus of non-white staff after months of bullying (where were those 'allies' who proclaimed 'solidarity' when you need them?). White accomplices who attended late-night Zoom sessions and helped turn strategies into action and used their privilege to express dis-quiet to those higher up at the food-chains, but whose actions were sabotaged by yet other allies naively threw minoritised body-minds under ballistic, speeding double-decker buses. Oh, and sudden 'postponement' in Spring 2023 of the MA Creative Arts Leadership Programme which I'd been developing. I'd found out only because an applicant I'd been working with for several months phoned up to cry 'I'm shocked!'. So was I. Was it because the MA had 'too much EDI', as a gate-keeper 'advised'?

*Q) Bullies and bull turd. What kill-joys. Can you tell us a joke?*

Sure! Brown and Black people walk into a ~~pub~~ university and become the first to break the familial/social cycle. Instead of champagne and oysters, they're served life sentences.

The labour of the 'subversive intellectual' as 'necessary as it's unwelcome', and the university 'needs what she bears but cannot bear what she brings', argue Harney and Moten.[423] Many minoritised academics bear witness to horror stories—their own and others'—who'd hit the wall. Some make the decision to locate meaning elsewhere, prioritise their health, or create niches where they can ~~thrive survive stay unharmed~~ stop watching their backs. Others' contracts aren't renewed, like that of Linda Tuhiwai Smith, after co-authoring a 13-page letter to the Ministry of Education exposing the University Waikato's casual and structural racism.[424] Several sign Non-Disclosure Agreements while cock-and-bull stories are devised and disseminated to demonise them. Others who's had enough of limp cocks whip-lashing their faces quit academia, as did boat-rocker and trouble-maker Sara Ahmed,[425] although why on earth should they be the ones to *move on*? As Bambara's close friend Toni Morrison clarifies, racism is a distraction that 'keeps you from doing your work', because it 'keeps you explaining, over and over again, your reason for being [...] be it your language, how 'your head isn't shaped properly', how you have 'no art"—there's 'always be one more thing'.[426]

It's a high price to stay and survive with your dignity intact inside spaces that systematically violate minoritised body-minds. You navigate the Catch-22 situation of working doubly hard to prove that you *aren't* the minority hire, earning more qualifications to silence the white noise, but also keeping your head down so as not to rouse jealousy by being 'too good', and playing the game enough in order to help nudge the diagram of power and crack the vicious cycle.

Silly us, with so much good-will, volunteering ourselves to do labour over and above our contracted tasks and hours, to teach others about an issue—anti-racism—that *literally isn't our problem*. We were the worker bees doing the Dirty, Dangerous and Demeaning work. Cock-less *and* sting-less, our labour gets usurped by the lazy Willies who ruled/rule the colonies.

Hilarious!

*Q) Not bad. Encore!*

A) Here's another. During this time, I took the pub quiz for wanna-be Brits, called 'Life in the UK'. That was how I learnt about the roses rivalry. When I was finally granted 'indefinite leave to remain', I puked.

## Bees' Knees (Boom Boom!)

June 2023. I'm cycling along St Peter's Square for the last time, having cleared my office to leave Manchester.

And there he was—the magnificent 'Boombox Barry' cycling past, blasting his favourite '80s post-punk music on a speaker fixed to his bike. I wave at him. He waves back, and is soon gone, although his music lingers on.

The fifty-something Black man with the surname of Barrington has personified 'surround sound' for more than ten years[427] while cycling around Manchester. 'It's loud', he grins.[428] The little that's known about him reveals that he, like Squeaky and Paw, is a carer, and that he cycles out of loneliness. He does 'bring a smile' to people's he rides past, and 'it's always such a nice little boost'.[429] This includes during the lockdowns, when he cycled during his allocated time for daily exercise. Boombox Barry has even been immortalised in a crowd-sourced dictionary[430] entry to describe people who are 'loud' and 'entertaining'—and I'd add 'defiantly'.

Cycling—where you use your knees to pedal forward—can enhance a sense of ownership of sites that you transit by and/or in-habit. For minoritised body-minds, this becomes inherently political and poetic. As the grand-daddy of electronic music and endurance cycling Kraftwerk have shown, cycling is an eloquent expression of human and machine working hand-in-hand to negotiate time and space.

But we've heard enough of and from MAMILs glorifying their heroic feats. That's why we're celebrating those making a difference from the ground up, and how they're disrupting and dismantling destructive cycles. Boombox Barry is the Bees Knees of leadership. The buzz he generates deafens practices and policies that persecute, police and murder Black body-minds, by mobilising his body-mind-world-on-the-move as a public 'site/sight of protest'.[431] Boombox Barry remind us that the struggle for freedom, self-governance and emancipation isn't just a political endeavour, also but a social, economic and educational, as well as aesthetic one, as the delegates of the Pan-African Congress had already made clear 75 years prior:

'The object of imperialist powers is to exploit. By granting the right to Colonial peoples to govern themselves that object is defeated. Therefore, the struggle for political power by Colonial and subject peoples is the first step towards, and the necessary prerequisite to, complete social, economic and political emancipation. [...] We are determined to be free. We want education. We want the right to earn a decent living; the right to express our thoughts and emotions, to adopt and create forms of beauty.... We will fight in every way we can for freedom, democracy and social betterment.'—*Pan-African Congress delegates 1945*[432]

Barrington's anthems drown out the flying sperm's cock-and-bull stories amid the ongoing double pandemic. They remind those imprisoned inside and outside of the buildings that he cycles by, to bang our heads to music, and not against walls or ceilings.

*Boom boom! Be the Bees Knees of leadership. Follow Boombox Barry. Express your thoughts and emotions, to adopt and create forms of beauty. Break cycles of maiming and murder of Black body-mind-worlds. Fight the double pandemic, imperialism and exploitation. No one is safe until everybody is safe. Generate a stinging Buzz!*

# CHAPTER 19

# S: Stim and Self-Soothe

*Are you shaking with anger? Let's have a pit-stop, not a melt-down. Set the timer to be silent for 4 minutes and 33 seconds. Critically-distance yourself from other body-mind-worlds for 3 breaths, 300 hours or 3000 days. Take and make time and space. Be still. Sure, Lao Zi states that humans are 'soft and nimble when living, but firm and rigid when dead'.[433] Mobilities founder John Urry said as much, as did a sixteenth-century mathematician and a contemporary evolutionary biochemist.[434] At the same time, we know that immobility is part of mobilities.[435] Rests are also a critical part of endurance running and other physical and/or mental discipline, to digest and process what we have learn, and to leap further* (Figs. 19.1 and 19.2[436]).

© The Author(s), under exclusive license to Springer Nature Switzerland AG 2024
K. S. Tan, *Neuro-Futurism and Re-Imagining Leadership*, Studies in Mobilities, Literature, and Culture, https://doi.org/10.1007/978-3-031-55377-6_19

**Fig. 19.1**　Self-Soothing

**Fig. 19.2**   Stim Room

*Stim and self-soothe. Fishes out of water, get back to swim and soak till your skin wrinkles like prunes. Cat-nap to nip the un-rest and re-set. Hide in the cubicle. Close your eyes. Rock your body. Create your own calm before, after, and amid the shit-storm. Wind down. Gather your second wind and conjure your ninth life. Cleanse your palate and detox—or puke it all out. Reflect— or empty your mind. Put on your noise-cancelling head-phones. Shut out the white noise. Kill small talk, chit chat, masking, passing, compensating, cam- ouflaging. Allay the dis-quiet. Let others with stronger knees take over the re-lay. This is a long slow distance.*

# CHAPTER 20

# I: Island-Hop: Insure Against Insularity

*In what ways can hopping between islands physically and poetically work as a critical and clumsy meaning-making process to counter island-mentality?*

## Processes & Processing In-Between

No person is an island. From contested geo-political sites (Ireland/Taiwan) and flights of imagination (Utopia/Lilliput) to live eco-disaster horror movies (Maui/Tuvalu), islands have always been powerful pawns, products and producers of change, as both geological and cultural constructs.

When I lived in and travelled around the archipelago of Japan, I made *Island-hopping*. This was a large, busy-body of artworks. It's also the name of a psycho-geographical framework I developed *en route*, which activates the 'island' as a creative jumping-board.

The programme mobilises the Japanese aesthetic concept of 間 *'ma'*,[437] which pays attention to the 'in between'. This includes spaces usually delegated as unimportant in Western terms, such as intervals, intersections, margins, corridors, or pauses between utterances, but which *ma* renders as powerful precisely because of how they up-hold that which is usually assigned more value.

The 'hopping' *between* islands is key, as the process that takes and *makes* place. Island-hopping invites the viewer/audience/reader to seek, locate

© The Author(s), under exclusive license to Springer Nature Switzerland AG 2024
K. S. Tan, *Neuro-Futurism and Re-Imagining Leadership*, Studies in Mobilities, Literature, and Culture, https://doi.org/10.1007/978-3-031-55377-6_20

and/or co-create meaning by physically and/or metaphorically travelling on and across islands.

## LIMINAL LEAPS OF TIME, SPACE AND FAITH

*Pub quiz: How could a yellow hair-less chimp feel out of place when surrounded by fellow yellow hair-less chimps?*

*Response: When 'fellow' yellow hair-less chimps assign themselves more value than others.*

The good old days of death penalties prescribed by the Tokugawa shogunate for foreigners who dared enter the island (or nationals who left it) when it isolated itself from the world for 265 years are gone. Nonetheless, how Japan doesn't consider itself part of 'Asia' continues to underpin its psyche. This thinking underpinned its 'Greater East Asia Co-Prosperity Sphere' campaign of 1931–1945. Don't be honey-trapped by the fancy label. This was a 14-year 'liberation' of Asia that murdered over 30 million civilians, which far rivalled the figure for the Holocaust.

*Pub quiz: Could the ghosts of imperialism be why there was no honey-moon period for me in Tokyo?*

Black dogs and I have been locked-in by umbilical cords from day zero, but the 10,000 black dogs seemed dead set to murder when I was first trans-planted to Tokyo. It didn't help that I was on a conveyor belt not of sushi but exams and rote-learning at a cram school, alongside other lowly Asians. I had to learn the Japanese language from scratch.

When I reached postgraduate fluency in the space of one year, I decided that I'd had enough. I hit the road, or rather railway tracks. For the following two years, I visited several of the 47 prefectures and 14,125 islands with my video camera and back-pack. I juxtaposed footage and objects I collected, including from the north (like Hokkaido, where indigenous Ainu people were/are deemed too hairy by the invaders), to the south (like Okinawa, where US military still pervades), and everywhere in between (including Hiroshima, where the aggressor's narrative was repackaged to that of victim-hood)—all the while passing as a 'native' with my by then fluent local lingo. My perfect hearing and perfect pitch might have enabled my mastery of copy-catting.

My 'island-hoppings' weren't just leaps of time and space, but faith too. To process what I was learning, I approached other creative inhabitants, including 'laptop musicians' and noise artists,[438] many of whom knew nothing about Japan's campaign of ethnic-cleansing. We co-created live performances in art spaces, *ala* DJs and VJs. Between footage of far-right locals donning military garb and praising Japan's war heroes at the notorious Yasukini shrine, I'd splice in that of my late aunt's testimony of running away from Japanese soldiers to escape rape, to which my collaborators responded with beeps, screeches and yelps.

The 'archipelago' or aggregate outcome of these disparate isles of sights and sounds was invariably dis-cordant and dis-concerting. These concerts outed my identity as a 外国人 *'gaikokujin'*, meaning foreigner, which is often shortened to 外人 *'gaijin'*, literally 'outside person'. Middle-aged men in the audience would man-splain the notions of decorum which this out-side person was de-void of. Let by-gones be by-gones, they instructed, and/or asked if I would act out their wet-dream of cartoonish tentacle sex with them.

## ITINERANT INTERSECTIONALITY TO RESIST INSULARITY

I'd invite my audiences to put their tails between their legs and instead consider island-hoping as a tentacular, clumsy, mobile leadership strategy against insularity.

Island-hopping is a clumsy method as it's neither elegant, linear nor coherent, but instead pragmatic and make-shift.[439] Users are less a master crafts-person than a 'do-it-yourself craftworker' engaged in bricolage, which collage as an art form derives from, and which links us to one of the head-feet of tentacular pedagogy.

As a creative mobilities method, island-hopping encompasses 'methods for researching the sensory, experience in co-production and participation, approaches to visualising and making things public', as well as 'engagement with the environment and landscape and a deep practical understanding of materiality'.[440] With its capacity to highlight 'im/mobilities that are happening now, and that lay ahead in uncertain, turbulent futures',[441] creative mobilities processes can enrich mobilities. Ergo, creative mobilities processes can also augment critical leadership studies—and island-hopping can bridge these islands of thought together.

Indeed, we can *perform* island-hopping to the politic and project of *neuro-futurising leadership*, to hop between the islands/chapters and make *subterraneous* connections across the various strategies shared, as well as the diverse schools of knowledge that they each jump from and contribute to. This capacity to relate distinct knowledges correlates island-hopping with a descendent, productive antagonism (Fig. 20.1). The latter's descriptors—a

**Fig. 20.1**   Island-Hopping Island-Hopping

'potential space' and 'fertile path' in which 'artistry, trust, creativity and ill-discipline' that enable 'antagonistic disciplinary knowledges' to 'rub up against each other'[442]—seem to apply to island-hopping, too.

The tension seems echoed in the notion of 'constructive dissent' in clumsy approaches as discussed in leadership studies—except that this actively excludes consent, which is described as 'destructive', 'enfeeble' and 'irresponsible' of 'subordinates'[443] How destructive, feeble and repulsive is that?

This is where other meanings of *ma* come in: the intersection and the margin. This is also the juncture where the corresponding notions—of intersectionality and the marginal—come in, which also allow me to clarify for the record, again, how our leadership project departs from standard leadership studies, and the accompanying irresponsible and unethical standards.

Christina Lee extends the notion of the intersection by arguing that it is 'not an island', and instead a dynamic site 'for resistance'.[444] The disability scholar, who is also a female migrant who uses a wheel-chair, compares intersectionality to a busy juncture where 'cars called "Sexism" from the right, "Racism" on the left, and "Ableism" coming at you head on'. Intersections are productive spaces for 'hesitations, decisions, clashes, and redirections'. Instead of feeling vulnerable,

**'Being in the middle gives me a vantage point for seeing where the cars are coming from and who they are heading towards. I see the bigger picture of oppression as part of a system created by capitalism and neoliberalism. All forms of oppression are interrelated and seeing this gives new meaning to the intersection. It is where advocates and allies come together to cause disruption.'**

In other words, island-hopping is a positionality of big-picture varifocal intersectionality. You're on your toes, checking in with and bouncing off ever-changing isles of meanings with another. This relational approach allow you to have an over-sight of how respective as well as the inter-relation of respective forces (such as sexism, racism and ableism) work. It counters your invasive introspection, like my 10,000 blood-thirsty Black dogs, as well as assumptions and complacency. Instead of being static or sticking with—and ossifying—with particular stances, you're Alice with *access* to multiple wonder-lands, learnings and findings simultaneously.

## WHERE ADVOCATES, ALLIES AND ALICES COME TOGETHER TO CAUSE DISRUPTION TO NORMATIVE TEA PARTIES

The same way my island-hopping had enabled me to find and join forces with others, we can invite many wonderful characters to the tea party of our Alice-slash-island-hopper.

Sara Ahmed would be one of our guests. The UK-Australian queer and brown scholar has argued that intersectionality is a 'starting point' to grasp both 'how we come into existence' and how power works.[445] hooks would be invited too, as she reminds us about the margin is a 'space of resistance and hope', or else 'one's creativity, one's imagination is at risk, there that one's mind is fully colonized, there that the freedom one longs for is lost'. As would hooks' contemporary Audre Lorde, who describes herself as a 'black, lesbian, feminist, socialist, mother, warrior, poet'—a trouble-some, inter-sectional mouth-ful, which is diametrically opposed to the 'mythical norm', and also not just an 'other'.[446]

Our other dream guest would be another Black feminist mover and shaker, Octavia E. Butler.

The power of claiming the marginal and intersectional as starting points to explore power as well as to generate hope is captured in Butler's *Speech Sounds* and more. After all, Butler's status as an oracle is built on how her work *sees and helps us see* not just sexism and racism, but ableism and classism, as well as different—*better*—roads ahead. Butler's 1979 *Kindred* similarly exploits such a vari-focal and multi-directional prism—and performs multiple somersaults—with the story of a young Black woman who travels back in time to *protect* her white slave-master.[447] Butler's observation in 2006 about how humans' harmful relationship with the environment is related to everything else also captures her 'bigger-picture' approach:

> 'I want to write about what's going to happen if we keep doing what we've been doing, if we keep recklessly endangering the environment, if we keep paying no attention to economic realities, if we keep paying no attention to educational needs, if we keep doing a lot of the things that are hurting us now.'[448]

Our other guests will include local heroes whose leadership is driven by their multi-perspectival approach, such as Belinda Everett and her Bee Pedals. Belinda's multi-cultural background provides the stand- and jumping points for effort, which is a community for 'women and girls to learn, fix, repair and ride bikes'.[449] The mechanic explained that she'd been a double minority in the cycling world, being both a woman, and of white, Jamaican and Nigerian roots. Belinda isn't just changing how we cycle. She's pro-actively engaging global majority women ~~who're 'hard-to-reach'~~ whom most organisations can't be arsed to care about. Apart from making cycling a fun and affordable activity, she teaches them valuable vocational skills while up-cycling otherwise condemned bicycles. Belinda also tells me that using the worker bee in their logo and name is their way to re-claim the classist implication of northern workers labouring to serve the Queen. Belinda's efforts has made her 'Greater Manchester Bicycle Mayor'. This Queen Bee is giving us hope that the revolution—pun intended—can happen. Just before I left Manchester, I donated items to Bee Pedals. Belinda and I met by a migrant-led barber shop at the foot of my apartment block named—you guessed it—Bee Barbers.[450]

Before I left, I'd also caught *(Un)Defining Queer*[451] which is one of the most genuinely inclusive exhibitions I have seen, and which is invited to Alice's party.

Curated by Dominic Bilton, the exhibition exemplifies island-hopping as an intersectional, marginal site to gather and galvanise resistance to cause disruption. The show at the Whitworth provides a tour of LGBTQIA+ history through art, and artfully does so by juxtaposing royalty (cult filmmaker Derek Jarman) alongside exciting contemporaries (the wicked dad jokes of Chester Tenneson, whom I had the privilege of being research mentor to), as well as testimonies from multiply-minoritised people (such as a story about forbidden love from a queer Muslim woman). As you walk through the gallery, you hop from island to island of stories, to collide and collage them into yet further meanings. You aren't just a match-maker, but a mid-wife, as your input is required to ignite sparks between the 'islets' of artwork. You're also invited to co-create a glossary to define, re-define and re-imagine the possibilities of queerness—hence the title of the show. The archipelago or aggregate feeling is one of productive antagonisms and hope. *Un)Defining Queer* seems to exemplify a different, intersectional and visual form of leadership through dissent that's *actually* constructive and *respectful*.

## Long Slow Distance Island(-Hopping) Sea-Parties

These exciting guests to our ~~tea-party long-island tea-party~~ long, slow-distance island-hopping sea-party show how island-hopping can function as a form of intersectional leadership strategy that's portable, elastic, critical and clumsy, and guard against singularity and reductionism.

Our 'hopping'—actual, metaphorical—enables the encounter and embodiment of multiple, conflicting viewpoints. While we'll never achieve the octopus' 360 vision, this pro-active movement can help alleviate the sense of blocked vision experienced by frogs trapped in a well (who consider what they see of the sky as the entire world), prisoners in Plato's cave (who're trapped by their own shadows), and Foucault's self-policing workers (who turn in on themselves by monitoring and restricting their own behaviour).

Island-hopping also resonates with Anne Douglas' call for artistic leadership to have what she similarly describes as a '360° vision'.[452] This refers to being 'interested in the complexity of the world' and taking an interest in different, 'non-linear' roles and skills. Examples includes artist, artistic director, bureaucrat, administrator, manager, entrepreneur, activist, policy-maker, 'public intellectual' and 'incidental person'.

In offering neither easy (re-)solutions or convenient conclusions to skip onto, and instead inviting/inciting the audience to do the leg-work, island-hopping as a relational, embodied, intersectional leadership approach is asking/tasking them to dart between different perspectives and registers, so that their assumptions are constantly challenged and mediated, useful for our stormy sea-changes ahead.

## An Anti-Boredom Starting Point and Jumping Board

We've darted across ideas, time and space in the last few paragraphs—but what of the artwork *Island-hopping* itself, and my own hopping?

After I left Japan, *Island-hopping* as a body of installation, film, text, performance and more went on to tour for the following two years. My own views developed too, such that I was to engage in co-creation more. Various iterations and 'islands' of the work has since have been enjoyed (sic) by people in various part of Japan and the world, including islands like New Zealand, UK and Australia (Fig. 20.2[453]).

**Fig. 20.2**   Live Here. Be Australian!

Does any of this matter to right-wing flying sperms? Probably not. Two decades on, unlike the Germans, Japan is still stone-walling calls to acknowledge—much less apologise for—any of its war crimes.

Perhaps more '*ma*'—more *passage* of time and space—is needed? After all, '*ma*' clarifies that the spaces *between* rocks in a rock garden and the silences *between* utterances of the kabuki actor are just as significant—if not more important—to what the rocks and utterances imply.

Or, perhaps I've also gotten even by using 'ma' in the first place, as a shame-less *gaikokujin*.

Still, to rival the fancy get-ups of the nationalist cos-players, and to remind myself against my own pride and myopia even if middle-aged and land-locked, I've recently had a drawing of an octopus-cum-cat inked on my body. Less radical than the body art of certain performance artists (Orlan, via invasive medical procedures; or Stelarc, growing a new ear on his arm amongst other interventions), but more embodied than theoretical pro-positions (and decidedly less extractive like the 'tentacular thinking' of Donna Haraway), making my body a 'sentient and conscious canvas'[454] enables me to permanently personify an inter-species itinerant island-hopper, and enact island-hopping as a mobile, creative and critical leadership strategy. While also a visual marker of my mid-life crisis, my tattoo will also help ensure that I don't just teach, but teach *through the skin*.

*Open your eyes, mind and heart. Island-hop clumsily, discordantly and defiantly.*

# CHAPTER 21

# J: Jeer-Leadership for Justice!

*Sick of cock-ups like claustrophobia, state-control, capitalism and Confucianism? Itching to foil imperialist zombies on the sceptred isle of Great (sic) Britain, the birthplace of Punch and Judy? Get ready to rock and LOL (sic)! Here's my smashing cock-tail of ~~dad~~ tiger-mummy jokes, Singapore Sling-shots and punch-lines.*

## IRON-FISTED EFFICIENCY

### *Sucker-Punch*

I was born in a sunny utopia, set in the sea, where pretty flowers bloom for you and me. The owners of this filthy-rich island-nation also brand it 'Lion City' and 'State of Fun'.

I certainly had fun.

I was 14 when I began to take global issues personally, viscerally. To protest the Chinese government's massacre of democracy-seekers led by 21-year-old Uyghur student-leader Örkesh Dölet, I began creating protest paintings, cartoons and mappings. This body-mind-world barometer of injustice didn't—*doesn't*—re-place, but to an extent re-purposes the turmoil I feel from my everyday reality.

K. S. Tan, *Neuro-Futurism and Re-Imagining Leadership*, Studies in Mobilities, Literature, and Culture, https://doi.org/10.1007/978-3-031-55377-6_21

Nonetheless, I felt home-sick—as in sick of 'home' (sic). My existential weight ballooned like lead, or iron. Iron-filings fill every atom[455] of my body. It's an over-sized baggage I drag along wherever I go. Still, my doctor insisted that I had iron-deficiency. Eat more meat, Dr Tan said. You're annoying, I said, and nearly punched him. Later, I asked another Dr Tan for a hysterectomy. He said I was hysterical. You're annoying, I said, and nearly punched him. A little later, I became a Dr Tan myself. Whenever a tannoy asks, 'Is there a doctor in the house?', I step in, and share how the arts and culture heal.

You're welcome.

'Iron-fisted' is often used to describe the leadership style of the island's founding father—let's call him 'Daddy'. Daddy sugar-coated his paternalistic-patriarchal-parochial leadership by pitching it as the anti-dote to Western debauchery, and aligning it with Confucius' teachings of 'gentlemanly' (sic) values. Unsurprisingly, Confucius looked down on our Lao Zi, whose name has been mis-interpreted to refer to 'old child', which I do like, and whose disciples are depicted as drunken tramps. The dyslexic, Cambridge-trained law graduate and his party, which has ruled the isle since its independence from Great Britain, are artful law-makers. They invent or tweak laws at will, like banning chewing gum, performance art, 'unlawful assembly' and 'political films'.

About the latter: Films that sing praises about Daddy aren't illegal. Those about what Daddy disliked were, like one about his arch-nemesis and *de facto* Leader of Opposition, whom we shall term 'Under-Dog', who was the star of a film I made with two colleagues at a film school I taught at. My camera had found the University College London (UCL) law graduate in his late 70s, peddling his self-published book outside one of many shopping malls that litter the mother-land (sic). Three years prior, an artwork of mine was censored at the same university for its volume of vulgarities, leading to coverage on UK's *Times* newspaper,[456] but this was the first time my art made it to the front pages of the national newspapers. I became famous because the film had the honour of being the island's first 'illegal film'.[457] Although made in a workshop organised by the school with a European cultural institute, the school denied knowledge/responsibility of the film. We were fed to the lions. This being 2001, my landline was tapped, my home visited, video tapes confiscated, and I rocked a buzz-cut.

Just as we were almost charged, and I momentarily entertained unsolicited career advice by about using my 'sharp teeth' to study law, everything died down. Daddy hated the doggedness of the Under-Dog, and would have been keen to use us to teach others a lesson, but he probably disliked the international press and face-loss more.[458]

Also, Daddy had bigger ambitions for the likes of me. Likely a fan of eugenicists like Francis Galton—who was UCL's poster-boy until recently—Daddy's other pet project was to be match-maker-cum-KY-jelly for single, educated paler women of the population to pump out kiddies.

### Punch-Line

To disrupt destructive cycles imposed, I won a scholarship to study over-seas,

Joyously and flagrantly child-free, I live, and will likely die, in Great Britain, the (is-)land of irony.

Bye Bye Daddy.

## IRONY-DEFICIENCY

### Sucker-Punch

Surprise surprise: the grass isn't greener when we hop to other (is-)lands. This is especially for body-mind-worlds that used to—and are used to—violating others' like yours. Flying-sperms and ghosts of imperialism not so much haunt, but openly up-hold institutions and constitutions in these spaces. Monuments (that celebrate people who enslaved your ancestors), museums (that eulogise the 'great explorers'), and monarchy (with a £100m coronation showing off looted bling during the cost-of-living crisis) aside, you're navigating layers and palimpsests of (un-)written rules and codes of conduct. You turn from white- to blue-collar, zero-hours 3D workers in the mother-land (sic). You're infantilised (Confucius and tiger-mummies, move aside!), rendered desirable (as mail brides and 'exceptional talents'[459]), and/or threatening (stealing jobs and spouses when not instigating global pandemics). You're hyper-visible (sticking out like a sore-thumb with your smelly food) *and* invisible ('I don't see colour!'). Behave! Stay in your lane! Don't run! Be grateful! If you're so un-happy, why don't you *go home*?

That and more have been hauled at me when moving through the UK and beyond. Great Britain is the birth-place of bull-dogs, Brexit, Braverman, brazen blocking of cease-fires, backing of butchery in occupied territories. Nope, I didn't sign up for these either. But I did make sacrifices and selfish decisions to call this island 'home'. That's why I'm even more invested, and am joining others in the under-commons who also live here, to battle these injustices and more. Still, being of the default colour for emojis (although that, like the inhabitants of Springfield and most things, denotes whiteness), what I rub up against is nothing that my brown and Black colleagues endure. When called 'Kung-fu Kai' on day one at UCL, I found it *funny*—both hilariously lazy as an alliteration, and weird (what if dressage was my cup of bubble-tea?). A couple months in, my tutor proudly did what he did to many other non-white female students. The lesbian-feminist professors scoffed, 'Why didn't you say no?' (like how the professor-slash-towering-genius' students didn't say no when he painted and bedded them). Other highlights include: local kids blocking my entry into my council flat at pre-gentrified Elephant and Castle because I looked like I liked fisting. 'Ching-chong' noises spectators made when I went running in Leeds. Hounded by ten policemen in a room in the Rimini airport due to 'issues' with my passport—shortly after escaping from the driver who'd repeatedly suggested stopping over at a 'disco' with him because we had 'sympatico'. Bumble dates bragging about their (con-)quests of petite submissive orientals. Estate agents in Winchester fawning over my status as a crazy cat-less single lady-slash-'the right kind of migrant'. Being praised for beansprouts (all of them), and my 'nice' eye-lids and command of English. Yours aren't too awful either, I giggled coyly. Here, have some (bitter-)sweet and sour-puss bat-soup with flied lice.

## Punch-Line

Joshua Bethania's come-back what he calls 'amateur' racism is anything but. When told that 'immigrants coming to this country should become more English', the comedian decided to exercise 'empathy', and thought:

> *'Can you imagine if someone came into your country, forced their culture, refused to learn the language, started stealing your things, [...] introduced racism, caused a community divide that would last for decades and decades, and when they left they took those stolen things and put them on display in a museum for you to come and see? That would be insane wouldn't it?'*[460]

With that, Bethania lands a killer triple blow: using stand-up comedy (a format that originated in US minstrel shows that also birthed both Black-face and Golliwogs), as an Indian-born comedian in a London club full of white audiences, and jeering at the absurdities of the world that jolt us out of the status quo. Discourses within leadership are increasingly interested in the capacity for humour to encourage creativity and innovation, gener-ate a sense of safety and wellbeing, improve self-efficacy and receptiveness to culture change, especially during crisis.[461] Bethania's killer-punches leap-frogs these discussions, by demonstrating how workers and leaders from minoritised backgrounds can use humour as KY jelly for tricky dis-cussions. By pulling the carpet from perpetrators of aggression, humour can shift diagrams of power within hostile spaces and workplaces. Affects are 'contingent',[462] explains Sara Ahmed, and 'humour is contagious'.[463] Hitting the guts and brain simultaneously, at once primal yet also sophis-ticated, humour is a 'tactic for countering hegemonic power, coping, and resisting geopolitical conflict, structural violence, and identity-based mar-ginalization'.[464] Bethania's writing and delivery is dead-panned, in con-trast to the emotiveness of the taunt hurled at him. His story's twist-turn-trip-trap are Kung-fu moves by stealth, that make you *break*, into laughter. Within this cathartic release/relief, the sting of the punch-line lingers on.

Bethania's mobilisation of wit as sling-shot to the feeble-witted recalls the anarchism of Lao Zi and satirist Jonathan Swift alike. How he ~~yells~~ *laughs* back at the 'insanity' of the norm aligns him with the efforts of other hyphenated UK movers and shakers, like British-Pakistani spoken-word poet Suhaiymah Manzoor-Khan, who similarly, dexterously, punches-up above her weight is *Post-Colonial Banter* and performance *LOL, Inshallah*, the titles of which already squeeze cold sweat from pale pores. Through uncanny juxtapositions of words and ideas, Bethania and Manzoor-Khan both, in the latter's words, 'destabilise' lazy binaries of 'moderate/extreme, liberal/conservative, oppressed/liberated, afraid/brave, victim/villain', demonstrating at once how 'complex' but also 'mundane, messy and boring' humans are.[465] Particularly at 'times of adversity', humour 'becomes a medium through which to live alternative realities', generating spaces for 'moments of solidarity' for 'vulnerable populations' to resist or oppose 'state territorialization'.[466] Within stand-up comedy—incidentally a career path-way recommended for ADHD-ers like Bethania since hyper-activity is the norm[467]—the most pungent mock-ery of white fragility have often come from comedians with migrant backgrounds. Like Margaret Cho (Korean/US) and Anisa Nandaulu (Ugandan/Australia), Bethania invents safe(r) spaces—physical, virtual and affective—for marginalised groups to congregate and cry collective tears of joy. This could be why, between March and June 2023 alone, Bethania's clip reached nearly 5 million views online. If this includes the person who'd inspired Bethania's routine, will they pull their socks up, and make their racism more 'professional'?

## CALLED TO THE (COLOUR-)BAR

### Sucker-Punch

'Things are getting on swimmingly well', starts the first line of my (un-banned) film, *Chlorine Addiction*. I'd picked up swimming to dry out my skin, numb my senses, and to drown my deadening 'life' back 'home'.

After all, 'if it ain't broke, don't fix it', Daddy, the 'Elder Statesman of Asia', had reassured his kids. Daddy's own bio-logical kid became his successor. Unsurprisingly, Successor-Son is heavy-handed with his iron-fisting too. To continue to project economic prosperity, it has upped the ante of the British tradition of hiring male labourers from India to work on its copious building sites strewn throughout the 710 square kilometre-big island, 22% of which is sand as re-claimed land. In 2022, the state hanged a mentally-disabled 'drug mule' to death for trafficking 42.72g of heroin, the same as the amount of sugar in a can of Coke.[468] Alas, unlike Musk or Kai, his neuro-divergence[469] wasn't a 'competitive advantage', but a direct liability, because this ADHD-er was a dark-skinned school drop-out-turned-security-guard from Malaysia, in a land where those on top of the ladder are yellow bees like the Daddy, Confucius and fecund jaundiced females. This land has form when it comes to making its brown migrant workers feel *in-secure*, like during the pandemic when the 'unevenness of resource distribution' to non-citizens uncovered the 'dangers' of its discriminatory ways.[470] If you are brown, foreign but cock-less, you're likely sentenced to servitude. Although live-in domestic workers from the region 'fill crucial care gaps' in local households, they're deemed un-skilled. With 'low-status, low-visibility, and low-pay', social protection for them remains 'uneven, uncertain, and indeterminate'.[471] Abuse, rape, imprisonment and other forms of human rights abuses aren't un-common.

Monkey see, monkey do. Aren't these islanders simply copy-catting their masters and former owners? During the Japanese Occupation

(1942–1945), the island's yellow rulers despised the darker yellow natives. They massacred tens of thousands of local Chinese to 'purge through cleansing', and re-named the island 'Light of the South'. Since then, the island has been delighting southern parts of anatomies, being both fetish-ised as a sexy utopia as well as the butt of jokes.

While 'repressive' and 'lobotomised' with any chaos 'authored', ugli-ness 'designed', and absurdity 'willed',[472] the city-state is also the 'Switzerland of Asia', and was even the Tories' wet dream for post-Brexit Great Britain.[473] Author William Gibson calls the isle 'Disneyland with the Death Penalty', where rebels must either have 'balls the size of durian fruit, or else be flat-out suicidal, or possibly both',[474] in reference to the pungent, thorny and effing delicious king of fruits.

A Kung-fu twist to the story is how the nation actively lures the pale-skinned, exposing how its anti-Western rhetoric is but a defensive cloak for its colonial hang-over. As 'Asia for beginners', the island remains a top destination for gap-year-travellers and ~~migrant workers~~ 'expatriates' from the global north. If they aren't 'finding themselves' or 'teaching English', they're disciplining former colonies about human/animal/environmental rights. Many are fast-tracked into roles of senior managers on 'expat' pay-scales and swiftly granted permanent visas. Arts and cultural organisations led by white neo-colonialists who mock the behaviours and diets of 'native' artists and low-paid brown technicians as 'barbaric' are open secrets.

### Punch-Line

One expat did have durian-like ballsy-ness. When teaching at a university on the island, the professor awarded all 169 of his business management students Grade 'A', and was fired.[475]

His name? Stefano Harney—one half of Harney and Moten.

But the barbaric natives have the last laugh. Asians describe these expats as 'low-skilled, cheap, thirsty, yellow fever pervs'[476] or LBHs (losers back home).[477]

The island's comedy royalty is also her most well-known Indian and LGBTQIA+ person, Kumar Chinnadurai. Having honed her skills in the trail-blazing cabaret bar Boom Boom Room, Kumar pokes fun at the State of Fun. In one sketch, while wearing a Union Jack dress, when Kumar complains that 'everywhere they dig dig dig dig, one day just going to go down',[478] she's likening the city-state's obsession with economic growth to digging its own grave. The crowd roars with laughter. She's killing it.

# PROFESSIONALISM BAR NONE

## Sucker-Punch

'Amateur racism' pales next to professional, white-collar versions, which shine the brightest in spaces that make humans human(e), i.e., the academy, arts, culture and humanities.

I've shared my own examples throughout the book, which is less than 1% of my experiences. I'll spare you boring stories about being 'kindly' advised by commissioners on how my discussion of BLM and the long history of imperialist looting 'don't go well aesthetically' with the rest of my film on thriving in 2050. Or the cultural unit of a branded university flagrantly and continually extracting, editing and publishing images from #MagicCarpet to publicise their own work without paying or crediting me.

Nevertheless, the sum total of my experience will be no more than 1% of the tip of harm and contempt that an other marginalised body-mind endures at any given time.

Take how one established Bandung art and activism collective, with which I underwent an artist-in-residency programme in 2004, was 'discovered' by the same neo-colonialists who'd mocked others as barbaric, for the German block-buster art show *Documenta* 2022 to much fanfare—only to then be gas-lit with accusations of 'anti-Semitism' and more.[479]

Those by badge-wearing 'liberal' self-proclaimed 'allies' are walking-talking master-classes in hypocrisy, oppression Olympics, and fragility.[480] They proudly wear their battle-scars fighting misogyny, sexism, ableism, earn Orders of the British Empire titles for such services, but refuse to engage in the discussion of the lasting (dis-)Orders of colonialism. Without batting an eye-lid, they manipulate or invent measures that are more prescriptive, pedantic and reductive than that which they purport to 'liberate' us from, and which often maim and slowly murder Black and brown body-minds. My favourite is when they accuse non-white body-minds as the ones that are un-professional or—get this—'racist'. The proclamations of summer 2020 are but white noise. When one mentee, an 'emerging' (sic) brown artist-curator, raised the issue of racism in disability arts, the regime-bots retort: 'Can't you see that I'm busy with childcare/saving the planet/ getting arrested for gluing my hands to paintings *on your behalf*?' The show must go on. Shush and watch 'Karen-s and Ken-s'—a short-hand by the Black community to describe white supremacist aggressions on Black body-mind-worlds[481]—take centre-stage and re-direct discussions around *their* victim-hood.

Those unhappy to join the conspiracy of silence and are able to move on pivot their narratives around just that—the *move*.[482]

The stubborn ones who stick around insist that this *is* home, and continue their struggle and run through pain to make this *home*—the arts and cultural industry, the academy, racist regimes etc—*work*.

### Punch-Line

Let's not waste the little time and space we have on lies, lice or distractions. Let's honour the truly artful, like Gina Yashere. Black people don't care about Ku Klux Klan and such-like, explains the UK-Nigerian queer comedian.[483] 'If I see some twat-biscuit in a bed-sheet with eye holes cut out, it's pretty obvious.' Instead, what's harmful is the racism that that is 'invisible to the naked white eye'.

Four decades prior, Yashere's predecessor Richard Pryor explained that racism is part of capitalism's ploy to stop people from understanding one another, to keep the wheels of the dominant order running.[484] In the same year, when he performed for 17,000 of these professional, naked white eyes at a fundraiser for gay rights, he'd yelled:

'This is the first time in my life I ever realised that faggots are prejudiced because I don't see no niggas out here! [...] When the niggas were burning down [...] you motherfuckers [...] didn't give a shit about it!'.[485]

The (white) press described this as an 'anti-gay rant'.[486] Did the grand-daddy of truth-telling care? No. He signed-off by saying:

'You can kiss my happy rich black ass.'

*Be neither shaken nor stirred. Lighten up your South. Ask twat-biscuits to kiss your ass. Kiss daddies and nepo babies good-bye. Bang on about opposition and under-dogs. Bang un-pro-creatively. Bang out of order. Down cock-tails of 42.72g of salt. Get punch-drunk. Punch up, with irony fists, and hit below the belt.*

# CHAPTER 22

# X: X-ray Yourselves

*Take a hard look inside-out. Cross-examine your own species, not just what but how you see. Have you got X-ray vision à la Super ~~man~~ baby? Can Specsavers make you spectacles to rival the Octopus' 360-degree eye-sight of radical empathy? Or are those xenophobic twat-biscuit views with blinkers? Are you a saviour or surveillance-bot? Are you saving hairless chimps from prisons? Or abolishing mindsets that entertain incarceration? Or a mercenary prison guard up-holding and magnifying the prison-system (Fig. 22.1[487])?*
*Will you come clean?*

© The Author(s), under exclusive license to Springer Nature Switzerland AG 2024
K. S. Tan, *Neuro-Futurism and Re-Imagining Leadership*,
Studies in Mobilities, Literature, and Culture,
https://doi.org/10.1007/978-3-031-55377-6_22

**Fig. 22.1**  Seeing-Through Twat-biscuits

# CHAPTER 23

# N: Neuro-Futurise & Collectivise

*Futurise, up-rise and prise open our imprisoned body-minds. Up our game to neuro-futurise. Join the dots and collectivise, so that we can fight all oppression and inch towards collective liberation.*

## RE-GROUP

Octavia Butler pulls no punches. But when a giant of one of the most elastic artistic genres acknowledges her limitation as a creative change-maker, we're reminded that endeavours like ours are necessarily flawed, under-developed and incomplete—and that we must collaborate with other alternative, oppositional aesthetic acts to shake things up and move things forward. As Butler states:

> *'I have written books about making the world a better place and how to make humanity more survivable. [...]. You can call it save the world fiction, but it clearly doesn't save anything. It just calls people's attention to the fact that so much needs to be done [...]'.*[488]

The need to collectivise is echoed by comedian Omid Djalili, who acknowledges that jokes alone aren't enough.[489] Even teaching can't build 'alternative futures', admit Harney and Moten. So much needs to be

K. S. Tan, *Neuro-Futurism and Re-Imagining Leadership*, Studies in Mobilities, Literature, and Culture, https://doi.org/10.1007/978-3-031-55377-6_23

done—*together*, *now*, in order to reap our harvest and earn our playtime tomorrow. A reminder of the advice of Butler's contemporary Toni Cade Bambara is timely: that the job of culture-workers is to make the struggle 'irresistible'.

*Neuro-Futurism and Re-Imagining Leadership: An A-Z Towards Collective Liberation* isn't—cannot be—a 'save-the-world' book. Instead of nirvanas, magic bullets or quick-fixes, it calls peoples' attention to enduring journeys and processes of meaning-, knowledge-, trouble-, change- and future-making, with/for/by diverse and divergent body-minds-worlds and bodies of knowledge to thrive. It highlights the work that needs doing collectively. That's why instead of divisiveness, or (hair-) splitting, I'll zero-in on connectedness here. With one eye on our deadline of 2050, and the other of the fact that we're at the final chapters of our (ad-)venture, let's remind us of what brought us here, what we've done, and where we can go, *together*. I'll run through the key ingredients of our (bitter-)sweet, sour and spicy (bat-)soup. I'll also highlight how my creative interpretations and interventions seek to add value to the respective fields we've learnt from. As Linda Tuhiwai Smith reminds us, making connections and affirming connectedness is essential. Reciprocity and solidarity are required to nourish our ultra-marathon ahead. To do and think *better* about *better* leadership, so much more needs to be done *together*.

## RE-CONNECT

We've asked, and addressed: *What can a more equitable and imaginative praxis of leadership look like? As odd times demand novel tactics, in what ways can marginalised and 'non-standard' perspectives and methods fill gaps, to disrupt, reveal insights, and generate new knowledge?*

My *A-Z* widens how we apprehend, engender and develop 'leadership', catalysing discourse and fostering alliances. We've speed-dated as well as mix-and-mis-matched with species, fields, practices that haven't properly met, to set our agenda. As an inter-disciplinary, ill-disciplined, intersectional, island-hoppy mapping for the value of *neuro-futurising leadership*, it generates new ways to problematise critical issues in around leadership. Gaps within and between the various fields—which are often already multi-disciplinary and contested—have enabled the sculpting of neuro-futurising leadership as a transversal and polycentric framework. In so doing, I've also outlined path-ways for *capacity-building*, which can also facilitate further connections. I invite my stake-holders and co-runners—you—to critically engage with the themes and tactics of *Neuro-Futurism*. More excitingly, I hope that my provocations have inspired you to assemble, grow and/or shift your own toolkit of creative approaches to re-place burning houses of knowledge and habits un-fit for purpose, slay stubborn zombies of imperialism, and yell back at canons with no bite or brio, to re-write and dys-play your own forms of *better* leadership.

What were the (under-)common grounds, gaps and opportunities in knowledge, practices and lived experience in the various fields? Let's sprint through what we have (dis-)covered.

## *Mobilities*

Since this book is in the *Mobilities, Literature and Culture* series, let's begin with mobilities studies.

*Neuro-Futurism* compiles and re-arranges through my non-normative interpretation the work of those on the move who have moved us, and are moving the world. These movers and shakers include people (Lao Zi/anti-adult running kids), communities (BeePedalReady/neuro-queering/RAN), non-humans (octopuses/tape-worms/killer-whales) and systems (DAIR/*Un-Defining Queerness*/the cunning coronavirus), historically (Lorde/Leonardo) and in fiction (Squeaky's running as sling-shot/Rye driving her own destiny). While bite-sized, this book has sharp teeth and elephantine ambitions, taking on troubling issues which are off-set with a pace and language that's light.

As an intellectually itinerant artist who has called mobilities studies a 'home' of sorts for nearly 15 years, I've been curious to find out how these stories, testimonies, survivance and envisionings can dialogue and dance with mobilities studies. The book showcases both products and processes of mobility studies. In addressing some of the lacunae through mobilities approaches related to creative practice, justice and futures, *Neuro-Futurism* seeks to deepen and widen the reach of the field. The *A-Z* fulfils the series' aims, which include examining the 'material means and structures of movement, as well as the infrastructures that surround such movement', with a focus on 'travel, postcolonialism, and/or embodiment'.

The book clarifies, through the mobilities compass, some of my recent explorations (such as neuro-divergence, including my own). My own experience of racial aggression in 2023 in a mobilities context has given the book's EDI focus a level of urgency. *Neuro-Futurism* advances mobilities' concern with subversive mobilities, and the 'kinopolitics of mobility' amid the 'triple mobility crisis' of 'climate change, migration and urbanization'.[490] If mobilities really cares about removing 'blockages, stoppage, friction' that have been assaulting the 'immobile, differently mobile, and stopped or managed',[491] it must learn from the intersectional, anti-oppressive and neuro-queer. It's not just a travesty to dis-regard odd thinkers and creative problem-solvers, or to continue to assume neuro-typicality as default, but a missed opportunity and failure to optimise and advance knowledge and human potential in a resource-poor world.

## *(Critical) Leadership*

Regarding the myth that autistic people don't have empathy, Jason Arday clarifies that the 'experts' aren't just wrong, but should grasp that empathy comes in 'different forms'.[492] Indeed, empathy underpins *Neuro-Futurising Leadership*. At its heart is not just one but *three* hearts—if that isn't enough empathy, what is?

Likewise, this *A-Z* clarifies that there are diverse and divergent forms of *different* and *better* leadership. We have run through how neuro-futurising leadership draws on, as well as counters and extends what, why and how of both 'classical' and critical leadership studies. I've shared various routes (making head-ways hyper-tactically; gently-anarchising; waking and shaking off smoke-screens), as well as (dis-)guises (cock-roaches; whiskers to escape from Japanese imperialists; mobile human-monuments; spaces for stimming and self-soothing).

Liminal, slippery and hyper-active, neuro-futurising leadership counters 'leadership' as an ossified or neutral ideology, and/or one fixated on individuals traits or birth-rights, or the leader–follower binary. Emphasising systems-, poetic- and process-thinking, action, (hyper-)activism, emancipation and en-visioning, through an iterative process of (re-)mapping entangled in and influencing larger socio-political contexts and cosmos, I've demonstrated neuro-futurising leadership as a (co-)creative praxis for positive structural, infra-structural, and intra-relational change.

## *Neuro-Diversity*

A key intervention and contribution will have been the meaningful embedding of creativity, art and artfulness not just as case studies (Butler/ Boombox Barry; Pankhurst/Paik) but also as applied methods (island-hopping/jeer-leadership for justice/running artfully), to broaden how leadership and neuro-diversity are discussed and understood. In entangling mobilities with leadership and neuro-divergence creatively, the book shows how a joint approach can help address outstanding issues in the respective fields. Neuro-Futurising leadership brings to life how creativity is a 'powerful force' that can 'shape and define all of our futures', and enable us to 'fulfil our human potential and to make positive changes to the world around us'.[493] In so doing, my project also brings rigour to the popular concepts of 'creativity', 'innovation', 'agility' in leadership and organisational studies.

In addition, the book critiques the dominant narrative of 'neuro-diversity' as a 'next talent opportunity', 'method for fostering innovation', or 'strong business case' to reap 'better financial outcomes'. My work nudges the diagram of power by re-moving the autistic white-supremacist cis-heterosexual 'Rain Man' from pedestals, and by neuro-queering leadership to facilitate the self-actualisation of body-minds marginalised within minoritised groups. In part created with/for/by neuro-divergent and QTIBIPOC movers and shakers, my book begins to fill key gaps in CLS and discussions around leadership and EDI, and ensures that knowledges and experiences around neuro-divergence are discussed in nuanced, intersectional ways, and are prioritised, not objectified or re-othered.

And, of course, a premise, driving force and key strategy of neuro-futurising leadership is the innovative aspects of non-standard ways of moving in the world. I have irritated normative approaches of and assumptions about leadership through methods like ill-disciplinary culture change and productive antagonisms, which draw on assets of neuro-divergence like divergent thinking, risk-taking and more.

### Psych-, Neuro- and Social Sciences

This *A-Z* invites researchers and practitioners in brain and mind sciences to (re-)view a-typical processes beyond deficits, disorders or abnormalities, and instead in creative, leadership terms, such as the proposal of 'ill-disciplined leadership' (Fig. 23.1[494]). Its qualitative and creative approach may inspire clinical—pun intended—researchers to improve the design of trials to make them more accurate. My endeavour may also spur researchers to collaborate with creative researchers and artists. Embedded in research, and as an exemplar of divergent thinking in action, the book goes further than memoirs or such-like to deepen the understanding of

**Fig. 23.1**   Mind-Wandering Mind-Wondering

those who explore differences as assets, or part of a 'normal' or 'more humane' ecosystem.

Neuro-futurising leadership teaches those in social science, cultural geography and other disciplines that make use of, extract from and exploit the creative arts and minoritised communities and efforts about respect and ethics. It highlights ways to engage with creative and neuro-divergent approaches and people in *leadership* terms, as thought-leaders and not as after-thought. Instead of instrumentalising them or regarding them as short-term contractors without agency, I've shown how the arts can artfully re-direct and lead (dis-)courses.

The book also teaches those in creative health the value of neuro-divergence, and how the false binary between 'community' and 'professional' arts practices is myopic. Furthermore, this work invites those in critical medical or health humanities to widen 'sites and scales of "the medical"' beyond the clinical encounter, and demonstrate how the arts is 'not in service to' the sciences but as 'productively entangled' beyond lip-service.

Those in critical pedagogy on the campaigns to 'decolonise the curriculum' or embed creativity are reminded to walk the walk, and engage with non-Western epistemologies (like Daoism) as well as creative and non-human approaches (like octopuses).

### Creative Arts

This book can offer insights for those keen to crack both chronic leadership and diversity issues in the research and practice of the arts and culture.

Its arsenal of neuro-queering adds a hitherto often-neglected area to the discussion, a travesty given the sector's over-representation of neuro-divergent and queer people. This work enriches discourse in public, social, political and live art, adds value to debates in creative research (and/or artistic research, practice-led research, practice as research et al.), as well as the role of creativity in research and the academy more generally. Those in art history and theory practice, cultural and museum studies, and arts management may be prompted to re-examine the arts in leadership terms, or develop yet other artful modes of encounters with players outside of the arts, to gain new audience and funding.

Notions and practices of care and self-care are increasingly mainstreamed, and my work reveals insights on neuro-divergent perspectives, as well as shed new light to understand empathy. Organisations that mimic the ways of Big Business or worship abusive Towering Geniuses may be inspired to create policies and practices that enact inclusive leadership, by developing cultures and spaces that aren't just safe(r), but are anchored in love and kindness, and *prize* difference.

My book sticks out by calling out on professional racism and oppression. Issues of essentialism, exceptionalism, tribalism and territorialisation are still under-researched and under-discussed, as those guilty of such practices are in positions of power, and those less powerful often have to toe the party-line. This work invites a re-consideration of the uncritical approach to the social model of disability, simplistic demonisation of the medical, and the fetishisation of trauma that re-hashes the lazy 'artist as mad genius' tropes. Intersectional, nuanced yet candid about its own myopia, my work urges us to x-ray ourselves *sans* polite air kisses.

### Those Who Feel Blocked

More generally, *Neuro-Futurism* may benefit those engaging in inter-disciplinary and inter-species thinking and making. Concepts like 'gate-crashing' (the arts into psychiatry) and 'clock-blocking' (con-joining 'crip' and Afrofuturist notions of time) advance discussions on how creative, practice-led methods challenge the boundaries of knowledge, while proposals like 'ill-disciplined culture change' extend inter-related notions like 'indisciplinary', 'undisciplined', 'transdisciplinarity'.

This *A-Z* can also be a reference for critical self-reflection for any field or body that feels stuck in its ways. It isn't a user-friendly read since your heavy-lifting is often required. But the rewards are tantalising if my trips and traps can intimate and animate dis-entanglements, or even trigger in-sights for nudges in position and/or paradigm.

### Those Who Are Blocked

I'm keen to hear feedback from fellow chimeras, composites and critical friends. Writing this book has been painful both physically and mentally, but which pales next to the trials and tribulations of these trail-blazers. The process of re-laying their enduring labour has filled me with anger, sadness as well as hope. That I'm able to have the resources and platform to share my interpretations, (un-)learnings and findings is humbling. I'm in-debted to many who have guided and pushed me. I seek to bring the path-finders' work to the attention of 'mainstream' audiences.

I will be thrilled if the book can help equip colleagues to advocate for themselves and assert their own leadership for the tough road ahead. If that is too risky or costly, I hope that you can point to stubborn line-managers and systems that up-hold the status quo, 'my human rights/lived experience/perspective/time-out is important—look, this (serious) book says so too'. Cite and make full use of what I have written, so that I can be your co-runner, and act as your body-blocker vicariously.

I've argued that we must futurise, up-rise, enterprise, synthesise and visualise something *better*. I hope that the strategies can help re-position issues and values ignored or deemed deviant/surplus/troublesome as assets. I've been clear about the need to be our glorious, monstrous, clunky intersectional and mouth-fully hyphenated selves when moving out of our home/lane/margin/ghetto. We've worked through ways to call out on white elephants, and sticking out as shame-less sore thumbs when/where you can. By activating tactics like neuro-queering and jeer-leadership, we can Kung-fu twist-turn-trip-trap the regime-bots/twat-biscuits/flying-sperms and crack violent cycles and chains memorised by colonialist muscles and rusty/dusty institutions. I've also run through ways for us odd-balls to mobilise our oddity, de-formity and non-conformity, to make our balls the size and, I'd add, smell and spikiness—of the of durians. Like Octavia Butler, I've written ourselves into dominant narratives, to kill feeble-witted cartoon representations. At the same time, I'd made no bones about the need to walk the tight-rope of code-switching, flip-flopping, as well as to be assertive about your boundaries. I've expressed the importance to take time out to rest and quell un-rests through stimming and self-soothing, or even walk out and run away when needed, and let others with stronger knees and thicker, elephant-like hide to body-block, pick up the baton and lunge forward.

In re-framing the life/work hacks of marginalised/minoritised communities and under-commons in leadership terms, neuro-futurising leadership seeks to fire us like sling-shots to into spaces/rooms/tables where the power-suited are, to productively antagonise, turn the tables show them how we party. With our beansprouts, bat-soup and other smelly food on new tables that we've re-designed, we'll show the pale/stale what they've been missing out. I hope that my candour and care can alleviate the clunkiness of my approach, and help fore-ground our fore-runners' grit, sweat, blood, tears, toil, as well as coups, runner's highs and joys.

## Those Who Block

Last but not least, *A-Z* is for all glove compartments, and inside the mobile devices of the mythical 'general public' and those who are 'standard' and set standards. I will send copies of the book to 10 Downing Street, the *White* House, amateur and professional racists, fake 'allies', butt-lickers who 'have a Black friend', and the proud 'un-woke', so that you can do the work and do your effing home-work. Pressing in its arguments, energetic in tone, quick in wit and pace, colourful in its language and images, and with 26 chapters in bite-sized chunks of no more than 3000 words each that you can dip in and out of, what excuses have you got?

But if you're still wondering why you should care, or if everything's Peachy for you, *you* are the Problem with capital P.[495] I'll swipe left and ask you to move along. Yep, it's *you*, not me. But thank you for shoving sewage into the open wounds of my oddly-shaped pre-mature skull to spur me to write this book.

You're always welcome.

## RE-COVER

*Neuro-Futurism* has been my invitation for other workers, colleagues, collectives, classrooms, and cosmoses, to join forces with myself and yet others. I've shown how it draws on and can add value to disparate schools of knowledge, and how, in creatively filling gaps, the book can generate new knowledge around leadership, as well as mobilities, the creative arts and social justice. I've also shown how our exercise is necessarily in-complete, and that the work continues. That's why we have, and will continue to, cast our tentacles far and wide and deep, and to seek one another out in the '*ma*' and liminal spaces, to continue and up the game of our endeavour. We'll continue to seek out, solidarise, and form alliances with one another beyond erect structures we are confined in. We'll lock hands with heads, hearts with horns, and soul with sole, to run the long slow distances or LSDs ahead, to break the harms of the non-consensual hallucination, to comfort and push one another, and celebrate wins when(ever) we can.

'*If you want to know what the undercommons wants, what Moten and Harney want, what black people, indigenous peoples, queers and poor people want, what we (the "we" who cohabit in the space of the undercommons) want, it is this—we cannot be satisfied with the recognition and acknowledgement generated by the very system that denies a) that anything was ever broken and b) that we deserved to be the broken part; so we refuse to ask for recognition and instead we want to take apart, dismantle, tear down the structure that, right now, limits our ability to find each other, to see beyond it and to access the places we know lie beyond its walls.'—Jack Halberstam 2013*[496]

# CHAPTER 24

# A: Agitate as Artful, Agile & A-Typical Cheer-Leaders

*The 'subversive intellectual enjoys the ride and wants it to be faster and wilder', state Harney and Moten 2013.*[497] *Instead of a room of her own, she 'wants to be in the world, in the world with others and making the world anew'. Hand-in-hand with others, she is making and re-making the world a-new, with new models of leadership and new role models, cheering one another on, cheerfully, defiantly.*

## WILDER JOY-RIDES

It's late summer 2023, Winchester, UK. Things are going on swimmingly well. I'm cycling about on my kiddy push-bike, waving to on-lookers curious about the new pleb in the posh village.

I'm also packing my bag for my visit to Japan in Autumn. A lot has *moved on* in the last two decades in and around Japan—or have they not? I'll be a juror of 'New Asian Currents' of the Yamagata International Documentary Film Festival which has, since 1989, shared 'new ways of expression'. This includes *Chlorine Addiction* in 2001.[498] I'll be screening the film again, plus other efforts. I'm thrilled to see how a new generation of movers and shakers navigate our stormy current and past, and envisage our future, through *moving* images.

© The Author(s), under exclusive license to Springer Nature Switzerland AG 2024
K. S. Tan, *Neuro-Futurism and Re-Imagining Leadership*,
Studies in Mobilities, Literature, and Culture,
https://doi.org/10.1007/978-3-031-55377-6_24

199

I'll also discuss my proposal for a TV series based on this book. The 7-part programme will feature highlights from the 26 chapters, and more. We'll island-hop across time, space and imagination. Each episode will be head-lined by an exemplar of artful, agile and a-typical leadership, like the innovators from Neurodiversity In/& Creative Research Network, Paw (who'll return to Myanmar to join the Karen National Liberation Army to fight the junta once she ends her contract as my dad's carer) and hopefully leaders like Jason Arday. Scenes will un-fold in bee colonies and the Chauvet Cave in France. Dressed as an octo-pussy, I'll ask why people 50,000 years ago wasted their time to scribble cartoons on the caves' walls, and explore the emerging field of neuro-aesthetics to investigate how art alters brain chemicals.[499] We'll also pop over to Chile to ask why Augusto Pinochet Ugarte, like Pol Pot and other despots, feared the power of imagination and the arts, and went on to kill artists through his 'Caravan of Death'. Animated sequences will compare the runner's high and with the 'motor' of ADHD. I'd like to ask ADHD-er gymnast Simone Biles about overcoming 'twisties' or blocks personally and collectively. We'll end with a sequel to *Speech Sounds*, featuring the kids who are now teenagers and mates of Orion.

It will be wild.

## BEYOND 2050 (TO CIRCA 2175)

While in Japan, I hope to hop to the island of Shikoku, to visit the Research Institute for Future Design in Kochi University of Technology,[500] to widen my horizons beyond 2050—to around 2175. Developed by economist Tatsuyoshi Saijo, the institute champions a form of participatory decision-making that counters the short-termism endemic in political decision-making, by enabling residents to discuss and set long-term plans for their towns and cities.

Future Design is inspired by the principle of 'seventh-generation decision-making', a form of back-casting, where decisions are made to result in a sustainable world not just one, but *seven*-generations into the future. This concept originated from the ancient Haudenosaunee philosophy of the First Nations peoples in northeast North America and Upstate New York. Haudenosaunee refers to a confederation or alliance among six Native American nations, and means 'people who build a house'.[501]

Clearly, I'd need to get to the root of this. I find out more about the Haudenosaunee way, not just through design or Japan.

## BUILDING DIFFERENT HOUSES
## WITH DIFFERENT LEADERSHIP

Learning about the Haudenosaunee way will be an area of further research I should under-take. Reflecting on the findings and feedback that I will receive from this book, and extending my time-line to not just one but *seven* generations ahead, will be thrilling.

My research process will include co-building a research-resource-renewal centre or house with other workers, dreamers, doers, movers, shakers and makers. I imagine this to be a different type of house with the different leadership that Audre Lorde, Octavia Butler and Michelle Evans have also talked about. The working title? 'House for Artful Cheer-Leadership'.

In this set-up, there we'll explore and push the possibilities of thinking, experimenting, making, and making change through art and artistry. We'll investigate artful agitation as a hyper-active and hyper-tactical process to respond to issues of the day in an agile way, as well as to set visionary agen-das for the future. Itinerant and de-centralised, our home is think-tank-cum-playground-slash-bus. The bus is powered by clean fuel, as well as running artists with stronger knees, who hold the (s)pace for one another and direct the conversations to ensure that we're on track.

Our bus has three hearts, and its nine tentacles tours Davos, dumps, oceans, online, mountains, moons and Mars. The house welcomes and fosters the leadership of members of diverse species, connecting politics and physics with philosophy and poetry, children with C-suites, and money with mathematics, music, and more. Body-minds-worlds hop on and off as desired, to co-create imaginative processes, outputs and outcomes with a focus on inter-generational justice and projecting 150 years ahead. Exploiting the power of art to provoke, problematise, evoke and entangle with other disciplines, we'll ask new questions and re-imagine new possibilities.

We're continually in a process of emergence and self-actualisation, neuro-queering normativity and quieting imperialist habits by recognising and facilitating the malleability and fluidity of diverse body-minds. To generate insights and impacts that are different—because we see differ-ently—and can catalyse 10,000 changes at individual, cultural, institu-tional or structural levels, story-telling will be a key theme and method. We'll per-use fiction to learn about anti-colonial and anti-oppressive pro-cesses of 'recovery' and self-determination'. We'll consult Butler's *A*

*Necessary Being*, for instance, as a treatise on governance, incarceration and race. We'll also commission stories by a-typical artists from the global south who'll up-cycle pre-colonial frameworks that transcend the limitations of neuro-developmental or neuro-divergence, for our beyond-colonial new future. These stories will re-place 'master' narratives with new, co-created ones that can in-form, re-form and trans-form policy and practice.

## HOPE AND CHEER-LEADERSHIP

Our house will have no walls, ceilings or gates, so that we can find, work and cry with, as well as cheer on one another. Instead of prisons, slavery or wage, our house/home is built on love and kindness, to exemplify a cheerful eco-system of working collaboratively.

Hope and its cousin of the long-range vision are key fuels for our LSD ahead. In asking us to believe in the possibility of making the world a better place that we can re-make anew through the revolution, Toni Cade Bambara, our Gen Z and Baby Boomer art teachers, as well as other guides have been reminding us of the value of optimism in our endeavour. Octavia Butler was always forth-coming in expressing her internal turmoil. Yet, her insistence on hope is evident in how she ends *Speech Sounds*, which she confirms in the story's Afterword:

'I'm not pessimistic about much of anything. No, I'm hopeful.'[502]

This is powerful, given that over and above collective and personal trauma that beset the marginalised body-mind-world,[503] those who are also neuro-divergent as well as creative within this are often doubly, triply disadvantaged, as attested by the complex correlation between neuro-divergence, creativity and ill health.[504] In fact, Butler often acts as her own cheer-leader—a further testament of her artfulness. Her pink note-book is filled with life-affirming war-cries. They include: 'This is my life. I write bestselling novels'; 'I will help poor black youngsters go to college'; 'I will find the way to do this. So be it! See to it!'[505]

Hope as a means to transform the pain of the past and present and to leap us to a better future has been a recurrent theme in our exercise. With the populist tide of fundamentalist and regressive over-tones of 'nostalgia' and 'taking back control', the role of hope as resistance and change- and meaning-making is more needed than ever. Hope is 'essential to any political struggle for radical change', adds Butler's contemporary bell hooks, especially 'when the overall social climate promotes disillusionment and despair',[506] such as now. It's by 'moving through that fear, finding out what connects us, reveling in our differences' and taking risks that 'brings us closer, that gives us a world of shared values, of meaningful community'.[507] Like our house.

## CHEERFUL, QUEER JOY

Our house/home will also move through pain and fear with hope's cousin, joy. hooks has frequently evoked the notion of joy in her work as part of a transformation, as have other Black feminists.[508] New generations of imaginations of joy requires attention. Black queer joy isn't just to counter fear, or 'battle fatigue' in a 'normalized violent collectives of heteronormative, cisgender White supremacist ideologies'.[509] Instead, it's the 'grand ridiculer creating possibilities for organisms to collaborate, fracture, rock with, and throw shade', clarifies humanities scholar Reagan Patrick Mitchell. What a joyous proposition through such a rousing arrangement of words! Other marginalised communities have also been fired up to explore their own iterations. Artist Jack Tan for instance is working with other of East and Southeast Asian (ESEA) artists to explore a 'cosmology' of 'ESEA joy' in creative practice and knowledge-making.[510] Hope and joy also drive *The Transformation* by UK theatre company Actors Touring Company (ATC). Playing in London in Autumn 2023. The iconic London bus is the stage—literally—for one of its segments, 'The Architect'. Audiences are seated on the same bus and watch up close as the story, which is based on Stephen Lawrence, unfolds. The Black teenager was murdered by a group of white men while at a bus stop in 1993. Fittingly, the trilogy asks: 'how can we transform the painful legacies of history into a future of hope and possibility?'[511]

Joy has been metabolising[512] our campaign too in many ways, including the euphoric process of monster-mapping, the runner's high and thriving (Fig. 24.1[513]). A sense of joy under-pins #MagicCarpet and the 75th Anniversary of the Pan-African Congress celebrations alike. Transforming that which dominant culture assigns as deficits, disorders or deviant into assets, positives and powerful—which is a key premise of *Neuro-Futurism* too—is a grand ridiculer creating possibilities for organisms to collaborate and rock (boats) with. Drawing on feedback that I'll get from this book, joy will be another area of research I'm keen to further develop. I'd like to

**Fig. 24.1**    Mind-blowing work-outs for a neuro-futuristic 2050

do so with my many mentees and students over the years, who have brought me joy as they share ways they counter fear, battle fatigue and ridicule normativity through QTIBIPOC, refugee-asylee compasses and more.

## DIFFERENT MASTERS

Speaking of teaching, tentacularly and through the skin, another group of people I'd invite to our house-home will be students I'm teaching in a new Masters programme at a different university that I've just joined. Anchored in social justice, sustainability, and inclusion and belonging, the MA Arts and Cultural Leadership advances innovative approaches to leadership. I'm embedding my learnings from the MA I'd developed in Manchester in the module I'm leading, called 'Ideas and Debates'.

I'm excited to find ways to develop further iterations like MBA, MASc (Masters in Arts and Sciences) and free public programmes, too. I'm also keen to engineer productive antagonisms between the MA and other programmes I have been teaching on, including Master of Science courses in Affective Disorders and Health Humanities.

As we continue to build dream(ies) of better futures, I'll continue to learn from my students, as well as from great teachers, about the role of teaching. How can we teach leaders of/with/for/by not just the next, but the following *seven* generations ahead? My efforts, like my physical frame, are slight. We'll continue to pay homage to those who have broken the colour bar as well as resolutely raised the bar, like Jason Arday, as well as W.E.B. Du Bois. Du Bois wasn't just the first African-American to receive a PhD from Harvard in 1895; he was also the first sociologist to articulate the agency of the oppressed, and his work elevated sociology to an 'emancipatory social science' and, thus, encouraged a more open and inclusive academia for the good of all.[514] Such exceptional role models give you high hopes about the classroom and ivory tower as a location of possibility, and where paradises can be created.

Once again hooks can clarify. According to our poet-teacher, 'as teachers we believe that learning is possible, that nothing can keep an open mind from seeking after knowledge and finding a way to know'.[515] The title of her book? *Pedagogy of Hope*. It's when we are cowered, resources are scarce, minds are closed, news is faked, and people more tribal, that we need to re-centre teaching and the re-learning of the creative arts and humanities.[516]

## DIFFERENT LEADERS

Our seven-generation house/home welcomes yet other leaders in the making, whom generations of teachers, protectors and other 'other mothers' have been nurturing. Through various pro bono and paid roles I undertake, I'm excited to help nurture new role models and leaders.

I consider keynote lectures, master-classes and media engagement as not just dissemination vessels, but an extension of my social art practice. The platforms may be high-profile (like one with 870 mental health specialists from 17 countries in Berlin which was more fabulous than Eurovision), or intimate (like a workshop which let philosophers and psychiatrists get intimate, with a chimeric philosopher-slash-psychiatrist long-term-partner-in-crime[517]). The impact of creative intervention is often impossible to trace, measure or quantify. That is also its power. I relish every opportunity to call people's attention to the fact that so much needs to be done, *together*, as well as for people to critique my work.

Co-creation is key in a role that I volunteer in. We are keen to find ways for psychiatrists to view patients as collaborators, instead of ab-normal or un-healthy vessels to re-pair. As the first artist on the Editorial Board of a UK professional body founded in 1841 that's responsible for education, training, and setting and raising standards in psychiatry, the stakes are higher, but the rewards can hopefully be high too. In an invited commentary, I urge its readers, which includes psychiatry professionals and researchers, to move beyond art therapy and 'inspiration porn', and instead collaborate with 'patients' and artists.[518] We've also started conversations with other key actors to make mental health training, research and practice more inclusive.

At another charity I volunteer in, we're opening up our ways of working to genuinely embed co-creation and (co-)leadership. The organisation prides itself as being sector-leading and, in the words of a key member, 'non-white-sliced-bread' in its innovative approaches to creating music with/for/by refugees and asylum-seekers locked up in prison-like conditions in the UK, and has anti-semitism as a key building block. However, its governance and staff profile don't deviate from that of third sector organisations, where salaried decision-makers are middle-class, and which can unwittingly fall into white saviour-ist and colonialist tropes—and which 'do-good' organisations can precisely fail to recognise. As trustee, I have helped drive efforts to radically transform the organisation by embedding co-creation and anti-oppression practices throughout. This includes power-sharing right at the top, with efforts to employ an artistic director with lived experience of detention and/or racial inequity. We're formalising processes to make recruitment more equitable, accommodate for dis-abled and neuro-divergent staff and participants, as well as ways to value—including financially—lived experience and more. Unsurprisingly, there have been push-backs and set-backs. I've also faced direct racial harm at board level and more. I've wanted to move on many times. But as this is a voluntary role, and I have nothing to lose in speaking out compared to salaried staff or the vulnerable participants we work with, I'm not going anywhere, just yet.

Also I'm an endurance runner, and artist,

I am proud to have played a key role in the work that has led to the appointment of its first, Black neuro-divergent female Artistic Director in 2023.

Building new worlds in the shell of the old is what anarchists as well as anarchic artists like the Dadaists and Butler excel in, and what artfulness expresses. Just as making art is about (re-)making worlds, artfulness is about (re-)making worlds by applying the same cunning and imagination into the broader systems. As Anne Douglas reminds us, artists should (pro-)actively and productively engage with non-arts organisations and, more generally, larger socio-political-economic systems.[519] This guards against a cartoon-like, 'routinized language of anti-institutionalism and anti-statism', which can be counter-productive, as we can end up 'unexpectedly colluding with neoliberal impulses that want to dismantle public institutions of human welfare'. Particularly in a time of 'palpable' yet 'uncertain' transformation, where people feel 'disempowered' to affect change in a global system, Douglas states that art—and I will add artfulness—'has a role in asking and envisioning what kind of world we want to create', and can 'help us imagine sustainable social institutions'.[520]

## Wilder, more Joyous Worlds and Rides to Come

Our roving House for Artful Cheer-Leadership will be warm not because it's on fire, but because it's sustained and nourished by joy, hope, love and kindness. The spectacular spectra of participants and perspectives visiting, squatting, staying or para-siting in our mobile-mongrel-multi-hyphenated-many-running-legged monster-octo-pussy-bus will propel us with better, long-range vision. The inter-generational moving-collage and entourage of a-typical thinkers, agile doers and creative problem-solvers who thrive in unknowns will help lead the conversations and actions for change. We look out for and look after one another too, opening windows of opportunities for yet others to ride and triumph the storms to come. As our different body-minds who see things differently grow, individually and collectively, we will also become more visible as a critical and creative mass that expresses the creative possibilities of *better* leadership.

I'll reflect on some of these new works-in-progress in two other books that I'm also working on. Like *Neuro-Futurism*, they explore creativity, futurity, anti-oppression and leadership. I'm co-editor for a hand-book that's co-created with members of the Neurodiversity In/& Creative Research Network. I'm author for the other, which is a full-length monograph with a scientific publisher, to reach readers in business, management and more. The latter will include details that I haven't been able to discuss in this short book, such as a speed-date with Nick Walker, in which she describes a neuro-queered future as one of 'creative liberation and transformation'.[521] I also propose to under-take a research trip to visit Aboriginal artist-knowledge-maker Gullawun Daniel Roque Lee in Australia, in order to learn more about Larrakia knowledge systems. To probe how these systems map with the '*dao*', I'll invite Lee to co-create an octopus-themed mapping. Octopuses are already map-like, arousing the curiosity of—and correlating between—diverse cultures and fields. I'll leave our map incomplete, with tentacles radiating outwards, across shelves and collections. Our map will guide us outside our colonised minds, and re-centre the stories of Lee and others.

Just as how mobilities studies generates 'different theories, methods, questions and solutions'[522] I'd be joyous if the sum of these books with *Neuro-Futurism* can contribute to 1% of those by other colleagues this ~~generation~~ *minute* who are also working towards a creative liberation and transformation. I also speculate—*hope*—that after these three books, instead of having to hatch artful ways to abolish harmful knowledge and practices of leadership, myself and other dogged under-dogs free to explore other adventures.

Like making a speculative fiction book starring some gigantic Octo-Pussy.

*I'm cheering for you.*

# CHAPTER 25

# O: Octo-Pussify. Oxygenate

*Is it a bird? Is it a plane? Is it a helicopter, or Leonardo da Vinci's 8-limbed Vitruvian Man? Look far ahead! It's a multi-legged bus! It's Your House for Artful Cheer-Leadership! It's faster than moon-walkers and more pungent than the smelliest durians with the sharpest stings, and able to hop islands, mountains and mars in a Single Bounce! To help us picture our new House/ Home, I've gathered a handful of elements, but have run out of time (Fig. 25.1). Can you cut out or re-arrange the components, add more ingredients etc. to collage your own octo-pussy?*

*If you need another hand, here's another up-dated definition of leadership.*

**Leadership: A buzzy, beyond-colonial, more-than-verbal, kinetic poly-centric and promiscuous politic, poetic, path-way of way-finding, re-direction, and change-, sense-, meaning-, trouble-, knowledge-, and future-making.**

To think about and do leadership in this way is to neuro-futurise leadership. Neuro-futurising leadership draws on and shows (off) the value of neuro-divergence, as well as body-mind-worlds that 'deviate' from the dominant. It dismantles the master's (sic) dangerous story of leadership, as an application of innovative, non-standard ways of processing, surviving and thriving in the world, such as hacking normative systems, problem-solving with limited resources, big-picture thinking, risk-taking, joining up hidden dots, and making novel connections.

© The Author(s), under exclusive license to Springer Nature Switzerland AG 2024
K. S. Tan, *Neuro-Futurism and Re-Imagining Leadership*,
Studies in Mobilities, Literature, and Culture,
https://doi.org/10.1007/978-3-031-55377-6_25

**Fig. 25.1**    Your House for Artful Leadership

Thus, instead of the individual, managerial or hierarchical, leadership encompasses the (intra-)relational, organisational, socio-political, collective, ethical, aesthetic, environmental and more. Instead of providing answers, leadership is about asking better questions. Instead of quick-fixes and being fixed, leadership is mobile, malleable, multi-scalar, multi-dimensional, clumsy and always in the process of becoming.

Leadership is sharp, bared teeth and monstrous excess of suckers and limbs. With not one but three hearts, leadership is governed by love. Leadership en-tails tentacular learning, un-learning and re-learning. With nine head-feet, leadership celebrates 9C's: Critical Creativity; Co-Creation; Collage; Can-do, Curiosity; Community + (under-) Commons; (Cosmic) Circulation; Curating Change through Care (and Com-passion); and Courage.

Leaders come from all walks. We are Deviant, Defiant Dare-Devils. We're ill-disciplined culture-workers, creative-activists, civic-animators, chimeras, octo-pussies, dogged under-dogs, hair-less chimps, stinky odd-balls the size of durians, wiggle-worms, queen-stinged bees, cockroaches and un-beached killer-whales. We work hand-in-hand, heart-beat-to-heart-beat, and holding (s)paces for one another as critical friends.

We're crafting and co-creating and fostering better strategies, stories, (infra-)structures, systems, and yet other new, alternative, oppositional aesthetic acts. We move hyper-tactically, to play the game insofar as to em-power us to tweak and transform the system, in order to profit people (of all walks and ilk), planet, play, and power-sharing, and to abolish prisons. We generate unlimited access to the pleasure and power of knowing, to transform external cacophonies of flows, write sideways, and move mountains of power and knowledge, moons and Mars.

Diverse and divergent, de-colonised, and neuro-queered, leadership comprises and nurtures artful, agile and a-typical approaches and actions. Leadership is sweaty, embodied and visceral. Running and agitating artfully, yelling back, island-hopping, clock-blocking, boat-rocking, monster-mapping, re-designing tables, flipping arm-chairs, constructing new monuments of workers, gate-crashing, making headways hyper-tactically, gently-anarchising, irony-fisting, zinging and stinging, pivoting, futurising, up-rising and collectivising, stimming and self-soothing, x-raying selves, speed-dating, gently-anarchising, lunging forward, dys-playing your difference, jeering for justice, cheer-leading, waking and shaking off smoke-screens and re-writing canons demand wit, grit, guts, tears and toil.

As well as hope, and joy.

Long story short, leadership is a love-led Practice of Freedom.

*And here we are. Remember, the above, neuro-futurising leadership and Neuro-Futurism aren't the final or only word about leadership. Equally, feel free to tear up my sketch, and create your own House/Home on a blank canvas from scratch, at your own drawing board. Come One, Come All, Have a Think, and Have a Ball!*

# CHAPTER 26

# K: Kick-Start 10,000 Oppositional Aesthetic Acts

*That has been some ride. What surprised or hit you the most? What have you felt troubled by? Here are the key references for the chapters. Use them as resources and rabbit holes for you to run further research on. Find out more about what titillated or troubled you. Expand on points I've touched on. Hack my strategies. Come up with complementary-/counter-strategies. Give my run of neuro-futurising leadership a run for its money. Make leadership more mongrel and monstrous. Outline new, alternative, oppositional aesthetic acts. Apply your long-range vision. How would you neuro-futurise leadership? Can you (re-)invent yet other creative and co-creative neuro-diversity-led (eco-)systems for all? What are your courageous actions, to re-imagine our collective destiny where people and planet prosper via play, poetry, and (com-)passion? Go forth and make art, trouble, change, future, knowledge, and meaning. Kick up a storm! Kick-start your adventures.*

K. S. Tan, *Neuro-Futurism and Re-Imagining Leadership*, Studies in Mobilities, Literature, and Culture, https://doi.org/10.1007/978-3-031-55377-6_26

# NOTES

1. This chapter and book develops ideas from Tan, Kai Syng. 2021. *How to Thrive In 2050! 8 Tentacular Workouts for a Tantalising Future, commissioned for BBC Culture in Quarantine.* https:// www.bbc.co.uk/iplayer/episode/p09sgyjy/culture-in-quarantine-how-to-thrive-in-2050; Tan, Kai Syng. Since 2016. *Notes on Leadership and New Leadership Postgraduate Programme.*
2. Urry, John. 2007. *Mobilities.* 1 edition. Cambridge: Polity.
3. Tan, Kai Syng. 2019. 'Running (in) Your City'. In *Mobilities, Literature, Culture,* edited by Marian Aguiar, Charlotte Mathieson, and Lynne Pearce, 1st ed., 163–86. S.l.: Palgrave Macmillan.
4. Carter, Evelyn R. 2022. 'DEI Initiatives Are Futile Without Accountability'. *Harvard Business Review.* https://hbr. org/2022/02/dei-initiatives-are-futile-without-accountability.
5. This article offers a sharp insight: Bero, Tayo. 2022. 'Why Are Black Rappers Aligning Themselves with the Right?' *The Guardian,* sec. Opinion. https://www.theguardian.com/commentisfree/2023/ aug/10/black-rappers-aligning-right-conservative-ice-cube.
6. Concern Worldwide US. 2022. 'The Rohingya Crisis, Explained: Five Things to Know, Five Years On'. Concern Worldwide. https:// www.concernusa.org/story/rohingya-crisis-explained/.

© The Author(s), under exclusive license to Springer Nature     215
Switzerland AG 2024
K. S. Tan, *Neuro-Futurism and Re-Imagining Leadership*, Studies
in Mobilities, Literature, and Culture,
https://doi.org/10.1007/978-3-031-55377-6

7. Austin, Robert D., and Gary P. Pisano. 2017. 'Neurodiversity as a Competitive Advantage'. *Harvard Business Review*. https://hbr.org/2017/05/neurodiversity-as-a-competitive-advantage.

8. Orduña, Nahia. 2019. 'The Next Talent Opportunity for the Digital Workplace? Neurodiversity'. *World Economic Forum*. https://www.weforum.org/agenda/2019/08/neurodiversity-workplace-opportunity/.

9. Baron-Cohen, Simon. 2020. *The Pattern Seekers: A New Theory of Human Invention*. 1st edition. Penguin.

10. Tan, Kai Syng. 2018. 'What Else Could "Neurodiversity" Look Like?' *Disability Arts Online*. http://disabilityarts.online/magazine/opinion/else-neurodiversity-look-like/.

11. I have raised these arguments since 2018, including ibid.

12. Warrier, Varun, David M. Greenberg, Elizabeth Weir, Clara Buckingham, Paula Smith, Meng-Chuan Lai, Carrie Allison, and Simon Baron-Cohen. 2020. 'Elevated Rates of Autism, Other Neurodevelopmental and Psychiatric Diagnoses, and Autistic Traits in Transgender and Gender-Diverse Individuals'. Nature Communications 11 (1): 3959. https://doi.org/10.1038/s41467-020-17794-1.

13. Judy Singer has since deleted her social media accounts, but the thread by another neuro-diversity thought-leader provides a summary: Walker, Nick. 2023. @WalkerSensei. 'Judy Singer Made....' Tweet. *Twitter*. https://twitter.com/WalkerSensei/status/1670470047700230144. On Singer's positioning: Singer, Judy. 2020. *What Is Neurodiversity?* (blog). https://neurodiversity2.blogspot.com/p/what.html.

14. Sheller, Mimi. 'Mobility Justice'. 2020. In *Handbook of Research Methods and Applications for Mobilities*, 11–20. Edward Elgar Publishing. https://www.elgaronline.com/display/edcoll/9781788115452/9781788115452.00007.xml.

15. Supran, G., S. Rahmstorf, and N. Oreskes. 2023. 'Assessing ExxonMobil's Global Warming Projections'. *Science* 379 (6628): eabk0063. https://doi.org/10.1126/science.abk0063.

16. On how systems conspire to harm the most vulnerable: Caffarra, Cristina, Matthew Elliott, and Andrea Galeotti. 2023. "Ecosystem' Theories of Harm in Digital Mergers: New Insights from Network Economics, Part 1'. *Centre for Economic Policy Research*. https://cepr.org/voxeu/columns/ecosystem-theories-harm-digital-mergers-new-insights-network-economics-part-1.

17. Runkevicius, Dan. 2020. 'How Amazon Quietly Powers The Internet'. *Forbes*. https://www.forbes.com/sites/danrunkevicius/2020/09/03/how-amazon-quietly-powers-the-internet/.

18. Belay, Million, and Bridget Mugambe. 2021. 'Bill Gates Should Stop Telling Africans What Kind of Agriculture Africans Need'. *Scientific American*. https://www.scientificamerican.com/article/bill-gates-should-stop-telling-africans-what-kind-of-agriculture-africans-need1/.

19. Hyde, Marina. 2023. 'What Does Jeff Bezos's New Fiancee See in the World's Third-Richest Man? Must Be His Enormous Philanthropy'. *The Guardian*. https://www.theguardian.com/commentisfree/2023/may/26/jeff-bezos-money-lauren-sanchez-europe.

20. European Space Agency (Lisa Denzer). 2023. 'Session 1: Key Space Achievements and Challenges for Pharma, Cosmetics, Nutrition, Advanced Materials'. In *Health from Space*. Cannes, France.

21. Burns, James MacGregor. 1978. *Leadership*. Harper & Row: 1–2.

22. Riggio, Ronald E., ed. 2018. *What's Wrong With Leadership?: Improving Leadership Research and Practice*. 1st edition. New York: Routledge.

23. World Economic Forum, and Klaus Schwab. 2016. 'The Fourth Industrial Revolution: What It Means and How to Respond'. *World Economic Forum*. https://www.weforum.org/agenda/2016/01/the-fourth-industrial-revolution-what-it-means-and-how-to-respond/.

24. LaRosa, John. 2021. '$10.4 Billion Self-Improvement Market Pivots to Virtual Delivery During the Pandemic'. https://blog.marketresearch.com/10.4-billion-self-improvement-market-pivots-to-virtual-delivery-during-the-pandemic.

25. Sims-Schouten, Wendy, and Patricia Gilbert. 2022. 'Revisiting "Resilience" in Light of Racism, "Othering" and Resistance'. *Race & Class* 64 (1): 84–94. https://doi.org/10.1177/03063968221093882.

26. An extreme version of this is played out in the notion of 'self-responsibility' in Japan, which manifests in intolerance and violence towards elderly: Lazzarini, Sylvie. 2022. 'Chie Hayakawa'. *Cineuropa*. https://cineuropa.org/en/video/426101/.

27. Tan, Kai Syng 2023. Image created from artworks 2007–2009, and adapted from a drawing by a #MagicCarpet participant.

28. hooks, bell. *Outlaw Culture: Resisting Representations: Volume 83*. 1st edition. New York: Routledge, 2006.
29. Tan, Kai Syng. 2020. 'TRANSCRIPT: 10 Reasons to Collaborate with Neurodiverse & Creative Allies'. *Artists Information (blog)*. https://www.a-n.co.uk/blogs/transcript-10-reasons-to-collaborate-with-neurodiverse-creative-allies/.
30. Tan, Kai Syng. 2017. 'Hand-in-Hand'. edited by Luc Gwiazdzinski, Guillaume Drevon, and Olivier Klein, Chronotopics. Readings and Writings on a World in Movement: 59–71. Elya Éditions.
31. Heinrich, Bernd. 2002. *Why We Run: A Natural History*. Reprint. Harper Perennial. 177.
32. One of 93 A4 hand-drawn mappings from: Tan, Kai Syng. 2017. '#MagicCarpet Website'. #MagicCarpet. 2019 2017. http://wesa-tonamat.weebly.com/blog/kais-speedy-sketch.
33. Tan, Kai Syng. 2014. *The Physical and Poetic Processes of Running: A Practice-Related Fine Art Discourse About A Playful Way To Transform Your World Today*. University College London. http://discovery.ucl.ac.uk/1420270/1/Tan_Kai_Syng_Thesis_Redacted.pdf.
34. WordSense Dictionary. 2023. 'Lithan'. https://www.wordsense.eu/lithan/.
35. Carroll, Brigid, Jackie Ford, and Scott Taylor, eds. 2019. *Leadership: Contemporary Critical Perspectives*. Second edition. Thousand Oaks, CA: SAGE Publications Ltd.
36. Carroll, et al. *Leadership*.
37. Smith, Linda Tuhiwai. 2012. *Decolonizing Methodologies: Research and Indigenous Peoples*. 2nd Revised edition. London: Zed Books Ltd. Access useful summary by social designer Sarah Fathallah here: https://twitter.com/sft7la/status/1257159589448962048.
38. Obasi, Chijioke. 2022. 'Black Social Workers: Identity, Racism, Invisibility/Hypervisibility at Work'. *Journal of Social Work* 22 (2): 479–97. https://doi.org/10.1177/14680173211008110.
39. Sheller, Mimi, and John Urry. 'The New Mobilities Paradigm Sheller'. *Environment and Planning A* 38 (2006): 207–26. https://doi.org/10.1068/a37268.
40. Urry, John. 2016. *What Is the Future?* 1st edition. Cambridge, UK ; Malden, MA: Polity.
41. Tan, Kai Syng. 2020. *Catalysing Change Through Artful Agitation: Be Ill-Disciplined*. https://howlround.com/happenings/catalysing-change-through-artful-agitation-part-i-be-ill-disciplined.

42. Ciulla, Joanna B. 2018. 'Leadership and Ethics: You Can Run, But You Cannot Hide from the Humanities'. In *What's Wrong With Leadership?: Improving Leadership Research and Practice*, edited by Ronald E. Riggio, 1st edition, 107–210. New York: Routledge. 119.

43. Tan, Kai Syng. 2020. 'Novel Viruses Require Artful Solutions'. *Royal Society of the Arts* (blog). https://www.thersa.org/discover/publications-and-articles/rsa-comment/2020/05/novel-viruses-require-artful-solutions.

44. Tan, Kai Syng, and Jen Southern, eds. 2018. *The Art & Mobilities Network Inaugural Symposium Instant Journal*. London and Lancaster. https://issuu.com/kaisyngtan/docs/2018august_cemore_instantjournal_ka.

45. Szerszynski, Bronislaw. 2016. 'Planetary Mobilities: Movement, Memory and Emergence in the Body of the Earth'. *Mobilities* 11 (4): 614–28. https://doi.org/10.1080/17450101.2016.1211828.

46. Southern, Jen, and Rod Dillon. 2023. 'Living with Deadly Mobilities: How Art Practice Takes Care of Ethics When Anthropomorphising a Medically Important Parasite'. *Mobilities* 18 (3): 391–407. https://doi.org/10.1080/17450101.2022.2111224.

47. I've been developing a framework of leadership around artfulness since at least 2019, in for instance: Tan, Kai Syng. 2019. 'TRANSCRIPT: Too Much/ Not Enough "Neurodiversity" in UK Art & Academia?' *A-N Blogs*. https://www.a-n.co.uk/blogs/transcript-too-much-not-enough-neurodiversity-in-uk-art-academia/.

48. Tan, Kai Syng. 'Using Tentacular Pedagogy to Change the HE Culture'. 2022. *The Society for Research into Higher Education* (blog). https://srheblog.com/2022/11/16/using-tentacular-pedagogy-to-change-the-he-culture/.

49. hooks, bell. "Choosing the Margin as a Space of Radical Openness." Framework: The Journal of Cinema and Media, no. 36 (1989): 15–23.

50. Ibid.

51. Martins, Luiza Prado de O. 2023. 'Privilege and Oppression: Towards a Feminist Speculative Design'. https://www.academia.edu/7778734/Privilege_and_Oppression_Towards_a_Feminist_Speculative_Design.

52. Dunne, Anthony, and Fiona Raby. 2013. *Speculative Everything: Design, Fiction, and Social Dreaming.* Cambridge, Massachusetts ; London: The MIT Press.

53. Definitions of neuro-divergence diverge, and more updated research is required to capture a clearer picture, but the figure for dyslexic students in art and design is consistently over 30% in UK HE formal records, as affirmed by this paper: Bacon, Alison M., and Samantha Bennett. 'Dyslexia in Higher Education: The Decision to Study Art'. *European Journal of Special Needs Education* 28, no. 1 (1 February 2013): 19–32. https://doi.org/10.1080/0885625 7.2012.742748.

54. Tan. *Physical and Poetic Running.*

55. Tan, Kai Syng. 2021. 'COMMISSION: How To Thrive In 2050! BBC Film Press Kit'. *Artful Agitation.* https://kaisyngtan.com/artful/bbc-film-press-kit/.

56. The term 'Neurofuturism' has various iterations Relating to autism: Gray-Hammond, David. 'David's Divergent Discussions', 5 June 2023. https://www.davidsdivergentdiscussions.co.uk/; relating neurodiversity with Afro-futurism: Ebizie, Nwando. *Neurodiversity, Afro Futurism & Superpowered Creativity, London.* 2018. https://www.list.co.uk/event/20990868-nwando-ebizie-neurodiversity-afro-futurism-and-superpowered-creativity/; vis-à-vis AI: Proger. 'Neurofuturism. What Else Will AI Adapt to in the near Future?' *Prog.World* (blog), 25 January 2023. https://prog.world/neurofuturism-what-else-will-ai-adapt-to-in-the-near-future/; as graphic novel and music: Rosenberg, Jonathan. 'Harvey Seldman, Inventor Of Neurofuturism'. *Scenes From A Multiverse* (blog), 19 May 2011. http://amultiverse.com/comic/2011/05/19/harvey-seldman-inventor-of-neurofuturism/.and Cybermode Beats. 'Neurofuturism'. cybermode, 19 April 2023. https://cybermode.bandcamp.com/track/neurofuturism.

57. Tan, Kai Syng. 1994. *Chewing Not Swallowing* (carried out at the Slade School of Fine Art studios days after I arrived in the UK, to protest my mother-land's ban of both performance art and chewing gum).

58. Egner, Justine E. 2019. '"The Disability Rights Community Was Never Mine": Neuroqueer Disidentification'. *Gender & Society* 33 (1): 123–47. https://doi.org/10.1177/0891243218803284.

59. Walker, Nick. 2015. *Neuroqueer: An Introduction.* https://neuro-cosmopolitanism.com/neuroqueer-an-introduction/.

60. Lowens, Randy. 2011. 'How Do You Practice Intersectionalism? An Interview with bell hooks'. *Northeastern Anarchist*, 2011. https://web.archive.org/web/20211215200516/https://blackrosefed.org/intersectionalism-bell-hooks-interview/.

61. Harney, Stefano, and Fred Moten. 2013. *The Undercommons: Fugitive Planning & Black Study.* Wivenhoe: Minor Compositions. 154.

62. Balagun, Kazembe. 2016. Interviewing the Oracle : Octavia Butler. https://indypendent.org/2006/01/interviewing-the-oracle-octavia-butler/.

63. National Museum of African American History & Culture. 2023. 'Remembering Afrofuturist Octavia Butler'. National Museum of African American History and Culture. https://nmaahc.si.edu/explore/stories/remembering-afrofuturist-octavia-butler.

64. Tan. *Physical and Poetic Running.*

65. Büscher, Monika, Malene Freudendal-Pedersen, and Sven Kesselring. 'AAG 2017: CfP Moving Methods. JISCMail – GLOBAL-MOBILITIES Archives', 10 October 2016. https://www.jiscmail.ac.uk/cgi-bn/wa-jisc.exe?A2=ind1610&L=GLOBAL-MOBILITIES&P=6449.

66. Latham, Alan, and Kai Syng Tan. 'Running into Each Other: Run! Run! Run! A Festival and a Collaboration'. *Cultural Geographies* 24, no. 4 (1 October 2017): 625–30. https://doi.org/10.1177/1474474017702511.

67. Collins, Patricia Hill. 2008. *Black Feminist Thought: Knowledge, Consciousness, and the Politics of Empowerment.* 1st edition. New York: Routledge.

68. Tan, Kai Syng. 'Run Riot! On Mobilities, Life, and Death (of Civilisation), and the Reveries of Running Artfully : Handbook of Research Methods and Applications for Mobilities'. In *Handbook of Research Methods and Applications for Mobilities*, 303–14. Edward Elgar Publishing, 2020. https://doi.org/10.4337/9781788115469.00038.

69. Urry. *Future?* Chapter 6.

70. Ibid. 53.

71. Smith. *Decolonizing Methodologies.*

72. Urry. *Future?* 64–73.

73. Djalili, Omid. 2023. '@omiddjalili: We Stand with the People...' *Instagram*. https://www.instagram.com/reel/Csb-cHkpJbv/.

74. Ladkin, Donna. 2021. 'Problematizing Authentic Leadership: How the Experience of Minoritized People Highlights the Impossibility of Leading from One's "True Self"'. Leadership 17 (4): 395–400. https://doi.org/10.1177/1742715021999586.

75. Lao Zi, and D.C. Lau. 1963. *Tao Teh Ching*. Penguin Classics. Ch. 20.

76. Tan, Kai Syng. 2020. 'Power, Play and Pedagogy through the PowerPoint Performance-Lecture'. *International Journal of Management and Applied Research*, Exploring visual representation of concepts in Learning and Teaching in Higher Education. https://doi.org/10.18646/2056.73.20-028.

77. Holtzbrinck Publishing Company. 'What We Stand For'. https://www.holtzbrinck.com/about/.

78. Lorde, Audre. 1984. 'The Master's Tools Will Never Dismantle the Master's House', Sister Outsider: Essays and Speeches:110–14. Berkeley, CA: Crossing Press.

79. I've been particularly moved by the fearless, anti-colonial efforts of multi-hyphenate Jacob V Joyce. Joyce, Jacob V. 2023. '@jacobvjoyce https://www.instagram.com/jacobvjoyce/.

80. Tan, Kai Syng, and Philip Asherson. 2018. 'How "lofty" Art Can Help the Medical World Reimagine Mental Health'. *The Conversation*. http://theconversation.com/how-lofty-art-can-help-the-medical-world-reimagine-mental-health-105689.

81. Collins. *Black Feminist Thought*.

82. Walker, *Neuroqueer*.

83. Haraway, Donna J. *Staying with the Trouble: Making Kin in the Chthulucene*. Experimental Futures. Durham, NC: Duke University Press, 2016.

84. Nam June Paik Center. The Consultant: Paik's Papers 1968–1979, NAM JUNE PAIK ART CENTER. 2022. https://njpart.ggcf.kr/the-consultant-paiks-papers-1968-1979/; Paik, Nam June. "Media Planning for the Postindustrial Society—The twenty-first Century Is Now Only 26 Years Away," 1974. http://www.medienkunstnetz.de/source-text/33/.

85. Tan, Kai Syng. 2021. Let's Imagine A Neuro-Futuristic 2050 Together (Commissioned Installation, Participatory Art (Speed-

Dating and Wish-Making), Performance, as Part of Group Show Including Artist Bob and Roberta Smith, in *The World Is a Work in Progress*, Attenborough Arts Centre. September 2021–January 2022. Film, performance, furniture, plants. Photographs by curator Rachel Graves. See Padlet of wishes here. https://padlet.com/rlg30/what-would-a-neurodiversity-led-2050-look-like-tell-us-and-a-z4ve8etyw7funqkf.

86. Washington, Booker T., William E. B. DuBois, James Weldon Johnson, and John Hope Franklin. 1999. *Three Negro Classics*. Reissue edition. New York, NY: Avon Books.

87. New African. 2013. 'W.E.B. Du Bois—The Father of Modern Pan-Africanism?' *New African Magazine* (blog). 3 December 2013. https://newafricanmagazine.com/4091/.

88. Morris-Rosendahl, Deborah J., and Marc-Antoine Crocq. 'Neurodevelopmental Disorders—the History and Future of a Diagnostic Concept'. *Dialogues in Clinical Neuroscience* 22, no. 1 (March 2020): 65–72. https://doi.org/10.31887/DCNS.2020.22.1/macrocq.

89. Deleuze, Gilles, and Félix Guattari. *A Thousand Plateaus: Capitalism and Schizophrenia*. London New York Oxford New Delhi Sydney: Bloomsbury Academic, 2013, p. 5.

90. Law, John, and John Urry. 'Enacting the Social'. *Economy and Society* 33, no. 3 (1 August 2004): 390–410. https://doi.org/10.1080/0308514042000225716.

91. Leban, Sebastian. 2014. In Pictures: Palestinian Parkour. https://www.aljazeera.com/gallery/2014/3/4/in-pictures-palestinian-parkour.

92. Matika Wilbur, Desi Small-Rodriguez & Adrienne Keene. 'Indigiqueer: Joshua Whitehead and Billy-Ray Belcourt'. All My Relations. https://www.allmyrelationspodcast.com/podcast/episode/47547617/indigiqueer.

93. This article is useful as an introduction to how some of these ideas and practices differ and overlap: Bishop, Claire. 2020. 'Claire Bishop in Conversation with Tania Bruguera', January. https://www.academia.edu/44755969/Claire_Bishop_in_conversation_with_Tania_Bruguera.

94. Fremantle, Christopher N., and Anne Douglas. 2009. 'The Artist as Leader'. *The Artist as Leader Research Report, AHRC*. https://www.academia.edu/4489268/The_Artist_as_Leader.

95. Douglas, Anne. 2013. *Values and Assumptions in the Concept of Cultural Leadership*, January. https://www.academia.edu/80348117/Values_and_assumptions_in_the_concept_of_cultural_leadership.

96. Fremantle and Douglas. *The Artist as Leader*.

97. Douglas. Cultural Leadership.

98. Fremantle and Douglas. *The Artis as Leader*.

99. Ryan, Frances. 'As a Billionaire King Is Crowned, He Urges Us to Do Some Charity Work. Welcome to Britain'. *The Guardian*, 28 April 2023, sec. Opinion. https://www.theguardian.com/commentisfree/2023/apr/28/billionaire-king-crowned-charity-work-funding-public-services.

100. *'Punching Up': The Secrets Of Dalit Stand Up Comics | Article 14*, 2023. https://www.youtube.com/watch?v=IVD9Z3DwqIA.

101. Tan. 'Novel Viruses'.

102. Tan, Kai Syng. 10 Reasons to Collaborate with Neurodiverse + Creative Allies (Commissioned Masterclass for 2020 CoCA Annual Meeting. CoCA—Comorbid Conditions of ADHD—Was a 50 m Euro EU Horizon 2020 Funded Consortium Comprising 17 Partners from 8 European Countries and the US), 2020. https://www.youtube.com/watch?v=7p5g3tt4rPg&feature=youtu.be.

103. Regine. 2012. 'The Individual and the Organisation: Artist Placement Group 1966–79'. *We Make Money Not Art* (blog). 25 October 2012. https://we-make-money-not-art.com/the_individual_and_the_organis/.

104. Southern, Jen, Emma Rose, and Linda O Keefe. 'Art as a Strategy for Living with Utopias in Ruins'. In *Mobile Utopia*. 2–11.

105. Ciulla. 'Leadership and Ethics'.

106. Barrett, Estelle. 2007. 'Experiential Learning in Practice as Research: Context, Method, Knowledge'. *Journal of Visual Art Practice* 6 (October): 115–24. https://www.researchgate.net/publication/249918879_Experiential_learning_in_practice_as_research_Context_method_knowledge.

107. Barry, Kaya, Jen Southern, Tess Baxter, Suzy Blondin, Clare Booker, Janet Bowstead, Carly Butler, et al. 'An Agenda for Creative Practice

in the New Mobilities Paradigm'. *Mobilities* 18, no. 3 (4 May 2023): 349–73. https://doi.org/10.1080/17450101.2022.2136996.

108. Southern and Dillon. 'Living with Deadly Mobilities'.

109. See note 10 above.

110. Büscher, Monika, Jen Southern, and Linda O Keefe. 2017. 'The Mobile Utopia Experiment'. In *Mobile Utopia: Art and Experiments. An Exhibition Curated by Jen Southern, Emma Rose, Linda O Keefe*, 12–18. United Kingdom.

111. Büscher, Monika. 2020. 'Covid-19: Other Mobilities Are (Im) Possible | CEMORE'. 25 March 2020. https://www.lancaster.ac. uk/cemore/covid-19-other-mobilities-are-impossible/.

112. Tan, Kai Syng. A 'Tentacular Pedagogy' to Lead 2050 (Commissioned Keynote Lecture in the Form of a Performance-Lecture for European League of Institutes of the Arts Teachers Academy or ELIA, Which Comprises 300,000+ HE Stakeholders from 282 Institutions in 48 Countries). 26 November 2021; https://kaisyngtan.com/artful/ tentacularpedagogy/; Tan. 'Using Tentacular Pedagogy'.

113. UNESCO International Institute for Higher Education in Latin America and the Caribbean. 'Pathways to 2050 and beyond: Findings from a Public Consultation on the Futures of Higher Education', 2021. https://unesdoc.unesco.org/ark:/48223/ pf0000379985?3=null&queryId=f456a96a-5fa8-4925-8f27- a0ab2810f2e2.

114. Godfrey-Smith, Peter. *Other Minds: The Octopus, The Sea, and the Deep Origins of Consciousness*. 1st edition. New York: Farrar, Straus and Giroux, 2017.

115. Smithsonian Ocean. 'Cephalopods', 30 April 2018. https://ocean. si.edu/ocean-life/invertebrates/cephalopods.

116. Nakajima, Ryuta, Shuichi Shigeno, Letizia Zullo, Fabio De Sio, and Markus R. Schmidt. 'Cephalopods Between Science, Art, and Engineering: A Contemporary Synthesis'. *Frontiers in Communication* 3 (2018). https://www.frontiersin.org/arti- cles/10.3389/fcomm.2018.00020.

117. Documentaries on streaming channels aside, there is a network for non-linear thinkers: The Octopus Movement. 'Manifesto'. https:// www.theoctopusmovement.org/manifesto.

118. Jones, Owain Smolovic, and Brad Jackson. "Seeing Leadership: Becoming Sophisticated Consumers of Leadership." In *Leadership*, 290–309.

119. Jones, Owain Smolovic, and Brad Jackson. "Seeing Leadership".
120. Grint, Keith. 2001. *The Arts of Leadership*. Illustrated edition. Oxford: Oxford University Press, USA.
121. Sinclair, Amanda, and Michelle Evans. 'Difference and Leadership.' In *Leadership*, 160–81.
122. Ibid.
123. Tan, Kai Syng. What Could a Neurodiversity-Led 2050 Look like? (Premiered for Royal Society of Art's 'Virtual Coffeehouse Conversation: Neurodiversity and the Future of Work'. 9 July 2020. Performance-lecture. https://www.academia.edu/43602890/2020_What_could_a_neurodiversity-led_2050_look_like_Royal_Society_of_Arts_.
124. Tan, Kai Syng. 'Neurodiversity In/And Creative Research Network'. Mailing list archive, February 2020. https://kaisyngtan.com/artful/neurodiversitycreativeresearch/.
125. Altered image from *Hand-in-Hand, 2018* with General Practitioners. King's Undergraduate Medical Education in the Community, Faculty of Life Sciences & Medicine King's College London.
126. For instance Lesch, Klaus-Peter. '"Shine Bright like a Diamond!": Is Research on High-Functioning ADHD at Last Entering the Mainstream?' *Journal of Child Psychology and Psychiatry* 59, no. 3 (1 March 2018): 191–92. https://doi.org/10.1111/jcpp.12887, LaFrance, Edith (Dee) Bird. 'The Gifted/Dyslexic Child: Characterizing and Addressing Strengths and Weaknesses'. *Annals of Dyslexia* 47, no. 1 (1 December 1997): 163–82. https://doi.org/10.1007/s11881-997-0025-7, and Sedgwick, Jane Ann, Andrew Merwood, and Philip Asherson. 'The Positive Aspects of Attention Deficit Hyperactivity Disorder: A Qualitative Investigation of Successful Adults with ADHD'. *ADHD Attention Deficit and Hyperactivity Disorders*, 29 October 2018. https://doi.org/10.1007/s12402-018-0277-6.
127. Tan, Kai Syng. Ill-Disciplined (ID): Creative Interventions in Mental Health through Visual Arts Processes with ADHD (Proposal). King's College London, 2018.
128. Examples include 'neurodiversity rong table' and 'disordering dance' by Network members, Oliver, Daniel. 2015. *Website*. https://www.danieloliverperformance.com, and Watson, Aby. 2020. *Disordering Dance*. https://disorderingdance.com/.

129. United Nations. 2015. 'THE 17 GOALS of Sustainable Development'. https://sdgs.un.org/goals.

130. Fuglesang, Christer. 2021. *Space in 2050*. Zero Pressure. https://open.spotify.com/episode/56aJRNAsMxyQeQmsxLNacZ.

131. For example: Donnelly, Gabrielle, and Alfonso Montuori, eds. 2022. *Routledge Handbook for Creative Futures*. Routledge.

132. Lek, Lawrence. 'Sinofuturism (1839–2046 AD)'. https://lawrencelek.com/Sinofuturism-1839-2046-AD.

133. Attenborough Arts Centre. 'Trans Futures: Trans Post Project', 2022. https://attenborougharts.com/commissioning/transpostproject/.

134. Khanna, Shama, ed. *Flatness: Queer Diasporic Futurity*. TBC, 2022. https://flatness.eu/.

135. Majid, Asif. 'Asylee Futurism as Political Aesthetic? Asif Majid'. 19 May 2022. https://www.eventbrite.co.uk/e/321418199487?aff=efbneb.

136. Iohe, Taey. Cli-Fi Writing with Taey Iohe—When Asian Queers Are Writing Cli-Fi, Saving Humans Isn't the Priority—Nunnery Gallery—Art Tickets. 23 July 2023. https://bow-arts.arttickets.org.uk/nunnery-gallery/2023-07-23-cli-fi-writing-with-taey-iohe-when-asian-queers-are-writing-cli-fi-saving-humans-isnt-the.

137. Smith. Decolonizing Methodologies. 8.

138. Ospina, Sonia, and Celina Su. 2009. 'Weaving Color Lines: Race, Ethnicity, and the Work of Leadership in Social Change Organizations'. *Leadership* 5 (2): 131–70. https://doi.org/10.1177/1742715009102927.

139. 'An Interview with Toni Cade Bambara'. 2012. In Conversations with Toni Cade Bambara, by Toni Cade Bambara, 35–47. Literary Conversations Series. University Press of Mississippi.

140. Tan, Kai Syng. *The Never-Ending Underwater Adventure* (the First Video Art Installation Commissioned for the Circle Line's Bras Basah Station in the Arts and Heritage District, of 29 Quizzes in a 29-Chapter 29-Minute Film). 2008. http://kaisyngtan.com/3rdlifekaidie/2010/08/bbs-art-1/.

141. BBC News. 2021. *Greta Thunberg Mocks World Leaders in 'Blah, Blah, Blah' Speech*. https://www.youtube.com/watch?v=ZwD1kG4PI0w.

142. There is extensive documentation online, like Tan, Kai Syng. *On Art, Neurodiversity';* Tan, Kai Syng. '#MagicCarpet Website'. #MagicCarpet, 2018. http://wesatonamat.weebly.com/.

143. Tan, Kai Syng, and Philip Asherson. 2017. 'Come Sit on a Mat with an Artist and a Psychiatrist to Have a Chat about Mind Wandering, Gingerbread Men, Shark Baits, and the Interface of Normal/ Abnormal Behaviour'. *Mind the Gap Blog* (blog). https://www.academia.edu/34132288/2017_A_practice_led_research_project_weaving_science_and_art_together_to_celebrate_mind_wandering_magic_carpets_mapping_making_making_small_talk_and_productive_antagonisms.

144. See my drawing in this position paper: Bozhilova, Natali, Giorgia Michelini, Jonna Kuntsi, and Philip Asherson. 2018. 'Mind Wandering Perspective on ADHD'. *Neuroscience & Biobehavioral Reviews* 92 (September): 464–76. https://doi.org/10.1016/j.neubiorev.2018.07.010.

145. ADHD in Adults. 2018. *ADHD Awareness Month 2018—Shine a Light on ADHD.* https://www.youtube.com/watch?v=XmS7jUhB74A&t=1s.

146. NICE. 'Attention Deficit Hyperactivity Disorder: Activity Disorder: Diagnosis and Management', March 2018. https://www.nice.org.uk/guidance/ng87/resources/attention-deficit-hyperactivity-disorder-diagnosis-and-management-pdf-1837699732933+&cd=1&hl=en&ct=clnk&gl=uk&client=firefox-b-ab.

147. For example: Tan. 'What Else'; Dr. Kai Syng Tan at King's Artists—New Thinking, New Making, 2018. https://www.youtube.com/watch?v=mTtJOs2S4O0&feature=youtu.be, and Tan, Kai Syng. *Brisk/Risks: Open Mic at Bush House, London UK. With BSL-Interpreted Film and Transcripts.* 2018. https://mind-the-gap.live/2019/06/19/risk-taking-and-adhd/.

148. Photograph by Marco Berardi commissioned for #MagicCarpet. 2018. *#MagicCarpet Launch.* Art Workers Guild. http://wesatonamat.weebly.com/2018-april-24-launch.html.

149. Tan, Kai Syng. 2019. On Art, Neurodiversity & Giant Octopussies. London, UK: King's College London. http://kaisyngtan.com/wp-content/uploads/2019/12/2019_MagicCarpet_booklet_DrKaiSyngTan.pdf.

150. Zatka-Haas, James. 'Kai Syng Tan #MagicCarpet'. *Disability Arts Online*, 20 September 2020. https://disabilityarts.online/maga-zine/opinion/kai-syng-tan-magiccarpet/.

151. Marlow, Sally. 'Arts in Mind'. *The Psychologist (The British Psychological Society)* 31 (August 2018): 68–69.

152. Tan, Kai Syng. 2019. 'Towards Cultural Change: Re-Imagining Mental Health through "Lofty" Art'. *A-N Blogs* (blog). https://www.a-n.co.uk/blogs/towards-cultural-change-re-imagining-mental-health-through-lofty-art/.

153. All Party Parliamentary Group on Arts Health and Wellbeing. 2017. *Creative Health: The Arts for Health and Wellbeing - Second Edition*.

154. Viney, William, Felicity Callard, and Angela Woods. 2015. 'Critical Medical Humanities: Embracing Entanglement, Taking Risks'. Medical Humanities 41 (1): 2–7. https://doi.org/10.1136/medhum-2015-010692.

155. Padfield, Deborah, and Joanna M. Zakrzewska. 'Encountering Pain'. *The Lancet* 389, no. 10075 (25 March 2017): 1177–78. https://doi.org/10.1016/S0140-6736(17)30756-0.

156. This section draws on Tan, *Ill-Disciplined*.

157. Büscher, Monika, John Urry, and Katian Witchger. 2010. *Mobile Methods*. Routledge.

158. The arguments here are from Douglas. *Cultural Leadership* and Fremantle and Douglas. 'The Artist as Leader'.

159. Philip Schlesinger, Director of the Centre for Cultural Policy Research, University of Glasgow (2008), in Fremantle and Douglas' The Artist as Leader, p. 34.

160. NCCPE. 2018. 'Culture Change Award'. https://www.publicen-gagement.ac.uk/sites/default/files/publication/images_of_pub-lic_engagement_2018_brochure.pdf.

161. Tan, Kai Syng. 'Neurodiversity In/And Creative Research Network'. Since February 2020. https://kaisyngtan.com/artful/neurodiversitycreativeresearch/.

162. hooks, bell. 1996. *Killing Rage: Ending Racism*. Reprint edition. New York: St Martin's Press.

163. Berger, Roni. 'Now I See It, Now I Don't: Researcher's Position and Reflexivity in Qualitative Research'. *Qualitative Research* 15, no. 2 (1 April 2015): 219–34. https://doi.org/10.1177/1468794112468475, and Hevey, David. 'From Self-Love to the Picket Line: Strategies for Change in Disability

Representation'. In *Disability, Handicap & Society*, 8:423–29, 1993. https://doi.org/10.1080/02674649366780391.

164. Manning, Erin. 'Me Lo Dijo Un Pajarito: Neurodiversity, Black Life, and the University as We Know It'. *Social Text* 36, no. 3 (1 September 2018): 1–24. https://doi.org/10.1215/01642472-6917742, and Egner. 'Disability Rights Community'.

165. Tan, Kai Syng. *Kai Syng Tan: Unreasonable Adjustments*. 2018. http://disabilityarts.online/magazine/showcase/kai-syng-tan-unreasonable-adjustments/.

166. Russell, Ginny. 'Critiques of the Neurodiversity Movement', 287–303. Springer Singapore, 2020.

167. A cartoonish example is seen in a UK neuro-diversity in business advocacy group, which posts near-daily photographs on LinkedIn of its founder in action. When not schmoozing with politicians or celebrities, there's the weaponisation of non-speaking autistic off-springs. When asked why a panel featuring Judy Singer lacked brown or Black body-minds, Singer's oft-cited background as a pensioner and descendent of Holocaust victims was repeated.

168. Barbarin, Imani. "On Today's Episode of 'I Know Why That Happens:' Why Are Marginalized White People like That? Https://T. Co/GCxC2H7yMB." Tweet. *Twitter*, June 14, 2021. https://twitter.com/Imani_Barbarin/status/1404441612286152706.

169. Zisk, Alyssa. 'Being the Curriculum'. *Ought: The Journal of Autistic Culture* 3, no. 1 (1 December 2021). https://scholarworks.gvsu.edu/ought/vol3/iss1/12 and aby watson. '*TICKETS GO ON SALE TOMORROW!* DYSCO Was Originally Developed at the Neurodiversity In/And Creative Research Network Headed by @kaisyngtan and @RanjitaDhital, and Was First Fully Shown at the Digital @weareunltd Festival at @southbankcentre in January 2021.' Tweet. *@abswatson* (blog), 11 February 2021. https://twitter.com/abswatson/status/1359912567846674436.

170. Battersea Arts Centre. 'ANNOUNCING THE 2022 FOYLE FOUNDATION COMMISSIONS'. Battersea Arts Centre, June 2022. https://bac.org.uk/2022-foyle-foundation-commissions/.

171. American Psychiatric Association. 2013. *Diagnostic and Statistical Manual of Mental Disorders (DSM-5®)*. https://www.appi.org/Diagnostic_and_Statistical_Manual_of_Mental_Disorders_DSM-5_Fifth_Edition.

172. Created with AI-functions on Photoshop, from Badge-Wearing Mind Wanderer In Action (MIA) series and 13 designs of badges from #MagicCarpet. Tan, Kai Syng. 2017–2019. *#MagicCarpet.* 2018. http://wesatonamat.weebly.com/.

173. hooks, bell. 1994. Teaching to Transgress: Education as the Practice of Freedom. New York; London: Routledge.

174. Ahmed, Sara. 2021. *Complaint!* Durham: Duke University Press Books; Sian, Katy P. 2019. *Navigating Institutional Racism in British Universities.* Palgrave Macmillan; Blell, Mwenza, Shan-Jan Sarah Liu, and Audrey Verma. 2023. 'Working in Unprecedented Times: Intersectionality and Women of Color in UK Higher Education in and beyond the Pandemic'. *Gender, Work & Organization* 30, no. 2: 353–72. https://doi.org/10.1111/gwao.12907.

175. Berg, Lawrence, Edward Huijbens, and Henrik Larsen. 2016. 'Producing Anxiety in the Neoliberal University'. *Canadian Geographer / Le Géographe Canadien* 60. 10 March 2016. https://doi.org/10.1111/cag.12261.

176. Laurencin, Cato T., and Joanne M. Walker. 2020. 'A Pandemic on a Pandemic: Racism and COVID-19 in Blacks'. Cell Systems 11 (1): 9–10. https://doi.org/10.1016/j.cels.2020.07.002.

177. Arday, Jason, and Christopher Jones. 2022. 'Same Storm, Different Boats: The Impact of COVID-19 on Black Students and Academic Staff in UK and US Higher Education'. Higher Education, October, 1–22. https://doi.org/10.1007/s10734-022-00939-0.

178. Ahmed, Sara. 2018. 'Rocking the Boat: Women of Colour as Diversity Workers'. In *Dismantling Race in Higher Education: Racism, Whiteness and Decolonising the Academy*, edited by Jason Arday and Heidi Safia Mirza, 331–48. Cham: Springer International Publishing. https://doi.org/10.1007/978-3-319-60261-5_19.

179. Havergal, Chris. 2022. 'Fight "Bonfire of the Humanities", Urges Mary Beard'. *Times Higher Education.* https://www.timeshigher-education.com/news/fight-bonfire-humanities-urges-mary-beard.

180. Phillips, Sam. 'Art under Threat: The Growing Crisis in Higher Education'. Royal Academy of Arts blog, 20 March 2019. https://www.royalacademy.org.uk/article/art-under-threat-crisis-britain-higher-education.

181. Pearce, Michael J. 2019. *Why Art Schools Are Disappearing.* https://fee.org/articles/why-art-schools-are-disappearing/.

182. Sharratt, Chris. 2017. 'University of Kent to Close Its School of Music and Fine Art'. *A-n The Artists Information Company*. https://www.a-n.co.uk/news/university-kent-close-school-music-fine-art/.
183. Elkins, James, ed. 2009. Artists with PhDs: On the New Doctoral Degree in Studio Art. New Academia Publishing, LLC.
184. BBC News. 2023. *Poor Quality University Courses Face Limits on Student Numbers*. https://www.bbc.com/news/uk-politics-66216005.
185. Annetts, Deborah. 2018. 'Arts Risk Becoming the Preserve of the Elite Once Again'. *The Telegraph*. https://www.telegraph.co.uk/education/2018/04/18/arts-risk-becoming-preserve-elite/.
186. Tan, Kai Syng. 2021. 'Towards an Anti-Racist Fine Art Ph.D.: "Anti-Racism Productive Antagonisms" (ARPA) for the Supervisor, Student and Examiner'. Art, Design & Communication in Higher Education 20 (1): 49–63. https://doi.org/10.1386/adch_00029_1.
187. Tan. Unreasonable Adjustments.
188. Tan. *Giant Octopussies*.
189. Gill, John. 'Omnicrisis? Or Just Business as Usual?' *Times Higher Education (THE)*, 26 May 2022. https://www.timeshighereducation.com/opinion/omnicrisis-or-just-business-usual.
190. Bhopal, Kalwant. 2015. The Experiences of Black and Minority Ethnic Academics: A Comparative Study of the Unequal Academy. London ; New York, NY: Routledge.
191. Mangione, Salvatore, and Rolando Del Maestro. 2019. 'Was Leonardo Da Vinci Dyslexic?' The American Journal of Medicine 132, no. 7: 892–93. https://doi.org/10.1016/j.amjmed.2019.02.019.
192. Catani, Marco, and Paolo Mazzarello. 2019. 'Grey Matter Leonardo Da Vinci: A Genius Driven to Distraction'. *Brain* 142, no. 6: 1842–46. https://doi.org/10.1093/brain/awz131.
193. Tan, Kai Syng, and Backdoor Broadcasting Company. 2019. 'Too Much/Not Enough: Neurodiversity and Cultural Production'. https://backdoorbroadcasting.net/2019/05/too-muchnot-enough-neurodiversity-and-cultural-production/.
194. Moten, Fred, and Stefano Harney. 'The University and the Undercommons'. *Social Text* 22, no. 2 (2004): 101–15. https://doi.org/10.1215/01642472-22-2_79-101.

195. Tan. 'Anti-Racism Productive Antagonisms'.
196. Bhopal, Kalwant. 2020. 'White Female Academics Are Being Privileged above Women- and Men- of Colour'. *Guardian*. http://www.theguardian.com/education/2020/jul/28/uks-white-female-academics-are-being-privileged-above-women-and-men-of-colour.
197. Grove, Jack. 2023. 'UKRI's Diversity Strategy "Doesn't Mention Race"'. *Times Higher Education*. https://www.timeshighereducation.com/news/ukris-diversity-strategy-doesnt-mention-race.
198. Adelaine, Addy. 2023. '@AddyAdelaine: Just Had a Catch up Meeting with @UKRI_News...'. Tweet. *Twitter*. https://twitter.com/AddyAdelaine/status/1656708272701812737.
199. Advance HE. 2023. 'Professional Standards Framework Review'. https://www.advance-he.ac.uk/professional-standards-framework-review#video.
200. Office for Students. 2020. *Degree Attainment: Black, Asian and Minority Ethnic Students*. https://www.officeforstudents.org.uk/advice-and-guidance/promoting-equal-opportunities/effective-practice/black-asian-and-minority-ethnic-students/.
201. Equality and Human Rights Commission. 2019. 'Tackling Racial Harassment: Universities Challenged Report'. 120.
202. University College London. 2014. *Why Isn't My Professor Black?*. https://www.ucl.ac.uk/play/ucl-talks/why-isnt-my-professor-black.
203. Arday, Jason. 2019. *E031: Growing up Black in the 90 s*. Surviving Society. https://open.spotify.com/episode/6ZOVzuBFgIAps4CNQs7N28.
204. Mahanty, Shannon. 2023. 'I Was Illiterate until I Was 18, Now I'm Cambridge's Youngest Black Professor'. *Evening Standard*. https://www.standard.co.uk/insider/jason-arday-cambridge-university-youngest-black-professor-b1065627.html.
205. Crenshaw, Kimberle. 1989. 'Demarginalizing the Intersection of Race and Sex: A Black Feminist Critique of Antidiscrimination Doctrine, Feminist Theory and Antiracist Politics'. *University of Chicago Legal Forum* 1989 (1). https://chicagounbound.uchicago.edu/cgi/viewcontent.cgi?article=1052&context=uclf.
206. Museum of Transology. 2023. 'QTIBIPOC'. In *Museum of Transology*. https://www.museumoftransology.com/qtibipoc.
207. Obasi. 'Black Social Workers'.

208. Kaufman, James C., and Ronald A. Beghetto. 2009. 'Beyond Big and Little: The Four C Model of Creativity'. *Review of General Psychology* 13, no. 1: 1–12. https://doi.org/10.1037/a0013688.
209. Moten, and Harney. 'The University'.
210. Harney and Moten. *Undercommons*. 31.
211. Krathwohl, David R. 2002. 'A Revision of Bloom's Taxonomy: An Overview'. *Theory Into Practice* 41, no. 4: 212–18. https://doi.org/10.1207/s15430421tip4104_2.
212. Freire, Paulo. 2000. *Pedagogy of the Oppressed*. 30th anniversary ed. New York: Continuum.
213. Pellegrino, James, M.L. Hilton, Board Education, Division Education, and National Council. 2013. *Education for Life and Work: Developing Transferable Knowledge and Skills in the 21st Century*. https://doi.org/10.17226/13398.
214. Thornton, Alan. Artist, Researcher, Teacher: A Study of Professional Identity in Art and Education. Bristol: University of Chicago Press, 2013.
215. Elkins, James. 2008. 'Who Really Needs Art PhDs?'. *Website*. http://www.jameselkins.com/index.php/essays/198-interview-with-elpida-karaba.
216. QAA for Higher Education. 2019. 'Subject Benchmark Statement: Art and Design'. *QAA*. http://www.qaa.ac.uk/Publications/InformationAndGuidance/Pages/Subject-benchmark-statement%2D%2D-Art-and-design-.aspx.
217. Tan. 2018. *Brisk/Risks (Full Film with BSL)*, 2018. https://vimeo.com/336958029.
218. Harney and Moten. *Undercommons*. 38.
219. UNESCO, *Pathways to 2050*.
220. hooks, bell. 1999. *Yearning: Race, Gender and Cultural Politics*. Boston, MA: South End Press. 213.
221. Harney and Moten. *Undercommons*. 37.
222. Singer, Judy. 2016. NeuroDiversity: The Birth of an Idea. 2 edition.
223. Patterson, Leslie, Shelia C Baldwin, Juan J Araujo, Ragina Shearer, and Mary Stewart. 2010. 'Look, Think, Act: Using Critical Action Research to Sustain Reform in Complex Teaching/Learning Ecologies'. 19.
224. Linan, Steve. 2012. 'USC Lab Encourages Participatory Learning'. USC News. https://news.usc.edu/45089/usc-lab-encourages-participatory-learning/.

225. Cormier, Dave. 2008. 'Rhizomatic Education: Community as Curriculum'. *Innovate: Journal of Online Education* 4, no. 5.

226. Haraway, Donna. 2016. 'Tentacular Thinking: Anthropocene, Capitalocene, Chthulucene—Journal #75 September 2016—e-Flux'. https://www.e-flux.com/journal/75/67125/tentacular-thinking-anthropocene-capitalocene-chthulucene/.

227. Branlat, Jennifer, Juan Velasquez, and Ingvil Hellstrand. 2022. 'Tentacular Classrooms: Feminist Transformative Learning for Thinking and Sensing'. *Journal of Transformative Education*. https://doi.org/10.1177/15413446211068556.

228. Zarabadi, Shiva, Carol A. Taylor, Nikki Fairchild, and Anna Rigmor Moxnes. 2019. 'Feeling Medusa: Tentacular Troubling of Academic Positionality, Recognition and Respectability'. *Reconceptualizing Educational Research Methodology* 10, nos. 2–3: 87–111. https://doi.org/10.7577/rerm.3671.

229. Branlat et al. 'Tentacular Classrooms'.

230. Bhopal, Kalwant. 'White Female Academics'.

231. Cargle, Rachel Elizabeth. 'When Feminism Is White Supremacy in Heels'. *Harper's BAZAAR*, 16 August 2018. https://www.harpersbazaar.com/culture/politics/a22717725/what-is-toxic-white-feminism/.

232. Etymonline.    'Curation'.    https://www.etymonline.com/word/curation.

233. Harney and Moten. *Undercommons.* 27

234. Tan, Kai Syng. 2022. 'STUDY WITH ME: Creative Arts Leadership MA from 09/2023'. *Artful Agitation*. https://kaisyngtan.com/artful/creative-arts-leadership-ma/.

235. Zineb Berrais. 2022–2023. Creative Arts Leadership MA audio-visual assets.

236. Manchester Metropolitan University. 2023. 'MA Creative Arts Leadership clip @mcrschart'. *Instagram*. https://www.instagram.com/reel/Co7nxAeAKYw/?hl=en.

237. Tan. 'Anti-Racism Productive Antagonisms'.

238. Amy Cuddy. 2012. 'Your Body Language May Shape Who You Are'. *TED Talk*, 2012. https://www.ted.com/talks/amy_cuddy_your_body_language_may_shape_who_you_are/comments.

239. Tan, Kai Syng. 2020. 'Accessing Kai'. Catalysing Change through Artful Agitation. https://kaisyngtan.com/artful/access/.

240. For instance Siddons, Louise. 2021. 'Notes for Callers (and More)'. 2021. http://louisesiddons.com/how-to.html#App6.
241. This 'inclusion rider' template was created by an academic with others in the film industry: Kotagal (Cohen Milstein Sellers & Toll), Kalpana, Stacy L. Smith, Fanshen Cox DiGiovanni (Pear Street Films), and Leah Fischman. 2018. 'Inclusion Rider Template'. http://assets.uscannenberg.org.s3.amazonaws.com/docs/inclusion-rider-template.pdf.
242. Egner. 'Disability Rights Community'.
243. Ibid.
244. Huxtable, Amanda, Rowan Rutter (High Tide), Richard Twyman (English Touring Theatre), Lian (New Earth Theatre) Wilkinson, and 15 UK touring theatre companies. 2021. 'Anti Racism Touring Rider (with Range of Accessible Options)'. https://antiracismtouringrider.co.uk/blog/.
245. Research Centre for Museums and Galleries. 2023. 'Trans-Inclusive Culture: Guidance on Advancing Trans Inclusion for Museums, Galleries, Archives and Heritage Organisations'. https://le.ac.uk/rcmg/research-archive/trans-inclusive-culture.
246. Jack, Tan. 2023. '@jackkytan: Anti-Racist Partnership Agreement'. Instagram. 1 September 2023. https://www.instagram.com/jackkytan/.
247. Tan, Kai Syng. 2022. 'Neurodiversity In/& Creative Research Network LIVE Community Guidelines'. https://docs.google.com/document/d/1xb6Krz576vcEOf8mdsdmfiLSgNmkcn3HWdYgbyEwX7c/edit?usp=embed_facebook.
248. *Peace and Love Studios Brand Video*, 2021. https://vimeo.com/510854324.
249. Harney and Moten. *Undercommons*. 42.
250. Clarke, J. J. The Tao of the West: Western Transformations of Taoist Thought. Routledge, 2000. X.
251. An earlier version premiered at a Running Artfully Network workshop 21 June 2023.
252. Musk, Elon, Steve Wozniak, Yoshua Bengio, and Deepmind. 'Pause Giant AI Experiments: An Open Letter', 22 March 2023. https://futureoflife.org/open-letter/pause-giant-ai-experiments/.
253. Gebru, Timnit, Emily M. Bender, Angelina McMillan-Major, and Margaret Mitchell. 'Statement from the Listed Authors of Stochastic

Parrots on the "AI Pause" Letter', 31 March 2023. https://www.dair-institute.org/blog/letter-statement-March2023.

254. Gebru, Timnit. 'DAIR (Distributed AI Research Institute)'. https://www.dair-institute.org/.

255. Ifeoma Ozoma (Pinterest), Owen Diaz (Tesla), Yasser Elabd (Microsoft) and Sophie Zhang (Facebook) are examples.

256. Ozoma has written a 'resource guide for building and using a slingshot, there when needed for battle with a Goliath': Ozoma, Ifeoma. *The Tech Worker Handbook*, 2021. https://techworker-handbook.org/.

257. This chapter draws on my writings since 2009, including: *Physical and Poetic Running*; 'Run Riot'.

258. Running Artfully Network, and Fermynwoods Contemporary Art. 'Running Artfully Network - Launch Event'. Fermynwoods Contemporary Art, 8 March 2021. http://fermynwoods.org/running-artfully-network-launch-event/.

259. Bambara, Toni Cade. 'Raymond's Run'. In *Gorilla, My Love*, New edition. The Women's Press Ltd., 1997. https://www.remsencsd.org/cms/lib/NY01913914/Centricity/Domain/46/RaymondsRun.pdf.

260. Tan, Kai Syng. 'DOCUMENTA (13), Kassel, Germany'. *Kaidie's 1000-Day Trans-Run: 12.12.2009–09.09.2012* (blog), 8 September 2012. http://3rdlifekaidie.com/2012/09/kaidie-documenta-kaisyngtan/.

261. Tan. 'Running (in) Your City'.

262. Tan. 'Power, Play and Pedagogy'.

263. Gibson, William. Neuromancer: The Groundbreaking Cyberpunk Thriller. 1st edition. London: Gollancz, 2016.

264. Image developed from those in: Tan. *Physical and Poetic Running*.

265. Tan, Kai Syng. 'Running Artfully'. In *The Encyclopaedia of Mobilities*, edited by Peter Adey, Kaya Barry, and Weiqiang Lin. Edward Elgar Publishing, 2024.

266. Tan, Kai Syng. 'An Exploration of Running as Metaphor, Methodology, Material through the RUN! RUN! RUN! Biennale #r3fest 2016'. In *Interrelationships Between Sport and the Arts*, 1st ed. Sport in the Global Society—Contemporary Perspectives. Routledge, 2022. https://www.routledge.com/Interrelationships-Between-Sport-and-the-Arts/Long-Sandle/p/book/9781032350387#.

267. 'Free Thinking, Running'. *BBC*, 2017. https://www.bbc.co.uk/programmes/b087yrll.

268. Tan, Kai Syng. 'Tough Ultramarathons and Life on the Run'. *Transfers* 6, no. 3 (1 December 2016): 130–37. https://doi.org/10.3167/TRANS.2016.060311; Tan, Kai Syng. 2022. 'An Exploration of Running as Metaphor, Methodology, Material through the RUN! RUN! RUN! Biennale #r3fest 2016'. In Interrelationships Between Sport and the Arts, 1st ed., 829–845. Sport in the Global Society—Contemporary Perspectives. Routledge.

269. Tan, Kai Syng. 2014. *The International Body for Running*. www.kaisyngtan.com; Tan, Kai Syng. 2014. 'Running Cultures'. https://www.jiscmail.ac.uk/RUNNING-CULTURES.

270. Tan, Kai Syng. *ANTI-Adult RUN! RUN! RUN! Masterclass*. September 2015. http://kaisyngtan.com/portfolio/antiadultrun/.

271. Muther, Elizabeth. 2002. 'Bambara's Feisty Girls: Resistance Narratives in "Gorilla, My Love"'. *African American Review* 36 (3): 447–59. https://doi.org/10.2307/1512208.

272. *Running Artfully Network—YouTube*, 2021. https://www.youtube.com/playlist?list=PLBnIr5jFWQujxPOezTK07Yhtowf3T0RVl.

273. Filmer, Andrew. 'Endurance Running as Gesture in Contemporary Theatre and Performance'. *Contemporary Theatre Review* 30, no. 1 (2 January 2020): 28–45. https://doi.org/10.1080/10486801.2019.1696322; Whelan, Gregg. 'Opening Words for the Sports, Art and Culture Presentation, ANTI Festival, Festival of Contemporary Art in Kuopio, Finland'. 2015. https://www.pechakucha.com/presentations/run-run-run.

274. Büscher, Monika. 'Handwritten Personal Letter to Kai Syng Tan', 5 January 2018.

275. Büscher, et al. 'The Mobile Utopia Experiment'.

276. *Abdelkader Benali in Conversation with Kai Syng Tan Running Artfully Network*, 2021. https://www.youtube.com/watch?v=SKNzH7v-Xq4.

277. Tan, Kai Syng. 'RUN RUN RUN Biennale 2018: Dangerous Movements'. RUN RUN RUN Biennale, 2018. https://kaisyngtan.com/r3fest/.

278. Braun, Robert. "Autonomous Vehicles: From Science Fiction to Sustainable Future." In *Mobilities, Literature and Culture*, 259–80.

Studies in Mobilities, Literature, and Culture. Palgrave Macmillan, 2019.

279. Tan, Kai Syng. 'What's Running Got to Do with the Climate Crisis?', commissioned for *Thames Run: Source to Sea* by Véronique Chance' 2022.

280. RAN artists. 2023. 'Running Artfully Network Hub'. www.runningartfullynetwork.com.

281. Zimmer, Ben. '"Hallucination": When Chatbots (and People) See What Isn't There'. *Wall Street Journal*, 20 April 2023, sec. Life. https://www.wsj.com/articles/hallucination-when-chatbots-and-people-see-what-isnt-there-91c6c88b.

282. See note 22 above.

283. Guy-Sheftall, Beverly. Commitment: Toni Cade Bambara Speaks, 1979. 'Commitment: Toni Cade Bambara Speaks', in Sturdy Black Bridges, Roseann P. Bell, Bettye J. Parker, Beverly Guy-Sheftall, eds., Anchor Press/Doubleday, 1979, pp. 230–49. https://www.enotes.com/topics/toni-cade-bambara/critical-essays/bambara-toni-cade-vol-88.

284. Romano, Aja. 2020. 'How Being "Woke" Lost Its Meaning'. *Vox*, 9 October 2020. https://www.vox.com/culture/21437879/stay-woke-wokeness-history-origin-evolution-controversy.

285. Tan, Kai Syng. 2023. Developed from an animated sequence I commissioned Zineb Berrais to create: Tan, Kai Syng. 2021. 'Exercise V: Killer Whale Biting Back and Kicking Butts'. *How To Thrive In 2050!*

286. Iszatt-White, Marian, Brigid Carroll, Rita Gardiner, and Steve Kempster. "Leadership Special Issue: Do We Need Authentic Leadership? Interrogating Authenticity in a New World Order." *Leadership* 17 (March 17, 2021): 174271502110001. https://doi.org/10.1177/17427150211000153.

287. Bass, Bernard M., and Paul Steidlmeier. "Ethics, Character, and Authentic Transformational Leadership Behavior." The Leadership Quarterly 10, no. 2 (1999): 181–217. https://doi.org/10.1016/S1048-9843(99)00016-8.

288. This point, as well as several others in this chapter, are from: Carroll et al. *Leadership*.

289. Sutherland, Neil. "Leadership Without Leaders: Understanding Anarchist Organising through the Lens of Critical Leadership Studies." In *Leadership*, 248–69.

290. Ibid.

291. Tan, Kai Syng. 2023. Collage with fragments from the influx of emails I've been receiving from ADHD-ers since 2017, whose stories about how they entangle creativity with neurodivergence exemplify ill-disciplined leadership. Details have been edited to protect the identities of the writers.

292. World Economic Forum, and Uschi Schreiber. "Three Big Challenges for the World in 2017." World Economic Forum, 2017. https://www.weforum.org/agenda/2017/01/three-big-challenges-for-the-world-in-2017/.

293. hooks. 'Margin'.

294. Ladkin, Donna. 2021. 'Problematizing Authentic Leadership: How the Experience of Minoritized People Highlights the Impossibility of Leading from One's "True Self"'. *Leadership* 17 (4): 395–400. https://doi.org/10.1177/1742715021999586.

295. Ibid.

296. Livingston, Lucy Anne, Punit Shah, and Francesca Happé. 2019. 'Compensatory Strategies below the Behavioural Surface in Autism: A Qualitative Study'. *The Lancet Psychiatry* 6 (9): 766–77. https://doi.org/10.1016/S2215-0366(19)30224-X.

297. Several ideas and data here are from: Tan, Kai Syng. *Ill-Disciplined*.

298. Tan, Kai Syng. "What Else Could 'Neurodiversity' Look Like?" Disability Arts Online, February 19, 2018. http://disabilityarts.online/magazine/opinion/else-neurodiversity-look-like/.

299. Lesch. *Diamond*.

300. Hartmann, Thom. 2016. Adult ADHD: How to Succeed as a Hunter in a Farmer's World. 3rd Edition, New Edition of ADHD Secrets of Success edition. Rochester, Vermont: Park Street Press.

301. Adey, Peter. *Mobility*. 2nd ed. London: Routledge, 2017. Abstract. https://doi.org/10.4324/9781315669298.

302. Tan and Southern. Inaugural Symposium Instant Journal.

303. Kelly, Simon. "Leadership Process." In *Leadership*, 203–22.

304. Urry. What Is the Future?.

305. Pearce, Lynne. '"Text-as-Means" versus "Text-as-End-in-Itself": Some Reasons Why Literary Scholars Have Been Slow to Hop on the Mobilities Bus'. *Transfers* 10, no. 1 (1 March 2020): 76–84. https://doi.org/10.3167/TRANS.2020.100109.

306. Discussions in this entry are from: Sheller, Mimi. 'Moving with John Urry, by Mimi Sheller'. *Theory, Culture & Society, Global Public Life* (blog), 20 April 2016. https://www.theoryculturesociety.org/blog/moving-with-john-urry-by-mimi-sheller; Sheller, Mimi. 'Mobility Justice'. In *Handbook of Research Methods and Applications for Mobilities*, 11–20. Edward Elgar Publishing, 2020, and Sheller, Mimi. *Mobility Justice: The Politics of Movement in an Age of Extremes.* Verso Books, 2018.

307. Sheller, Mimi. 2014. 'The New Mobilities Paradigm for a Live Sociology'. *Current Sociology* 62 (6): 789–811. https://doi.org/10.1177/0011392114533211.

308. Tan. 'Run Riot!'.

309. Egner. 'Disability Rights Community'.

310. Tan. *Notes.*

311. Henley, Darren. 2020. 'Kindness in a Time of Crisis | Arts Council England'. 20 March 2020. https://www.artscouncil.org.uk/blog/kindness-time-crisis.

312. This section draws on: Egner, 'Disability Rights Community', and Walker, *Neuroqueer.*

313. Tan, Kai Syng. 2023. Neuroqueering Leadership and the Future. Speed-date.

314. Carroll, et al. *Leadership.* 5–8, 11, 126.

315. Sheller. 'The New Mobilities Paradigm'.

316. Pei Hwa Secondary School. 2023. *Our Story.* https://moe-peihwasec-staging.netlify.app/we-are-pei-hwa/our-story/.

317. Tan, Kai Syng. @kaisyngtan. 2021. 'Chinatown'. Tweet. Twitter. https://twitter.com/kaisyngtan/status/1424425445441871873.

318. Himid CBE, Lubaina. 2023. *Found Cities, Lost Objects: Women in the City (Roving Exhibition of Works from the Arts Council England Collection).* Southampton City Art Gallery.

319. Ibid.

320. Pearsall, Phyllis. 1990. *A. to Z. Maps: The Personal Story – From Bedsitter to Household Name by Phyllis Pearsall*. Geographers' A-Z Map Co Ltd.

321. Lao Zi and Lau. *Tao Teh Ching*. Ch. 54.

322. Tan. *Physical and Poetic Running*.

323. Jensen, Ole B., Claus Lassen, Vincent Kaufmann, Malene Freudendal-Pedersen, and Ida Sofie Gøtzsche Lange, eds. 2020. *Handbook of Urban Mobilities*. London: Routledge. https://doi. org/10.4324/9781351058759. Back cover.

324. Smith. *Decolonizing Methodologies*. 68.

325. This pattern of cultural vandalism and genocide is chronic and prevalent. For instance, non-binary communities have thrived since antiquity in India but, criminalised under colonial rule, *hijra* became ostracised in India. Hinchy, Jessica. *Governing Gender and Sexuality in Colonial India: The Hijra, c.1850–1900*. Cambridge University Press, 2019. https://doi.org/10.1017/9781108592208. Pp95–109.

326. Leonard, Andrew. 2020. 'How Taiwan's Unlikely Digital Minister Hacked the Pandemic'. *Wired*. https://www.wired.com/story/how-taiwans-unlikely-digital-minister-hacked-the-pandemic/.

327. Tan, Jack. 2023. '@Jackkytan: DISPOSING FORESTS …' Instagram. 19 August 2023. https://www.instagram.com/p/CwIyO6OtVtr/.

328. One of 93 A4 hand-drawn mappings from: Tan, Kai Syng. 2017. '#MagicCarpet Website'. #MagicCarpet. 2019 2017. http://wesatonamat.weebly.com/blog/kais-speedy-sketch.

329. Presti, Laura Lo. 2020. 'The Migrancies of Maps: Complicating the Critical Cartography and Migration Nexus in "Migro-Mobility" Thinking'. Mobilities 15 (6): 911–29. https://doi.org/10.1080/17450101.2020.1799660.

330. Roberts, L., ed. 2012. *Mapping Cultures: Place, Practice, Performance*. Basingstoke, Hampshire New York, NY: Palgrave Macmillan. 4.

331. Dodge, Martin, Rob Kitchin, and Chris Perkins, eds. 2009/ *Rethinking Maps: New Frontiers in Cartographic Theory: 28*. 1st edition. London ; New York: Routledge. 17, 231.

332. Leonard. 'Taiwan's Unlikely Digital Minister'.

333. Verhoeff, Nanna, Heidi Rae Cooley, and Heather Zwicker. 2017. 'Urban Cartographies: Mapping Mobility and Presence'. Television & New Media 18 (1). https://doi.org/10.1177/1527476417705030.

334. Wilmott, Clancy. 2017. 'In-Between Mobile Maps and Media: Movement'. *Television & New Media* 18 (4): 320–35. https://doi.org/10.1177/1527476416663637.323.
335. Manning. 'Me Lo Dijo Un Pajarito'.
336. Kirby, Philip, and Margaret J. Snowling. 2022. 'Dyslexia Discovered: Word-Blindness, Victorian Medicine, and Education (1877–1917)'. In *Dyslexia: A History [Internet]*. McGill-Queen's University Press. https://www.ncbi.nlm.nih.gov/books/NBK588803/.
337. Dale Oen, Vibeke, Jeanett Svihus, Sara Helene Røyland Solberg, Anette Harris, and Jarle Eid. 2022. 'Crisis Leadership in COVID-19: A Qualitative Study of Norwegian Business Leaders'. *Frontiers in Psychology* 13. https://www.frontiersin.org/articles/10.3389/fpsyg.2022.937935.
338. Smith. *Decolonizing Methodologies*. 71.
339. Lee, Gullawun Daniel Roque. *The Final Hearing of the Kenbi Land Claim of 1995*. 1999. Turtle shell, H 950mm x W 750mm x D 260mm. National Museum Australia. https://collectionsearch.nma.gov.au/icons/images/kaui2/index.html#/home?usr=CE.
340. *Minoan Pottery Stirrup Jar Decorated with an Octopus, 1300-1200 BC (LM IIIb). Found in Tomb 50, Kourion, Cyprus. British Museum, GR 1896.2-1.265.* https://commons.wikimedia.org/wiki/Category:Octopuses_in_Minoan_pottery#/media/File:Minoan_pottery_stirrup_jar,_1300-1200_BC,_BM_Cat_Vases_C501,_142789.jpg.
341. Farquharson, Alex, and Martin Clark. 2013. *Exhibition Publication: Aquatopia: The Imaginary of The Ocean Deep*. https://cms.nottinghamcontemporary.org/site/assets/files/1934/nc_guide_aquatopia_1.pdf.
342. UC Museum of Paleontology. 2021. 'How Your Eye Works'. Understanding Evolution. https://evolution.berkeley.edu/how-your-eye-works/.
343. Katz, Itamar, Tal Shomrat, and Nir Nesher. 2021. 'Feel the Light: Sight-Independent Negative Phototactic Response in Octopus Arms'. *The Journal of Experimental Biology* 224, no. Pt 5. https://doi.org/10.1242/jeb.237529.
344. Gutnick, Tamar, Ruth A. Byrne, Binyamin Hochner, and Michael Kuba. 2011. 'Octopus Vulgaris Uses Visual Information to Determine the Location of Its Arm'. *Current Biology: CB* 21, no. 6. 460–62. https://doi.org/10.1016/j.cub.2011.01.052.

345. Russell, Ginny. 2020. 'Email Discussion between Ginny and Kai', circa 2020.

346. Cameron, Elizabeth. 2015. 'Is It Art or Knowledge? Deconstructing Australian Aboriginal Creative Making'. *Arts* 4, no. 2. 68–74. https://doi.org/10.3390/arts4020068.

347. See note 19 above.

348. Butler, Octavia E. 2021. 'Positive Obsession'.

349. Tan. 'Power, Play and Pedagogy'.

350. Tan, Kai Syng. 2012. 'KAIDIE'S FINAL 38 DAYS: Kai Dies. *Kaidie's 1000-Day Trans-Run: 12.12.2009–09.09.2012* (blog). https://kaisyngtan.com/3rdlifekaidie/.

351. Douglas. *Cultural Leadership*.

352. Ciulla. 'Leadership and Ethics'. 119.

353. Butler, Octavia. 1983. 'Speech Sounds'. *Asimov's Science Fiction Magazine*, 1983. http://future-lives.com/wp-content/uploads/2014/11/speech_sounds.pdf.

354. Pearce, Lynne. 2019. 'Trackless Mourning: The Mobilities of Love and Loss'. *Cultural Geographies* 26, no. 2. 163–76. https://doi.org/10.1177/1474474018792665.

355. Drawing by 11-year-old Marcus, from Tan. #MagicCarpet.

356. Balagun. *Interviewing the Oracle*.

357. Schalk, Sami. 2018. *Bodyminds Reimagined: (Dis)Ability, Race, and Gender in Black Women's Speculative Fiction*. Durham, NC: Duke University Press. 23.

358. Ferrández-Sanmiguel, María. 2022. 'Toward an Ethics of Affinity: Posthumanism and the Question of the Animal in Two SF Narratives of Catastrophe'. *Critique: Studies in Contemporary Fiction* 0 (0): 1–14. https://doi.org/10.1080/00111619.2022.2095248.

359. Murray, Lesley, Amanda Holt, Sian Lewis, and Jessica Moriarty. 2023. 'The Unexceptional Im/Mobilities of Gender-Based Violence in the Covid-19 Pandemic'. *Mobilities* 18 (3): 552–65. https://doi.org/10.1080/17450101.2022.2118619.

360. Sinclair and Evans. 'Difference and Leadership'.

361. Schalk, Sami. 2017. 'Interpreting Disability Metaphor and Race in Octavia Butler's "The Evening and the Morning and the Night"'. *African American Review* 50 (2): 139–51. https://doi.org/10.1353/afa.2017.0018.

362. See note 5 above.
363. Schalk, Sami. 2017. 'Experience, Research, and Writing: Octavia E. Butler as an Author of Disability Literature'. Palimpsest: A Journal on Women, Gender, and the Black International 6 (1): 153–77. https://doi.org/10.1353/pal.2017.0018. 157.
364. Rowell, Charles H., and Octavia E. Butler. 1997. 'An Interview with Octavia E. Butler'. Callaloo 20, no. 1: 47–66.
365. See note 5 above.
366. Fox, Margalit. 2006. 'Octavia E. Butler, Science Fiction Writer, Dies at 58'. The New York Times, 1 March 2006, sec. Books. https://www.nytimes.com/2006/03/01/books/octavia-e-butler-science-fiction-writer-dies-at-58.html.
367. See note 5 above.
368. Butler. 'Positive Obsession'; Octavia E. Butler. 2021. Kindred, Fledgling, Collected Stories: 725–31. Library of America. https://loa-shared.s3.amazonaws.com/static/pdf/Butler_Positive_Obsession.pdf.
369. Remington, Anna, and Jake Fairnie. 2017. 'A Sound Advantage: Increased Auditory Capacity in Autism'. Cognition 166. 59–65. https://doi.org/10.1016/j.cognition.2017.04.002.
370. See note 11 above.
371. Ibid.
372. Butler, Octavia E. 2021. 'Positive Obsession', Octavia E. Butler: Kindred, Fledgling, Collected Stories: 725–31. Library of America https://loa-shared.s3.amazonaws.com/static/pdf/Butler_Positive_Obsession.pdf.
373. Kafer, Alison. 2013. Feminist, Queer, Crip. Indiana University Press. https://www.jstor.org/stable/j.ctt16gz79x.
374. Eshun, Kodwo. 2003. 'Further Considerations on Afrofuturism'. Project Muse (Michigan State University Press), CR: The New Centennial Review, Volume 3, no. 2: 287–302. https://doi.org/10.1353/ncr.2003.0021.
375. Lord, Robert G. 2019. 'Leadership and the Medium of Time'. In What's Wrong with Leadership, 130–72. New York: Routledge.
376. Jonsdottir, Inga Jona, and Kari Kristinsson. 2020. 'Supervisors' Active-Empathetic Listening as an Important Antecedent of Work Engagement'. International Journal of Environmental Research and

*Public Health* 17, no. 21: 7976. https://doi.org/10.3390/ijerph17217976.

377. Reitz, Megan, and John Higgins. 2021. 'Speaking Truth to Power: Why Leaders Cannot Hear What They Need to Hear'. *BMJ Leader* 5, no. 4. https://doi.org/10.1136/leader-2020-000394.

378. Butler. 'Speech Sounds'.

379. Das Neves, Bonnie, Carolyn Unsworth, and Colette Browning. 2023. '"Being Treated like an Actual Person": Attitudinal Accessibility on the Bus'. *Mobilities* 18 (3): 425–44. https://doi.org/10.1080/17450101.2022.2126794; Szerszynski, Bronislaw. 2020. 'How to Dismantle a Bus: Planetary Mobilities as Method'. In *Handbook of Research Methods and Applications for Mobilities*, 398–410.

380. AFRICAN AND BLACK HISTORY. 2023. '@africanarchives: She Refused to Move…' 5 September 2023. https://www.instagram.com/p/Cw0GIJrg4Pu/?img_index=1.

381. Braun, Robert. 2019. 'Autonomous Vehicles: From Science Fiction to Sustainable Future'. In *Mobilities, Literature and Culture*, 259–80.

382. Sheller. 'Mobility Justice'.

383. Ibid.

384. Butler, Octavia. 2000. 'Visions: "We Tend to Do the Right Thing When We Get Scared"', 1 January 2000. https://archive.nytimes.com/www.nytimes.com/specials/010100mil-identity-octa.html.

385. Douglas. Cultural Leadership.

386. Schalk. *Bodyminds Reimagined*.

387. South London Gallery. "MICHELLE WILLIAMS GAMAKER: OUR MOUNTAINS ARE PAINTED ON GLASS." *South London Gallery*. https://www.southlondongallery.org/exhibitions/michelle-williams-gamaker/.

388. Afterword, in *Speech Sounds*.

389. Tan, Kai Syng. 2016. *(Dys)Service Cat(Suit): ADHD, Dyslexia and Dyspraxia, Conceptual Artwork*. https://wellcomecollection.org/works/kkng8gjs.

390. Tan, Kai Syng. 2016. *Hinder: An Unintuitive Dating App*. https://kaisyngtan.com/artful/hinder/.

391. Edited transcript of my chat with Bethany-Anne Arnold, from: Tan, Kai Syng. 2021. 'Exercise VI. Bright Stars Shining, Tantalising Times Coming'. *How To Thrive in 2050!*.

392. This section draws on: 'Tan Chin Hwee: Why You Should Be like a Cockroach', 2015. https://nextinsight.net/story-archive-mainmenu-60/927-2015/10059-tan-chin-hwee-why-you-should-be-like-a-cockroach. One of few openly-neuro-divergent high-profile person in East / Southeast Asia, Tan is the Asia-Pacific CEO of a global Fortune 25 company. His multiple awards include winning the World Economic Forum Young Global Leader twice, but has snubbed its founder's invitation to dinner.

393. hooks. *Outlaw Culture*.

394. hooks. 'Margin'.

395. Edited transcript of my 'speed-date' with artist-activist Bob and Roberta Smith aka Patrick Brill OBE RA. Tan, Kai Syng. 2021. 'Exercise II: Anthropoid Artfully Raising Fists and Hope', *How to Thrive in 2050!*

396. King's College London and Sue Hoyle. 2018. 'Changing Cultures: Transforming Leadership in the Arts, Museums and Libraries'. https://www.artscouncil.org.uk/sites/default/files/download-file/ChangingCulturesKCLACE.pdf; Hewison, Robert, and John Holden. 2002. 'An Investment in the Rising Generation of Cultural Leaders Is Necessary, and Timely'. The Clore Leadership Programme. 2002. https://www.cloreleadership.org/resources/investment-rising-generation-cultural-leaders-necessary-and-timely; Patten, Mags. 2018. 'Creating Cultural Leadership for the 21st Century'. 17 October 2018. https://www.artscouncil.org.uk/blog/creating-cultural-leadership-21st-century; Carty, Hilary. 2020. 'An Update on Clore Leadership Activities in Light of Covid-19 | The Clore Leadership Programme'. https://www.clore-leadership.org/news-events/news/update-clore-leadership-activities-director-hilary-carty.

397. Montserrat, Jade, Cecilia Wee, and Michelle Williams Gamaker. 2020. '"We Need Collectivity against Structural and Institutional Racism in the Cultural Sector"'. ArtsProfessional, 24 June 2020. https://www.artsprofessional.co.uk/magazine/article/we-need-collectivity-against-structural-and-institutional-racism-cultural-sector.

398. Nisbett, Melissa, Ben Walmsley, and Emma McDowell. 'Bullying Bosses, Broken Boards and a Crisis of Accountability'. *ArtsProfessional*, 23 February 2023. https://www.artsprofessional.co.uk/magazine/article/bullying-bosses-broken-boards-and-crisis-accountability.

399. Lachlan Patterson: DARK WHITE—Full Special, 2021. https://www.youtube.com/watch?v=Gub6fcm4n_k.

400. Marsh, Kate. 2016. 'Taking Charge—Dance, Disability and Leadership: Exploring the Shifting Role of the Disabled Dance Artist'  https://pure.coventry.ac.uk/ws/portalfiles/portal/42066580/Marsh2016.pdf.

401. Eltham, Ben. "We Are Witnessing a Cultural Bloodbath in Australia That Has Been Years in the Making." The Guardian, April 6, 2020, sec. Culture. https://www.theguardian.com/culture/2020/apr/06/we-are-witnessing-a-cultural-bloodbath-in-australia-that-has-been-years-in-the-making; Puffett, Neil. "Exodus of Artistic Directors 'Symptom of Sector Neglect.'" ArtsProfessional, August 17, 2023. https://www.artsprofessional.co.uk/news/exodus-artistic-directors-symptom-sector-neglect.

402. Gheerawo, Rama. *Creative Leadership: Born from Design*. Lund Humphries Publishers Ltd, 2022.

403. Developed from Tan. 'Novel Viruses'; Tan, Kai Syng, and Tom Northey. "Artful Leadership against a Clever Virus." ArtsProfessional, June 18, 2020. https://www.artsprofessional.co.uk/magazine/article/artful-leadership-against-clever-virus.

404. Henley, Darren. *Creativity: Why It Matters*. London: Elliott & Thompson, 2018.

405. Johnson-Nwosu, Chinma. "Artist Mary Evans to Be First Black Director of London's Slade Art School." *The Art Newspaper – International Art News and Events*, August 8, 2023. https://www.theartnewspaper.com/2023/08/08/artist-mary-evans-to-be-first-black-director-of-londons-slade-art-school.

406. Moorhead, Joanna. '"Lucian Wanted Us to Have a Baby"'. *The Guardian*, 12 October 2012, sec. Life and style. https://www.theguardian.com/lifeandstyle/2012/oct/13/celia-paul-lucian-freud-son.

407. See for instance Romer, Christy. 'Grantium: NPO Applicants Struggle with "Nightmare" Grantium'. *ArtsProfessional*, 27 January 2017. https://www.artsprofessional.co.uk/news/npo-applicants-struggle-nightmare-grantium.

408. Hill, Liz. 'Grantium "Impasse Hell Hole" Unleashes Twitter Storm'. ArtsProfessional, 17 April 2020. https://www.artsprofessional.co.uk/news/grantium-impasse-hell-hole-unleashes-twitter-storm.

409. For instance Hawkins, Harriet. "Geography's Creative (Re)Turn: Toward a Critical Framework." *Progress in Human Geography* 43, no. 6 (December 1, 2019): 963–84. https://doi. org/10.1177/0309132518804341. UCL; *Three UCL Researchers Honoured with Philip Leverhulme Prizes of £100,000.* UCL News, October 31, 2018. https://www.ucl.ac.uk/news/2018/oct/three-ucl-researchers-honoured-philip-leverhulme-prizes-ps100000.

410. World Wildlife Fund. 'Learn These Top 10 Facts about Bees'. WWF. https://www.wwf.org.uk/learn/fascinating-facts/bees.

411. Kovac, Helmut, Anton Stabentheiner, and Robert Brodschneider. 'Contribution of Honeybee Drones of Different Age to Colonial Thermoregulation'. *Apidologie* 40, no. 1 (January 2009): 82–95. https://doi.org/10.1051/apido/2008069.

412. Gravitz, Lauren. 'Animal Behaviour: Nested Instincts'. *Nature* 521, no. 7552 (May 2015): S60–61. https://doi.org/10.1038/521S60a.

413. Wikipedia. 2023. 'List of Unarmed African Americans Killed by Law Enforcement Officers in the United States'. https://en.wikipedia.org/w/index.php?title=List_of_unarmed_African_Americans_killed_by_law_enforcement_officers_in_the_United_States&oldid=1158130990.

414. The Newsroom. 2018. 'Wars of the Roses: How the Rivalry between Yorkshire and Lancashire Still Exists Today'. *Yorkshire Post*, 18 May 2018. https://www.yorkshirepost.co.uk/news/wars-of-the-roses-how-the-rivalry-between-yorkshire-and-lancashire-still-exists-today-47277.

415. Radio X. 2023. 'The Significance of the Manchester Bee Symbol'. Radio X, 22 May 2023. https://www.radiox.co.uk/features/what-does-manchester-bee-mean-symbol/.

416. Manchester City Council. 2023. 'The Manchester Bee'. https://www.manchester.gov.uk/info/100004/the_council_and_democracy/7580/the_manchester_bee.

417. MCPHH. 2020. 'Fifth Pan-African Congress 75th Anniversary Celebrations, 15-18th October 2020'. MANCHESTER CENTRE FOR PUBLIC HISTORY & HERITAGE (blog). 25 September 2020. https://mcphh.wordpress.com/2020/09/25/fifth-pan-african-congress-75th-anniversary-celebrations-15-18th-october-2020/.

418. Manchester Metropolitan University. 2020. 'PAC@75: Pan African Congress 75th Anniversary Celebrations Home'. https://www.mmu.ac.uk/pac75.

419. See this and other tweets by following #PAC75: Tan, Kai Syng. 2020. 'Finale Programme with Lemn Sissay OBE FRSL, Staff and Students'. Tweet. *Twitter.* https://twitter.com/kaisyngtan/status/1317859636557586434.

420. A visual expression of the Celebrations by UK-Algerian Zineb Berrais.

421. Like Chio Lin Tan, Simone Biles and the children in *Speech Sounds,* Sissay was adopted and has spoken powerfully about this. Of particular relevance to neuro-futurising leadership is his analysis of how the government effectively parents people who are fostered, adopted, and/or orphaned and treated them as a problem waiting to happen rather than as a solution'. Channel 4 News. 2023. ''Poet Lemn Sissay Explains How ..,''. Instagram. 15 September 2023. https://www.instagram.com/reel/CxNpFEjMv-V/.

422. 'BBC Radio 4. 2020. *Africa United in Manchester.* 27 November 2020. https://www.bbc.co.uk/programmes/m000ptb5; Manchester Metropolitan University, dir. 2020. PAC@75: Pan African Congress 75th Anniversary Celebrations Channel. https://www.youtube.com/channel/UC8f7ic4fO4UnoqLiLFuolfw/videos.

423. Harney and Moten. *Undercommons,* 26.

424. Gabel, Julia. 'Thousands Use Twitter Hashtag to Show Impact of Indigenous Scholar'. *NZ Herald,* 17 September 2020, sec. New Zealand, Education. https://www.nzherald.co.nz/nz/education/thousands-use-twitter-hashtag-to-show-impact-of-indigenous-scholar/EBZ76SMSWJNS7RZ5S6TGR75SOQ/.

425. Ahmed, Sara. *Complaint!* Durham: Duke University Press Books, 2021.

426. Morrison, Toni. 1975. 'A Humanist View'. May 30. https://www.mackenzian.com/wp-content/uploads/2014/07/Transcript_PortlandState_TMorrison.pdf.

427. Kinder_Surprises. 2012. 'A Short Video about the Boom-Box Bike Man of Manchester'. Reddit Post. R/Manchester. www.reddit.com/r/manchester/comments/10qhsn/a_short_video_about_the_boombox_bike_man_of/.

428. Townsend, Ben. 2020. 'Meet Barrington, Manchester's Boom Box Cyclist Who "Just Loves the Music"'. Manchester Evening News, 16 February 2020, sec. Greater Manchester News. https://www. manchestereveningnews.co.uk/news/greater-manchester-news/ meet-barrington-manchesters-favourite-boom-17753667.

429. Foursevenniner. 2019. 'How Long Has Boombox Bike Man Been Going up and down Oxford Road (and into St Peters)?' Reddit Post. Reddit. www.reddit.com/r/manchester/comments/cmtfh9/ how_long_has_boombox_bike_man_been_going_up_and/.

430. Urban Dictionary. 2021. 'Barry Boombox'. In *Urban Dictionary*. https://www.urbandictionary.com/define.php?term=Barry%20 boombox.

431. Tan, Kai Syng. 'RUNNING (IN) YOUR CITY Prezi. AAG2015 Chicago Premiere.' Prezi, 2015. https://prezi. com/8ozt2o5k013q/2015-gig-running-in-your-city-aag2015- chicago-premiere/.

432. Blankson, Perry. 2022. *When Africa's Future Came to Manchester*. The Challenge to the Colonial Powers. https://tribunemag.co. uk/2022/10/fifth-pan-african-congress-manchester- chorlton-1945.

433. Lao Zi, and D.C. Lau. *Tao Teh Ching*. Penguin Classics, 1963. Chapter 76.

434. Pascal, Blaise. *Pensées and Other Writings*. Translated by Honor Levi. Oxford Paperbacks, 1999; Lane, Nick. *Life Ascending: The Ten Great Inventions of Evolution*. W. W. Norton & Company, 2009.

435. Adey, Peter. 2006. 'If Mobility Is Everything Then It Is Nothing: Towards a Relational Politics of (Im)Mobilities'. Mobilities 1 (1): 75–94. https://doi.org/10.1080/17450100500489080.

436. Tan, Kai Syng. 2023. Digital collage created from various past work, including *Panda Hygiene* (1994).

437. Tan, Kai Syng. 2009. 'MA: THE CONCEPT OF IN-BETWEEN: PART 1 – Kaidie's 1000-Day Trans-Run: 12.12.2009–09.09.2012…' 12 December 2009. http://kaisyngtan.com/3rdlifekaidie/2009/ 12/in-between-1/.

438. Tan, Kai Syng. 2002. Islandhopping, Conflict, Difference, Meaning, Live-Ness. http://kaisyngtan.com/tokyo/; Tan, Kai Syng. 2004. 'One of the Greatest Shows on Earth: An Invitation to a Discourse about Our Pasts, Hard-to Define Present/Presence and Hereafter via a Not-yet-Defined Presentation Mode'. In *Twilight Tomorrow*, edited by June Yap. Singapore: Singapore Art Museum.

439. Grint, Keith. 2008. 'Wicked Problems and Clumsy Solutions: The Role of Leadership'. *BAMM Publications*, Clinical Leader, Volume I Number II (December). http://leadershipforchange.org.uk/wp-content/uploads/Keith-Grint-Wicked-Problems-handout.pdf.

440. Barry, et al. 'An Agenda'.

441. Ibid.

442. Latham, Alan, and Kai Syng Tan. 2017. 'Running into Each Other'.

443. See note 3.

444. Lee, Christina. 2019. 'Crossings: Reflections on Disability and Intersectionality'. 27 March 2019. https://blogs.kcl.ac.uk/english/2019/03/27/crossings-reflections-on-disability-and-intersectionality/.

445. Ahmed, Sara. 2017. *Living a Feminist Life*. Illustrated edition. Durham: Duke University Press Books. 5, 212.

446. Lorde, Audre. 1995. 'Age, Race, Class, and Sex: Women Redefining Difference'. In Campus Wars. Routledge.

447. Levecq, Christine. 2000. 'Power and Repetition: Philosophies of (Literary) History in Octavia E. Butler's "Kindred"'. *Contemporary Literature* 41 (3): 525–53. https://doi.org/10.2307/1208895.

448. Balagun. *Interviewing the Oracle*.

449. Everett, Belinda. 2023. 'Bee Pedal Ready Community'. Facebook. https://www.facebook.com/beepedalready/.

450. Tan, Kai Syng. 2023. 'With Bee Pedals & Bee Barbers in My Final Days in the City of Worker Bee.' Instagram. 30 June 2023. https://www.instagram.com/p/CuHkuwUoA9F/.

451. Bilton, Dominic. 2023. *(Un)Defining Queer*. | Whitworth Art Gallery. https://www.whitworth.manchester.ac.uk/whats-on/exhibitions/currentexhibitions/undefiningqueer/.

452. Douglas. *The Artistic Turn*.

453. Images from Tan, Kai Syng. 2006. 'ISLANDHOPPING (Sydney Leg)'. *Biennale of Sydney*.

454. McDade, Adam. "Beyond the Epidermis: A Practical Investigation into Contemporary Western Tattooing," 2021.

455. This term 'dragging' to describe existential weight is inspired by a conversation I had with a participant (a philosophy PhD candidate) of a workshop I gave at University of Oxford, 2022.

456. Holderness, Mike. 1998. 'Managers Reclaim the Sites'. Times Higher Education, 13 July 1998. http://www.timeshighereducation.co.uk/news/managers-reclaim-the-sites/108215.article.

457. Wikipedia. 2023. 'Media Censorship in Singapore: Party Political Films'. In Wikipedia. https://en.wikipedia.org/w/index.php?title=Media_censorship_in_Singapore&oldid=1147313585#Party_political_films.

458. Agence France Presse. 2002. 'Documentary on Jeya Withdrawn from Film Festival: Report'. *Agence France Presse*, 4 January 2002. http://www.singapore-window.org/sw02/020104af.htm.

459. Tan, Kai Syng. 2018. *Exceptional Talent, the State of Fun & Islands of after Death: A Story in 100 Slides.* https://kaisyngtan.com/portfolio/exceptional-talent/.

460. Bethania, Joshua. 2023. 'So You Think You're Funny? 2022 Grand Final'. Instagram (blog). 22 March 2023. https://www.instagram.com/reel/CqF1m1ooZrl/.

461. Hu, Lili, Long Ye, Ming Guo, and Yunshuo Liu. 2023. 'The Impact of Leader Humor on Employee Creativity during the COVID-19 Period: The Roles of Perceived Workload and Occupational Coping Self-Efficacy'. *Behavioral Sciences* 13 (4): 303. https://doi.org/10.3390/bs13040303; Rosenberg, Caroline, Arlene Walker, Michael Leiter, and Joe Graffam. 2021. 'Humor in Workplace Leadership: A Systematic Search Scoping Review'. *Frontiers in Psychology* 12. https://www.frontiersin.org/articles/10.3389/fpsyg.2021.610795.

462. Ahmed, Sara. 2010. 'Happy Objects'. In , 29–51. Duke University Press. http://hemi.nyu.edu/courses/sp2016-performance-and-activism/wp-content/uploads/sites/8/2016/02/02242016-Ahmed.pdf.

463. Shrestha, Rupak, and Jennifer Fluri. 2021. 'Geopolitics of Humour and Development in Nepal and Afghanistan'. In *The Palgrave Handbook of Humour Research*, 189–203. Springer Nature.

464. Ibid.

465. Paskett, Zoe. 2018. 'Get Your Spoken Word Fix at the Roundhouse's Last Word Festival'. *Evening Standard*, 21 June 2018, sec. Culture. https://www.standard.co.uk/culture/the-last-word-festival-at-the-roundhouse-shares-the-power-of-storytelling-and-spoken-word-a3856791.html.

466. See note 8 above.

467. ADHD UK. 'Comedian', 2023. https://adhduk.co.uk/category/career/comedian/.

468. Amnesty International. 2022. 'Singapore: Execution of Man with Learning Disability Is a "disgraceful Act" by the Government'. https://www.amnesty.org.uk/press-releases/singapore-execution-man-learning-disability-disgraceful-act-government.

469. Singapore Law Watch. 2017. 'Nagaenthran a/l K Dharmalingam v Public Prosecutor [2017] SGHC 222'. https://www.singaporelaw-watch.sg/Portals/0/Docs/Judgments/%5b2017%5d%20 SGHC%20222%20(amended).pdf.

470. Lin, Weiqiang, and Brenda S. A. Yeoh. 2021. 'Pathological (Im) Mobilities: Managing Risk in a Time of Pandemics'. Mobilities 16 (1): 96–112. https://doi.org/10.1080/17450101.2020.1862454.

471. Yeoh, Brenda S. A., Charmian Goh, and Kellyn Wee. 2020. 'Social Protection for Migrant Domestic Workers in Singapore: International Conventions, the Law, and Civil Society Action'. American Behavioral Scientist 64 (6): 841–58. https://doi.org/10.1177/0002764220910208.

472. Koolhaas, Rem, Bruce Mau, Hans Werlemann, and Jennifer Sigler. 2002. *Small, Medium, Large, Extra-Large*. 2nd edition. Monacelli Press. 1015–1041.

473. IFLR. 2021. 'Opinion: "Singapore-on-Thames" Model Is a Post-Brexit Fantasy'. *International Financial Law Review*. https://www.iflr.com/article/2a6466axp6qvytzvdg6ww/opinion-singapore-on-thames-model-is-a-post-brexit-fantasy.

474. Gibson, William. 1993. 'Disneyland with the Death Penalty'. *Wired*. http://www.wired.com/wired/archive//1.04/gibson_pr.html.

475. Ang, Jolene, and Amelia Teng. 2019. 'SMU Reviews "bogus" Grades for Module after Professor Gives All of His 169 Business Students an A'. *The Straits Times*. https://www.straitstimes.com/singapore/education/smu-reviews-bogus-grades-for-module-after-professor-gives-all-of-his-169.

476. Kiyankiriam. 2020. 'Would You Date White Guy Who Used to Teach English in Asia ?' Reddit Post. *R/FemaleDatingStrategy*. www.reddit.com/r/FemaleDatingStrategy/comments/g71538/would_you_date_white_guy_who_used_to_teach/.

477. Kaufmann, Rupert. 2016. 'Singapore – Asia for Beginners! DreamTravelOnPoints'. https://dreamtravelonpoints.com/singapore-asia-for-beginners/.

478. Kumar. 2020. *Coconuts and Commotion*. https://www.youtube.com/watch?v=hDvKxaULgBQ.

479. Ruangrupa. 2022. 'We Are Angry, We Are Sad, We Are Tired, We Are United.' *Ruangrupa* (blog). 10 September 2022. https://lumbung.space/pen/pen.lumbung.space/we-are-angry-we-are-sad-we-are-tired-we-are-united/.

480. Tan, Kai Syng. 2020. *This Is Not an Ally.* https://www.academia.edu/43399631/2020_This_is_Not_An_Ally_Manchester_School_of_Art_Research_hub_.

481. Williams, Apryl. 2020. 'Ken and Karen Are White Supremacists'. Berkman Klein Center Collection (blog). 1 July 2020. https://medium.com/berkman-klein-center/ken-and-karen-are-white-supremacists-eeb0b283be5d.

482. Youde, Kate. 2019. 'Younis Leaves Southbank Centre after Less than a Year'. *ArtsProfessional.* https://www.artsprofessional.co.uk/news/younis-leaves-southbank-centre-after-less-year.

483. Yashere, Gina. 2020. 'Clip from Live at Apollo 2018'. *Instagram.* https://www.instagram.com/tv/CBDGLu1n4HP/.

484. BillBoggsTV, dir. 1977. *Richard Pryor Interview with Bill Boggs.* https://www.youtube.com/watch?v=a-sCP_Vhnpk.

485. *Richard Pryor's Anti-Gay Rant*, 2021. https://www.youtube.com/watch?v=7jMUBrPpu1Q.

486. Ibid.

487. Tan, Kai Syng. 2023. Developed from earlier works including an oil painting and 16 mm films.

488. Balagun. *Interviewing the Oracle.*

489. Djalili, Omid. 2023. '@Omiddjalili: Speech at Westminster Hall'. Instagram. 26 June 2023. https://www.instagram.com/reel/Ct9n20wvNuK/.

490. Ibid.

491. Sheller, Mimi. 2018. Mobility Justice.

492. Channel 4 News, dir. 2023. 'Krishnan Guru-Murthy Interviews Jason Arday'.

493. Henley. *Creativity.*

494. Photograph from King's College London. 2018. 'Exhibition of Work from Artist-Academic Collaborations at Bush House'.

495. Tan. *Tentacular Pedagogy.*

496. Introduction by Jack Halberstam. Harney and Moten. *Undercommons.* 6.

497. Harney and Moten. *Undercommons.* 17.

498. Yamagata International Documentary Film Festival. 2023. 'YIDFF 2023: New Asian Currents'. https://www.yidff.jp/2023/program/23p2-e.html.

499. Gallo, Laura M. H., Vincent Giampietro, Patricia A. Zunszain, and Kai Syng Tan. 2021. 'Covid-19 and Mental Health: Could Visual Art Exposure Help?' Frontiers in Psychology 12. https://doi.org/10.3389/fpsyg.2021.650314.

500. Saijo, Tatsuyoshi. 2022. Designing the World with Future Generations in Mind'. *Intergenerational Foundation*. https://www.if.org.uk/2022/07/23/designing-the-world-with-future-generations-in-mind/.

501. Smithsonian's National Museum of the American Indian. 2009. *Haudenisaunee Guide for Educators*. 2009. https://americanindian.si.edu/sites/1/files/pdf/education/HaudenosauneeGuide.pdf.

502. Butler. 'Speech Sounds'.

503. The premise of the notion of 'double pandemic' for instance correlates Black racism with physical and mental ill health, in Laurencin and Walker. 2020. 'A Pandemic on a Pandemic'.

504. For instance: Katzman, Martin A., Timothy S. Bilkey, Pratap R. Chokka, Angelo Fallu, and Larry J. Klassen. 2017. 'Adult ADHD and Comorbid Disorders: Clinical Implications of a Dimensional Approach'. BMC Psychiatry 17 (1): 302. https://doi.org/10.1186/s12888-017-1463-3; Taylor, Christa L. 2017. 'Creativity and Mood Disorder: A Systematic Review and Meta-Analysis'. Perspectives on Psychological Science: A Journal of the Association for Psychological Science 12 (6): 1040–76. https://doi.org/10.1177/1745691617699653; Benedek, Mathias, Martin Karstendiek, Simon M. Ceh, Roland H. Grabner, Georg Krammer, Izabela Lebuda, Paul J. Silvia, et al. 2021. 'Creativity Myths: Prevalence and Correlates of Misconceptions on Creativity'. Personality and Individual Differences 182 (November): 111068. https://doi.org/10.1016/j.paid.2021.111068.

505. Halliday, Ayun. 2020. 'Behold Octavia Butler's Motivational Notes to Self'. *Open Culture*, 29 June 2020. https://www.openculture.com/2020/06/behold-octavia-butlers-motivational-notes-to-self.html.

506. The South End Press Collective, ed. 1999. *Talking About a Revolution: Interviews with Michael Albert, Noam Chomsky, Barbara*

*Ehrenreich, Bell Hooks, Peter Kwong, Winona LaDuke, Manning Marable, Urvashi Vaid, and Howard Zinn*. Cambridge, MA: South End Press.

507. hooks, bell. 2003. *Teaching Community: A Pedagogy of Hope*. 1st edition. New York: Routledge.

508. Dericotte, Toi. 2008. 'Joy Is an Act of Resistance, and: Special Ears, and: Another Poem of a Small Grieving for My Fish Telly, and: On the Reasons I Loved Telly the Fish'. *Prairie Schooner* 82 (3): 22–27. https://doi.org/10.1353/psg.0.0107.

509. Mitchell, Reagan Patrick. 2022. 'The Art of Ridicule: Black Queer Joy in the Face of the Fatigues'. *International Journal of Qualitative Studies in Education* 35 (9): 943–59. https://doi.org/10.108 0/09518398.2022.2035463.

510. Tan, Jack. 2023. "@jackkytan: A Small Group of ESEA Researchers..." Instagram, August 25, 2023. https://www.insta-gram.com/p/CwVJeDets4N/.

511. Xia, Matthew. 2023. 'The Transformation Season'. Actors Touring Company. 2023. https://www.atctheatre.com/production/the-transformation-season/.

512. The use of the term 'metabolising' is inspired by what UK curator Annie Jael Kwan spoke about in a discussion at esea contemporary Manchester UK, 2023.

513. Tan, Kai Syng. 2021. Publicity still for *How to Thrive in 2050*.

514. Morris, Aldon D. 2018. 'Scholarship Above the Veil: A Sesquicentennial Symposium Honoring W.E.B. Du Bois"'. October 29. https://news.harvard.edu/gazette/story/2018/10/lecturer-explains-du-boiss-role-as-eminent-sociologist/.

515. See note 11 above.

516. Tan, Kai Syng. 2019. 'Effecting Change in Perspective Is a Challenging (and Hence Critical) Endeavour'. *BMJ Blogs: Medical Humanities*. https://blogs.bmj.com/medical-humanities/2019/05/15/effecting-change-in-perspective-is-a-challenging-and-hence-critical-endeavour/.

517. Tan, Kai Syng and Rashed, Mohammed. 2022. *MASTERCLASS: At University of Oxford's Philosophy and Psychiatry Summer School 2022*. https://kaisyngtan.com/artful/oxford-uni-summer-school/.

518. Tan, Kai Syng. 2021. 'Art and Psychiatry in the 21st Century: Here's to More Messy – and Magical – Entanglements'. *British Journal of Psychiatry Bulletin*. 1–4. https://doi.org/10.1192/bjb.2021.93.
519. Douglas. *Cultural Leadership*.
520. Ibid.
521. Tan. *Neuroqueering Leadership*.
522. Urry. *Mobilities*.

# Index[1]

[1] Note: Page numbers followed by 'n' refer to notes.